California Maritime A

DATE DUE

Advance Responses to
*CyberUnion: Empowering Labor Through Computer Technology**

"The first truly definitive 'must read' paradigm of Labor's participation in the evolution of cyber communications."

—*Gary Cortes, Union Jobs Clearinghouse*

"A valuable book for all unionists. CyberUnion challenges the imagination and encourages us to tackle the future with confidence."

—*Nancy Brigham, Webmaster, Electronic Communications Specialists,*
UAW Interational Union (Auto Workers)

"Most exciting is the description of opportunities for greater and more effective union democracy... for how Labor can utilize technology to counter a corporate global agenda with a more humane one."

—*Allyne Beach, Ohio Civil Service Employees Association*
OCSEA, AFSCME Local 11

"Shows us the vibrant and creative side of American unions. Illustrates how the digital revolution has gone way beyond management."

—*Ross Koppel, Social Research Corporation*

"A 'must read' for anyone looking for a great way to amplify the 'move' in the labor movement."

—*Charles H. Laskonis, International Brotherhood*
of Electrical Workers (IBEW), Local 364

"Both mind-boggling and practical. Like the computer itself, [the] CyberUnion [book] is a resource for labor movement revival."

—*Paul Johnston, Sociologist/Organizer*
at the Citizenship Project and UC Santa Cruz

"This important volume [can be] used . . . to liberate [union] vision, and to challenge [unions] to rethink how they define and fulfill their mission."

—*Michael Eisenscher, Project for Labor Renewal, San Francisco*

"Shostak's taxonomy provides an excellent guidepost for unions to move from a 'gee whiz' use of technology to a purposeful integration of computers, CD-ROMS, and web sites into the fabric of the 21st-century union."

—*Rachel Hendrickson, National Education Association (NEA)*

*No necessary endorsement is implied by any of the organizations mentioned:
They are cited for identification purposes only.

CyberUnion

ISSUES IN WORK AND HUMAN RESOURCES

Daniel J.B. Mitchell, Series Editor

CYBERUNION
Empowering Labor Through Computer Technology
Arthur B. Shostak

WORKING IN THE TWENTY-FIRST CENTURY
Policies for Economic Growth Through Training,
Opportunity, and Education
David I. Levine

INCOME INEQUALITY IN AMERICA
An Analysis of Trends
Paul Ryscavage

HARD LABOR
Poor Women and Work in the Post-Welfare Era
Joel F. Handler and Lucie White

CYBERUNION

EMPOWERING LABOR THROUGH COMPUTER TECHNOLOGY

WITHDRAWN

Arthur B. Shostak

M.E.Sharpe
Armonk, New York
London, England

Library of Congress Cataloging-in-Publication Data

Shostak, Arthur B.
CyberUnion : empowering labor through computer
technology / Arthur B. Shostak
p.   cm.—(Issues in work and human resources)
Includes bibliographical references and index.
ISBN 0-7656-0462-0 (hbd. : alk. paper).   ISBN 0-7656-0463-9 (pbk : alk. paper)
1. Trade-unions—Computer networks.   2. Trade-unions—Computer
network resources.   I. Title.   II. Series.
HD6490.C616S56   1999
331.88′0285—dc21   99-10062
CIP

Printed in the United States of America

The paper used in this publication meets the minimum requirements of
American National Standard for Information Sciences—
Permanence of Paper for Printed Library Materials,
ANSI Z 39.48-1984.

∞

BM (c)   10   9   8   7   6   5   4   3   2   1
BM (p)   10   9   8   7   6   5   4   3   2   1

Dedicated to union brothers and sisters
busy helping
Organized Labor
make the most of computer power
and
in memory of
union brothers and sisters
who have helped mark the path
to CyberUnionism;

Jim Benson,
Business Manager, IBPAT, Kansas City, Kansas
developer of MODEM,
a listserve for union activists;

Alice Cook,
labor historian,
who revered labor traditions;

John T. Scally,
CWA Representative; head, CWA Staff Union;
a model of devotion
in the service of others;

and

John Sturdivant,
President,
American Federation of Government Employees
(AFGE-AFL-CIO),
a pioneer backer of
computer uses by unions.

Royalties from the sale of this volume have been assigned to the
Student Scholarship Fund of the AFL-CIO National Labor College
at the George Meany Center, Silver Springs, Maryland.

Contents

PART IV. WITH A LITTLE HELP FROM OUR FRIENDS: BUILD IT, AND THEY WILL COME

Series Editor's Foreword

Unions have faced difficult times over the last few decades. By the 1970s, union-represented workers as a proportion of the total work force had clearly begun to decline. The early 1980s saw sharp absolute drops in the number of unionized workers, and the erosion of membership continued into the 1990s. Not surprisingly, unions began to look at alternative approaches to organizing, bargaining, dispute resolution, political activity, and administering internal affairs.

Just as these perilous times for unions began to unfold, computers became accessible as a tool for individuals and organizations. How did unions apply this new tool to their special needs? How could they—or should they—apply computers in the future? These critical questions are the subject of this volume.

The view in the popular press is often that unions are dinosaurs left over from the Great Depression. In this view unions are gradually becoming less and less relevant to the national economy and to the new work force. Declining union membership has been at the root of this perception. But so, too, was a sense that the top leaders of the AFL-CIO and the major unions had become ossified. However, during the 1990s, dramatic changes have occurred in union leadership ranks, notably at the AFL-CIO. There is today much more receptivity among union leaders to new ideas and a conscious effort to reach out to the young. Use of computers simply has to be part of the changed approach.

A critical element in the need for unions to adapt is that their own members—and potential members—will be (or already are) using computers routinely in the workplace. Computers potentially provide a way to link up with these workers that calling a traditional membership meeting could never offer. Conversely, not to take advantage of computers means forgoing a vital communication link.

Enough said. Union leaders who want to meet the challenge of future organizing, bargaining, or other forms of representation will want to read on. So, too, will others interested in the future of labor relations in the United States. You may not agree with everything Professor Shostak has to say. But if not, you can always send him an e-mail! <shostaka@.drexel.edu>

Daniel J.B. Mitchell

Preface

*The future isn't coming in 2000 anymore. It's coming on Monday—
maybe every Monday.*

—Lester del Rey, *Analog*, 1976

While you would hardly know it from TV or the newspapers, where
Organized Labor is concerned—something remarkable is happening.

Experiments are going on with empowering computer systems that
just might help Labor transform its culture, redefine its mission, and
reinvent itself . . . possibly in time to help save itself. All of this is
happening awkwardly, to be sure, but urgently and even with some
flair.

Like many of you, I find all of this gripping and challenging. I have
watched the process, fostered it, and fretted over it for several decades.
A student of unions and a labor educator for nearly 45 years, I know
the pain of Labor's ominous slide in union density and clout. And yet,
despite the odds, I remain hopeful, knowing also of Labor's indispensability in the workplace, its iron will to survive, and its uncanny knack
for coming up with strategic reform aids (Shostak 1991).

Computers—Center Stage!

Like electricity decades ago, the computer has proven itself a transformational technology. It appears capable of radically changing nearly
everything. Called the "Big Bang of our time," it has unlimited prospects, bright and dark alike (Levy). Accordingly, its impact requires
Labor to fundamentally rethink everything about itself and its future.

In a most uneven and little-guided way, this process is underway. Far too few, however, in or outside of Labor, are helping as fully as they could. I want more people to know about Labor's effort to turn computerization to advantage, and I want far more to participate in that effort, for only as many insiders care and act can a mass movement possibly save itself.

CyberUnion Profile

Four nontechnological aids, if and when combined with computerization, could significantly help labor remake itself for the Information Age. Knit together in a novel model I call a *CyberUnion,* they beckon to unionists convinced that Labor must offer something different, something of quality that can attract and hold members who will only support a very modern, future-making organization.

The first such aid, *futuristics,* empowers as only foreknowledge can. The second, *innovations,* energizes as only creativity can. The third, *services,* engages as only rewards can. And the fourth, *traditions,* bonds as only emotional ties can. Equal components of a F-I-S-T model, the four could make a major difference in deciding Labor's fate.

Whether or not unions and locals will choose the CyberUnion option is anything but clear. Regardless, I believe enough cannot be done to encourage and support their reinvention of themselves. This book is one small way I have of paying down my debt to Labor for propping up our well-being . . . now, and hopefully for decades to come.

Background Explanation

For you to understand where I am coming from, especially my preoccupation with Labor's computerization process, is to know that in 1954, when I started my formal college study of unionism, I could not have imagined that in my lifetime:

• almost daily, several very different listserves would bring me more breaking news, commentary, and analysis of the labor movement than any library could ever hope to keep current with;
• the AFL-CIO would fax me (and thousands of others) a weekly, free two-page account of the important news Labor wants the public to know;

• rank-and-file activists, local leaders, labor educators, and varied others would meet often on an "electronic commons" in a vibrant dialogue, this a democratic exercise all too rare less than a decade ago;

• concerned parties around the globe would argue on listserves over the meaning of this or that new labor development—unionists likely never to meet in person;

• more union and labor-related Web sites would beckon on the World Wide Web than I ever imagined might be available to a researcher;

• almost weekly, a union student of mine from the AFL-CIO George Meany Center would use e-mail to exchange views, argue, ask questions, or in some other way continue our joint learning relationship;

• I could send my latest think piece to a wide range of union activists, Old Pols, staffers, rebels, and sundry other labor skates—profiting thereby from feedback in days, and sometimes only in hours . . . a review process that used to take weeks;

and—

• a bluecollar friend of mine would notice a volume of essays by Noam Chomsky, a world-class linguist and philosopher, contact him via e-mail, go to hear him speak, and begin an e-mail dialogue with him that is helping make them both better unionists.

More could tumble after this, but I'm sure you've got my point: Computers have changed my life, largely for the better, in my roles as a student of unionism, a participant in labor reform efforts, and a writer preoccupied with Labor's struggle to merit appreciation and respect.

Earning my Ph.D. as far back as 1961, when mammoth mainframe computers were still being introduced, I am pre-computer in every significant way, much to my everlasting regret. Indeed, I resisted using the infernal machines long after colleagues prodded, goaded, and snickered in front and behind. Not until 1982 did I give in and purchase a primitive Apple-E computer for our home, and then only at the insistence of my young stepsons, who could not live without access to certain trendy computer games.

In 1984, Drexel University, my employer since 1967, adopted the Apple Mac as a requirement of admission. Arguably the first university in America to take such a bold step, Drexel left me no turning back—and I began an odyssey of computer learning and relearning, of wonderful Mac highs and damnable Mac lows, seemingly without end (McCollum).

Labor and Computers

Throughout the 1970s, I saw little or no special interest paid by Labor to computer uses, save for prosaic mainframe data-management tasks connected with dues collection and the handling of health and welfare benefits.

While the origin of any special interest of mine here is increasingly vague, in 1980 I served for a year as the survey researcher for the Professional Air Traffic Controllers Organization (PATCO-AFL-CIO), the ill-fated federal union decertified after its disastrous 1981 strike (and reborn six years later when the replacements themselves unionized!).

My part-time role had me prepare my first large-scale computer-aided surveys of the attitudes of the union's 14,500 members. I was dazzled by the data's complexity, timeliness, and usefulness. After telling of this in my co-authored book on the PATCO drama, I begin to look elsewhere for like uses by Labor (Shostak and Skocik, 1986).

In 1991, for example, I noted in *Robust Unionism,* my study of over 200 labor innovations, the effective use the Air Line Pilots Association was making of teleconferencing options. ALPA's United division, in particular, matched every computer advance of the company, and other unions came to it for lessons in this high-tech format. Large-scale experiments by the Steelworkers Union and others also drew favorable reviews.

Similarly, in my 1994 book, *For Labor's Sake,* I introduced each of 28 grass-roots union activists and their project, as told by themselves. While I noted how interested these bold change-agents were in the work world turmoil around them—especially the dizzying uses and misuses corporate America was making of computers—I also noted their bewilderment about how to aid "future shock" casualties among the rank-and-file, and their puzzlement about how Labor might best respond.

Methodology: Searching for Clues

The research entailed in putting these three books together, and especially the pleasure of meeting a small cadre of computer enthusiasts in various unions, has had me ever since pursuing the subject in greater depth.

I have, for example, recently interviewed union computer advocates in Britain, Canada, Israel, Norway, and Sweden—and I continue to learn much from their counterparts here. In the summer of 1998, I sent a 10-item computer-use questionnaire via e-mail to many American unionists, and I have learned much of value from all who responded.

I have also taken advantage of teaching since 1975 at the AFL-CIO George Meany Center for Labor Studies. There, after class and over coffee, I have collected many tape-recorded accounts of computer adventures and misadventures. As well, in 1995 I initiated the first-ever e-mail listserve of Meany Center college-degree students and staff, and I have been both an eager participant and a close student of this resource ever since.

Best of all, in 1997 in San Francisco I attended a three-day Labor TECH Conference, the single best source of current information about the state of union use of information advances (radio and video got attention, along with computers). Held three times before, somewhere in America, by a rag-tag band of stalwarts, the conference attracted about 300 devotees, and its workshops covered a dizzying range of ongoing computer projects and wannabee schemes.

This was the first such gathering that earned brief (one session) attendance by a formal representative of the AFL-CIO, a fact that both heartened some attendees (others are at odds with officialdom), and yet also underlined the costly marginality of the conference.

Similarly, in late January 1999, I attended the first-ever East Coast–based two-day gathering of union proponents of computer use. Called by its New York academic sponsors the Labor Online Conference, it drew over 200 attendees from all over America (and others from Britain, Europe, and Korea). It gave me my first opportunity as an invited panelist to preview ideas in this book, and significantly influenced what I have written—especially my confidence in Labor's prospects of computer-aided recovery. While the AFL-CIO per se was not represented (due, perhaps, to the coincidence of the worst ice storm in years), the IT directors of several major unions served as stimulating "insider" panelists. New software and videos were demonstrated, hallway banter crackled with excitement, and in 1,001 ways the enthusiastic participants helped promote the Cause.

Naturally, I have also explored the entire matter on the Internet and through various labor listserves. This is an increasingly difficult task, so fast are relevant Web sites and listserves multiplying in cyberspace. Some stand out. The International Federation of Professional and Technical Engineers' Web site (www.ifpte.org), for example, offers help to affiliates in designing their own Web pages. The United Steelworkers (www.uswa.org) features streaming video and audio clips. And the United Transportation Union Web site (www.utu.org) contains an electronic bulletin board with job opportunities from around the country.

With every passing month, more such cyberspace sites earn admiration and visitors.

Focus of the Book

I begin in Part I by exploring conventional uses unions are making of computers—as in keeping track of dues and rallying the troops—the better to compare and contrast this in Part III with what unions might go on to do (my CyberUnion prescription).

As the American labor movement is too big and contradictory to fit into a single template, Part II examines three ongoing variations on the theme, three different ways unions are handling computers:

- the *Cyber Naught approach*, or direction without distinction; the situation of unions and locals making the least of the possibility;
- the *Cyber Drift approach,* or direction without a clear destination; the situation of unions and locals wandering in what may seem a digital desert; and the
- the *Cyber Gain approach,* or direction with distinction; the situation of unions and locals making the most of computerization—but still missing much of what the CyberUnion model offers.

Partisans of each view the world quite differently, and it is vital to try and understand where they are coming from, and where they would take Organized Labor.

Not to get too far ahead of myself, the rest of the book explains why I believe these three ongoing models will *not* suffice. I am convinced another we can only glimpse, the model I call *CyberUnion,* is the best choice if Labor in the early twenty-first century is to secure a popular and significant role.

Accordingly, I focus in Part III on the four components of a CyberUnion—futuristics, innovations, services, and traditions (F-I-S-T)—that set it apart.

I discuss, for example, rewards possible from reliable forecasts: rewards that innovations, such as computer data mining, can uniquely secure for risk-takers; rewards that computer-based services can best provide; and rewards possible from the computer-aided modernization of labor traditions (as in the production of interactive software rich with labor history material).

Computerization, in short, is necessary, but insufficient. It will not profit labor to pour old wine into new bottles, as is true of the Cyber Gain model: A new medium warrants new content, and the F-I-S-T model provides that—and more.

In Part IV, I begin by exploring the role change-agents are now playing, or could soon play, in advancing Labor's computerization process. I look at the AFL-CIO, the international unions, the locals, the Central Labor Councils, and the special role women unionists have in this situation. I go overseas in the next chapter to ask what can Americans learn from Labor elsewhere in this regard. And I close Part IV with both a chapter and an epilogue that ruminate on some tough choices Labor must make if it is to progress here as it must.

Summary

Labor has much of which to be proud: Union wages are 34 percent higher than non-union wages. Eighty-five percent of union members have health care and pension benefits. Seventy-three percent of unionists have short-term disability benefits. Eighty percent of unionists have defined benefit pension plans. And six in ten unionists have been on the job more than 10 years, where only three in ten non-unionists experience that kind of job security (Gittlen).

Thanks to its experimental use of computers, labor has a fresh opportunity to achieve even more. While no "magic bullet," the computer has already proven a valuable aid, an empowering device of great value (as in research, data management, communications, etc.), and its potential has barely been glimpsed.

To be sure, even after 20 years of development and sales, the personal computer still "remains the only common possession that makes smart people feel stupid and requires the constant ministrations of a priesthood of experts. Unless you own a really lousy car, it's likely that your PC is the least dependable device in your home or office" (Mossberg).

These gripes (which I share) notwithstanding, Organized Labor can go much further in benefiting from computerization by adopting a model I call a CyberUnion, a twenty-first-century organization of F-I-S-T distinction.

Whether this soon occurs or not remains for you to help decide . . . and then creatively promote.

Acknowledgments

There are a hell of a lot of us here. If we are going to make it, you had
better remember that the guy next to you is your brother.
—Opening announcement, Woodstock Music Festival, 1969

Prime among those who gave generously of their scarce time and
valuable ideas are unionists Carol Fehners (AFGE, CA), Karin Hart
(CWA Local 9415), Elly Leary (UAW Local 2324), Matthew C.
Marsh (AFGE, Local 4056), C. Perry Rapier (BMWE), Michael
Silberberg (United University Professionals, SUNY System), and Dan
Smith (Roofers and Waterproofers Local #95). Paul Balski (vice presi-
dent, Roofers Union) provided valuable leads, and, like the others,
offered encouragement throughout.

At a critical point in June 1998, I sent out a 10-item questionnaire
to many unionists with some link to my subject. Those who took time
from their hectic and very busy lives to answer include Bobby Brown
(Local 351, IUOE), Alex Cullison (MEBA member), Paul Finn (field
organizer, painters local in Minnesota), Ike Gittlen (USW Local
1688), John J. Griffin (IT consultant), Gary Angel Johns (UFCW
member), John Klusinski (contract administrator with the Clerical-
Technical Union of Michigan State University), Larry Kuehn (director, research and technology, British Columbia Teachers' Federation),
Charles Laskonis (IBEW member), Aikya Param (former publisher,
Women and Money: Economic Justice and Empowerment Report),
Carol Rodgers (Railway Workers Hazardous Materials Training Program, George Meany Center for Labor Studies), Ellen Starbird (Oak-
land Local 1603), and Reinhard U. Witiak (AFGE staffer).

Similarly, in late June of 1998 I sent out a draft of the preface to many unionists, and received back very helpful suggestions from Bobby Brown and Jenifer M., his daughter; Michael Eisenscher, Ross Koppel, Charles Laskonis, Mike Sacco, and Sharon Pinnock. Michael, in particular, helped to substantially improve the final version.

When I later sent out the first draft of the introduction, Ross Koppel, Sharon Pinnock, and my wife, Lynn Seng, helped sharpen the thinking and prose.

In mid-July of 1998, I spent an afternoon in focused conversation with four Chicago union "students" of union use of informatics—Rust Gilbert, Tom Hopper, Robert Yeager, and Mike Sacco. The dialogue ranged far and wide, but was especially valuable for its skepticism about the political impact of computers on institutions.

Similarly, at the July 1998 session at the Meany Center I interviewed Carl D. Cantrell (IBEW Local 2113), Kevin Gardner (National Letter Carriers Association), Jon Geenen (UPIU), Donald Giljum (IUOE Local 148), Shellie R. Green (UNITE), Chuck Hodell (director, GMC, Educational Design Unit), Mary Holman (URW, Local 285), Connie Johnsey (UNITE), David L. Lyons (International Association of Fire Fighters), Andrew Peterson (National Letter Carriers Association), C. Perry Rapier (BMWE), and Judy Yackee (BCTWU Local 19), all of whom were generous in sharing their special insights into the matter.

Late into this venture, I learned of the existence of an ad hoc group of major union Web masters. I e-mailed all ten of the members, and received helpful material back from Alan Spaulding (UFCW), Kris Raab (CWA), Nancy Brigham (UAW), and Peter Popock (SEIU). Kris also cooperated in a lengthy phone-call "interview."

In August 1998, I gave a day-long workshop on futuristics for the American Federation of Government Employees. That enabled me to interview at length a very creative pioneer, Ben Martin, president of Local 2317, and also the union's Web publisher, Mike Creech, one of the very few in labor in this position with an academic background and relevant schooling.

As twice before, Blair Calton of the AFL-CIO took time from his hectic schedule, went out of his way, and filled me in at length and in depth about the Federation's remarkable vision and blueprint for promoting informatics gains by its affiliate. This material has always been invaluable.

Five of my former students at the Meany Center generously agreed to let me edit and reproduce essays originally done for my courses: Joe Breedlove, Bobby Brown, Kim Evon, Sharon Pinnock, and Carol Rodgers. As well, Don Giljum allowed me to use an essay he had prepared for Jim Griffin's Meany Center course in computer utilization by unionists. And Jon Geenen did an independent study under my guidance that produced an excellent report, "Unions and Information Technology," from which I learned much of value.

Eight Drexel University students taking a 1998 fall term course that required field research interviewed Philadelphia unionists and assessed union Web sites on behalf of this book. I am grateful to Norizan Abdullah, Norhayti Azit, Shariza Maricar, Mohd Azlan Mohammad, Galina Nosik, Yelena Rozhitskaya, Nor Azita Yahaya, and Mazlan Mat Zain.

Jim Dator, a leading futurist, gave permission for me to adapt a talk he originally gave to a labor audience in Hawaii. I appreciate the opportunity to give his views a wider audience. Likewise, I appreciate being able to use an original essay by an IBEW friend, Charles Laskonis.

Ken Garson, a reference librarian at Drexel, came through every time, and then some. Would that every author had the backup of someone as reliable and persistent.

Charley Lewis, head of department, COSATU Information Technology Unit, in South Africa (charley@cosatu.org.za) was very helpful both in teaching me much about COSATU, a pioneer in computer uses, and in providing the longest, richest, and most relevant list of labor listserves and Web sites I could have hoped for.

As this is my 19th book, I have some familiarity with the ways and wiles of publishing houses, and I think I know a good one when I come across it: M.E. Sharpe, Inc., makes the grade. Esther L. Clarke, administrative assistant to the economics editor, handled the tricky start-up stage with calming assurance. Steven Martin did a fine job with myriad production challenges. Overseeing the entire process, Sean M. Culhane, the economics editor, was thoroughly supportive and quite cordial, the very model of a publishing industry professional with a keen sense of mission.

As often before over the past 20 years and its several book-writing projects, my wife, Lynn Seng, gave up a lot so that I could help tell this story. Hours that we could have spent together went instead into research, ruminating, and hunt-and-peck typing and retyping. Lynn remained patient, interested, and supportive—all of which I have come to count on and value beyond telling. Our lives together affirm a loving belief we share: "Come grow old with me, the best is yet to be."

Naturally, the entire crowd are guiltless where the book's various shortcomings are concerned: They're mine alone. If they vex you enough, please let me know—and together we may reduce their toll in a second, improved edition.

CYBERUNION

Introduction

"Please Fasten Your Seatbelts"

A new medium of human communications is emerging, one that may prove to surpass all previous revolutions. . . . The future is information technology, and it isn't just for propeller heads.

—Don Tapscott, *The Digital Economy,* 1996

In his 1995 book, *Navigating in Cyberspace,* Frank Ogden, a leading Canadian futurist, explains that the defining theme of our times is "continuous disequilibrium." Trends already on the horizon suggest that "the next decade will make the past look tame. . . . Within 10 years, the technology that is hardly out of the starting gate will change 90 percent of our culture and society" (Ogburn, 12, 3, 6).

Nowhere is Ogburn's point better demonstrated than in the case of *the* major lever for change at present, *informatics* (the marriage of telecommunications and information technologies, as exemplified by the Internet and the computer) (Karlgaard). Its exponential growth curves continue to produce bulletproof evidence that we live in a New Economy—one "all about . . . the ability to transform [organizations] into new entities that yesterday couldn't be imagined and that the day after tomorrow may be obsolete" (Tapscott, 43).

As if to underline that point, two global giants, General Electric and Microsoft, competed in 1998 for bragging rights as *the* most valuable company in the stock market, the highest-value firm of them all. Fifteen years ago Microsoft had no capital at all!

What a remarkable new world in which Organized Labor must find its way!

Information Options—Now!

Consider, for example, how unionists might soon satisfy their hunger for information, a key to whether or not one remains a significant player in the twenty-first century.

We can already customize our "page" on any one of several Internet search engines (AOL, Yahoo, Excite, etc.). This "personalization" option enables us to have our own computer-based "newspaper" with the morning coffee, complete with our choice of very current news stories, comics, sports scores, stock quotations, TV schedules, editorials, and even astrological forecasts. A tailor-made collection of valued information culled from over 650,000 sites on the Web alone, personalization "promises to re-emphasize the personal in personal computing" (Madrick).

Similarly, only a few years ago the idea of our "hiring" an electronic agent, or "knowbot," was "mostly the wishful thinking of fuzzy futurists." Now we can cruise the Internet and find the lowest-cost items, cheapest prices, and most accommodating merchants. Proponents believe that comparison-shopping software may help turn the Web "into a nirvana of 'frictionless capitalism,' where middlemen are obsolete, markups are pared to the bone, and consumers rule" (Quick).

Not surprisingly, a reporter for the *Wall Street Journal* frets that this "paradise for comparison shoppers," this "killer" application, could spark a cutthroat pricing war in cyberspace. Using this software makes beating down prices "a hobby, a sport, and almost an artform" (Wysocki).

Imagine how further along all this may be just a few years from now. By 2005 or so, our insatiable appetite for information may have us:

- wearing a compact picture-phone and computer on our wrist and dictating to it by voice, even as we enjoy listening to its "voice" in turn;
- using it to access any type of information, anywhere, at any time;
- using it to stay "in the loop" and stay in touch with significant others all the time;
- using it to send and receive messages in all languages;
- using it to surf the Internet and the Web with the stressless help of "smart" software that provides useful information even *before* we ask for it;
- and, feeling empowered by these information aids as never before!

Even if only half of this is realized in the next few years, the rest is likely to be close behind, and the impact is likely to prove mind-boggling.

A remarkable information future beckons ... though some will make far more of it than others. Labor can turn it to advantage, both for itself as a social movement and for its individual members, but the doing will not come easy, and the hour grows late.

Labor at Bat

Labor, in short, is challenged to renew itself once again, as not since the 1930s, when it had to "invent" large-scale industrial unionism, and the mid-1990s, when it opted for the invigorating "New Voice" vision of the Sweeney team. The head of that team, after taking "the hitherto taboo step of saying that Labor is in danger of becoming 'irrelevant,'" authorized an immediate step-up in the use of informatics (Heckscher, xv).

Accordingly, in 1996, the AFL-CIO held its first major meeting to discuss Labor and the Internet. In 1998, an ad hoc committee of 12 information technology officers of the most progressive unions published an unofficial White Paper on making the most of computer uses. Similarly, a group of specialists inside the AFL-CIO were busy that year studying how to offer an "Intelligent Agent" to unionists. But ... I get ahead of myself: More on this latter (see, for example, Chapter 8, "Innovations," and Chapter 11, "Change-Agents: Stateside").

Thanks in part to this effort, far more American unionists are on-line than most Americans and unionists appreciate. Carl D. Cantrell, a contributor to this book, offers this guesstimate:

> According to the AFL-CIO, there are 16.1 million union members in the United States. In virtually all occupational groups, union workers are making more money than non-union workers, and in some industries, union members may make as much as a 73 percent difference. That means union members have more spending power, and thus we can expect that more union workers are on the Internet than their non-union counterparts.
>
> If one takes the 131 million work force number from the 1997 U.S. census tables and assumes there are 57 million users, then 39 percent of the work force are participating. If we are conservative and only esti-

mate 25 percent of union members are on-line, that still means there are now more than 4,000,000 union members using the Internet.

As impressive as is this possible total, Cantrell also notes—with appropriate exasperation—that of the 74 international unions affiliated with the AFL-CIO, as late as the fall of 1998 only 44 had Web sites. Nearly half (30) were not yet participating in the biggest change in communications in modern times.

Accordingly, by about 2003 or earlier the matter should be clear: The American labor movement will either be employing computers with finesse, or it will have become an inconsequential has-been, the organizational equivalent of "roadkill on the Information Superhighway."

Reality Check

This sharp-edged possibility—either mastery or fade-out—is *not* the same thing as saying computerization can or will save Labor. As one of the most extensive pioneering users of computers, an overseas federation of 403 unions in 113 countries, maintains—"The computers are one possible medium, not the message" (ICEM, 56).

Computerization is no "silver bullet." It is a complex, demanding, and often exasperating tool, only as reliable and effective as the humans in charge. As well, it is no solo star. It is at its pro-Labor best when part of a mix that includes militancy, labor law reform, political action, and so on.

It would be a costly mistake to confuse computerization with a magic remedy, almost as costly as the present-day underutilization of its remarkable potential. Which *is* to say, that while computerization cannot "rescue" Labor, unless Organized Labor soon makes the most creative possible use of it, Labor probably cannot rescue itself.

Picking Up the Pace

I write as a labor educator who is persuaded that a genuine revolution in organizational and social reality is in the making. I believe huge issues must be tackled, from the changing nature of work all the way to fundamental changes in the nature of union organizational realities. Labor can, should, and *must* create a new way of "doing business," a substantial alternative to its current organizational culture. For a world being recast by computerization requires far more of Labor than ever before.

Accordingly, my book asks and tentatively answers three questions: First, what's happening where Labor and computerization are concerned? Second, so what? What are its implications? For whom? Why? And third, what could, or even should, be happening?

My attempt to answer these questions has me in Part I first describe the current scene, one rich in unrealized possibilities. Drawing extensively on excerpts from three years' worth of field interviews, I highlight the strengths and weaknesses of current uses of computer potentialities.

I move next in Part II to consider three distinct variations I label Cyber Naught, Cyber Drift, and Cyber Gain unions. The first, *Cyber Naught,* involves a very hazardous neglect of computerization. The second, *Cyber Drift,* is characterized by a costly sort of aimlessness. The third, *Cyber Gain,* shines with possibilities, but does not go far enough.

Over the next few years one of these three alternatives is likely to characterize the scene—a process I am fully intent on trying to influence, as my partiality in favor of a fourth possibility, CyberUnionism, could not be greater (a bias the reader will keep carefully in mind).

The Heart of the Matter

I am persuaded that Labor's overdue use of computers, while necessary, is insufficient. If Labor is to reinvent itself as rapidly, as thoroughly, and as meaningfully as appears necessary, far more seems required.

Specifically, I intend in Part II to make a case for experimenting with an ambitious and creative alternative to the status quo. My CyberUnion model would incorporate futuristics, innovations, services, and labor traditions (F-I-S-T)—all of which go better when they build on computerization.

Why this unusual set? Because as a futurist, a professional forecaster, I think Labor must take advantage of this ancient, and yet also avant garde art form. Similarly, as a labor educator, I believe innovation is a resource Labor urgently needs to make more of. And like most labor educators, I champion the extension of union-offered services and the celebration of labor traditions, for goods and lore can make a powerful combination—especially if facilitated by new-fangled computerization aids.

Together, then, these four additional items (F-I-S-T) should provide Labor with the foresight, the dynamism, the appeal, and the heart necessary to reverse its long-term decline . . . and prove itself a significant player in the early twenty-first century.

Pulling It Together

I go on in Part IV to consider, first, five types of change agents vital to the emergence of CyberUnions, and, second, the Labor-computer scene overseas.

In Chapter 11, I discuss four organizations—the AFL-CIO, international unions, district offices, and local unions—along with one special type of activist—women unionists—as these five change-agents are critical in shaping CyberUnion prospects.

In Chapter 12, among other aspects of the global scene, I cite plans unionists have to create the world's first Town Hall of empowered unionists. Intended to jump-start global union services, it may command attention from the powerful, as little Labor has previously attempted.

I use my book's closing chapter to share some questions that continue to vex me, recognizing as I do how my own ideas about Labor and computers remain in flux. Every day brings fresh developments in key aspects, for as futurists like to remind us, a seamless and ever-changing web connects everything to everything else.

At the end of each chapter, I list a few mind-stretching exercises, and some reading and Web site sources (an appendix list expands on relevant Web sites) to help you make better sense of what I have been trying to explain. If you look up the readings cited, you will learn where some of my ideas come from, and how my ideas often go their own way.

As well, after several chapters I offer short essays by others of like persuasion printed here for the first time. You will hear the voice of a thoughtful academic, futurist Jim Dator, and also of union activists, all but one of whom (Charles Laskonis) are current or former students of mine at the National Labor College of the AFL-CIO George Meany Center for Labor Studies.

Busy operationalizing ideas bandied about in the book, the union essayists "walk the talk." They enable me to see beyond the limits of my own experience. And their no-nonsense, get-on-with-the-job approach lends useful ballast to my sometimes airy approach.

Typical are the far-sighted ideas of Donald Giljum. He makes a strong case for getting beyond the Cyber Gain model by daring to try a virtual union approach, one that could serve as a pragmatic and appealing bridge to the CyberUnion option. Original, pragmatic, and convincing, Giljum's vision exemplifies the Labor reinvention possibilities explored throughout the book.

Similarly, I have had the privilege of reading a lengthy research report done by another contributor, Carl D. Cantrell, an IBEW member and the Web master of a site he created for his IBEW district. To meet degree requirements at the National Labor College, Carl surfed the Internet, interviewed many union users of computers, and produced the best unpublished general survey of the scene I came across while doing this book. I learned much of value from Carl's work, and with his blessings, I draw often on it.

Asking Your Help

Frankly, if all goes as well as I dare hope, I will be teased shortly after the book's publication about computer-and-labor gains that eluded my research, and the book will be outdated in five or fewer years. By then victims of the Cyber Naught model may have secured a sound new place in the sun. Hopefully, the Cyber Drift model may also be history. And most unions will have "graduated" into the Cyber Gain situation, even as rewarding experiments of the best of them will be promoting the CyberUnion option that I favor.

The better to move along this happy daydream, I have attached in an appendix a short version of the questionnaire I used in preparing this first edition. I earnestly invite your answers, along with any related thoughts stirred by this book, as I need that feedback if I am ever to prepare an even better second edition.

Plowing a Well-Plowed Field?

It only remains now to ask how much of this has already gotten attention—before we can get on with it.

Not surprisingly, a growing body of literature explores the impact of computerization on many major components of society. For example, a pioneering 1996 book, *Cybercorp: The New Business Revolution,* by

James Martin, got me started thinking about writing this one. Another book with a similar title, *Cyberschools: An Education Renaissance,* by Glenn R. Jones, came a lot closer in values to my own, and helped strengthen my resolve to undertake this one.

Any doubts I may have had about tackling this project were left behind when I discovered there was essentially no literature on the subject. This was quite surprising, as pundits are very busy suggesting Labor should do this, that, or the other thing. Occasional articles in *Challenge, Dissent, Mother Jones, New Labor Forum, Social Policy, The Nation, The New Left Review, The Progressive, Working USA, Z,* and others (including the likes of *Business Week* and *Fortune*), are generous with analysis, evaluation, and prescription.

Missing, however, is any attention in general to the infrastructure of unionism, and, in particular, to the effort Labor is (or is not) making to use computers to help renew itself (Bennett and Delaney). Missing also is any useful counsel in this critical matter (Hannigan).

Typical is the 1998 Labor Day feature in *The Nation,* a collection of eight essays by long-time labor friends and advisers eager to highlight "unmet challenges." Only once in eight pages was computerization even as much as mentioned, and then only to urge a use already well under way. Similarly, the Winter 1997 issue of *Social Policy* was entitled "Rethinking Labor." This notwithstanding, its 63 pages included but three fleeting mentions of computer uses (as for job retraining) and not one mention of the consequential labor-computer nexus.

Volumes by academics are no more relevant. The *Proceedings* of the 50th Annual Meeting of the Industrial Relations Research Association (January 1998), to cite one typical publication, offers valuable insights into numerous aspects of the current labor scene. But there is hardly any mention in its 382 pages of how computerization has, is, and may continue to alter major aspects of unionism here and abroad (Voos).

Ironically, a book which offers otherwise excellent analysis of union administration matters, at least from 1979 through the mid-1990s, concludes with eight progressive recommendations for union reforms, but no recognition of computer potential (Masters). Similarly, a unique 1998 guide to creating high-performance unions ignores computer use altogether (Hannigan).

This blackout is made all the odder by the remarkably early start intellectuals actually had here: In the very year (1972) that the world first learned of the existence of the Internet, a labor staffer, Charles Levinson, wrote a major article urging use of the new technology of computer communications. Unfortunately, his call went unheeded, by Labor and its intellectual friends alike (Lee, E. 45).

So, the library shelf is bare, though I trust not for long.

Info Age Prospects

We must remain open to amazing possibilities where computers are concerned, both of the appealing and also of the frightening variety.

Only a century ago, very few citizens imagined what a difference in their lives might follow from electricity, radio, film, TV, the PC, the cellular phone, the microwave oven, heart transplants, space exploration, cloned sheep, and the dazzling like. Or, imagined the harrowing possibilities posed by biological weapons, corporate mega-mergers, global warming, hydrogen bombs, and other such terrors.

Nearly 10 million youngsters—many of whom could navigate through a computer as toddlers—were using the Internet in 1998, a number projected to triple in the next four years (Stone). And Boston became the first big city to link its entire 128-school system to the Web, with others rushing after its example.

Our kitchen equipment can have a built-in bar-code scanner to read our favorite food choices, and use software "intelligent agents" to track on-line for related recipes and discount coupons, both of which are useful when we buy our groceries through the Net (Narisetti).

The average automobile now coming off the assembly line has the same computing capabilities as the first lunar module. Accordingly, the average auto mechanic is challenged to become a computer technician and electronic wiz (Joyce).

Similarly, a former track repair worker told me with keen appreciation:

> As every train goes across a computer-aided "hot-box" detector, the actual temperature of the wheel bearing is taken. This comes across a graph, at the train dispatcher's office, which is hundreds of miles away. He can look at every wheel that way, and learn what set of wheels on the trains needs to be looked at. He will immediately tell the engineer to stop his train, and check car so and so. That's to prevent a bearing burning out—and derailing the train, and wiping out a town.

Over and again, workers find at work technological breakthroughs that dazzle them (and most others they tell about it).

The average age of an Internet user is only 21 and declining (Tapscott, 20). Many college students say the Internet is a more popular pastime than drinking beer, the first time beer has been topped since the campus survey started in 1985 (Jasen). "Miss Manners" contends that the Internet has rescued manners, and points to the development of "netiquette" as evidence (Martin). And over 20 million Americans read parts of the 453–page Starr Report on line within 48 hours of its release (Harmon).

As if this were not enough, IBM announced in late October, 1998, the development of a new computer, arguably the world's fastest, capable of nearly 4 trillion calculations, or 4 teraflops, a second. This is 20 times faster than the wonder machine that defeated a human in the great chess match of 1997. Its purchaser, the U.S. Department of Energy, hopes to have a 10-teraflop model going by mid-2000, and a 100-teraflop computer operational by 2004 (Wald).

Among its other accomplishments, the "Pacific Blue" computer can perform enough complex calculations to maintain the reliability of the nation's nuclear weapons without conducting actual bomb tests. According to an admiring Vice President Albert Gore, it can also "lead to advances in and greater understanding of weather patterns, global climate change, medicine, manufacturing, and aviation safety" (Wald). Equal in power and speed to 15,000 PCs, the IBM supercomputer does in a second what it would take a pocket calculator 63,000 years to complete (Brokaw).

Labor Union Prospects

In light of these and 1,001 other Information Age possibilities, Organized Labor's familiar ways appear insufficient. Its conventional wisdom must give way to a new formulation of reality and a new plan of action.

Unions five years from now are likely to be very different from the present. Either they will draw handsomely on what I call CyberUnion attributes, or their hallmark may be their irrelevance. Either they will command respect as mature information-intensive powerhouses, fully the equal of anything the business world boasts, or they may be ossified relics.

I hope that this book's discussion of the Cyber Naught, Cyber Drift, and Cyber Gain models—along with my CyberUnion option—stirs fresh thinking about Labor's Information Age choices. At the very least it should help us ask whether Labor is *really* making the most of its twenty-first-century possibilities. At the very best, it may help show the way.

Recommended Resources

Davis, Stanley M. *Future Perfect*. Reading, MA: Addison-Wesley, 1987. A classic that ages well. Explains how to create a fundamentally new vision of how things work. Teaches how to regard time as a resource, rather than a constraint. Urges something more than incremental thinking, something like "transformative" thinking that imposes no limits on its results.

Kelly, Kevin. *New Rules for the New Economy: 10 Radical Strategies for a Connected World*. New York: Viking, 1998. A manifesto for creating strategy for a networked economy. Contends that the entire global economy will resemble Silicon Valley and the Internet. Believes "communication . . . is not just a sector of the economy. It is the economy." Labor must wrestle with the implications of Kelly's insights, especially his disdain for government and its regulatory role, as many "Netizens" allegedly share this bias.

Rawlins, Gregory J.E. *Slaves of the Machine: The Quickening of Computer Technology*. Cambridge, MA: MIT Press, 1997. Easily one of the most engaging, informative, and provocative explorations available of computers, artificial life, and Cyber Age possibilities. Dares to explore the possibility that the computer is not a "toaster," but a "kitten"—and all the awesome implications thereof.

To get a "personalization" service for yourself, and to construct your own "newspaper" on-line, contact www.excite.com OR www.yahoo.com OR www.netscape.com

A compilation of search engines is available at www.dogpile.com

An especially good search engine is at www.askjeeves.com

Special attention should be paid to the AFL-CIO Web site, available at www.aflcio.org, and called *Today's Unions*. It offers an "Executive Pay Watch" service that keeps tabs on exorbitant CEO salaries. It also has a "Congressional Page" with e-mail addresses and voting records of all the members of Congress.

Most recently a new AFL-CIO Web site focuses on the Social Security challenge (www.aflcio.org/socialsecurity).

Part I

COMPUTERS AND LABOR

The lesson of the last three decades is that nobody can drive to the future on cruise control.
—Rowan Gibson, *Rethinking the Future;* 1977

To their credit, the AFL-CIO, its especially progressive union affiliates, and their best locals are busy making more and better use of cellular phones, CD-ROMs, modem-aided computers, faxes, and videos, the "stuff" of informatics. Especially when they draw on what a modem makes possible and take off into cyberspace, the unionists involved enjoy a remarkable boost in empowerment.

Background

Unions have been using centralized mainframe and midsize computers for almost 30 years. Massive amounts of data on accounts payable, dues collection, health and welfare benefits, membership rolls, payroll, pensions, and voting records have long been handled by custom-tailored software, this a welcome change from the relatively crude business office equipment and punched cards previously used.

(While it gets harder to do with every passing year, it is good to pause once in a while and reflect back on how crude office techniques were before the advent of computers. A union staffer I interviewed recalled with a weary sigh that when he first started as a part-time union rep, in 1976, "nobody had computers. We did everything by hand. We used a lot of carbon paper. We used to buy it by the box. Had to carbon copy every damn thing! When we got to use copying machines, that was something! We got copying machines in our homes, and we thought that was something!")

While Labor in the 1970s achieved a successful integration of data-management tasks, no particular interest developed thereafter in more adventurous computer uses. Instead, an inappropriate sort of bureaucratic quietism settled over the scene. A top-down, noninteractive, host-based (not networked), and command-and-control model held sway.

Fortunately, however, the ranks harbored anonymous unionists who saw further. Who thought further. And who recognized this sort of bureaucratic quietism as a death sentence of sorts. Typical of the energetic response of those who declined to sleepwalk is this account from a Southern organizer I interviewed:

> I use it for research on companies. That's proved to be invaluable. We use Yahoo to get to Dun and Bradstreet, and other sources. I use it for mapping out the community I'm driving into for an organizing drive. I also use it to maintain a data base in my own organizing. And I use it for desktop publishing; that's proven to be invaluable for getting something out quickly. I don't have to go running around to get somebody else to put something together nice. I can individualize each flyer, or anything I have to do for a company. I use it constantly.

These change-agents experimented with uses that went far beyond mere data management. Their creativity stirred new interest in the computer's enormous untapped potential, and things began to stir.

In the Shop

Changes in the uses of computers initiated by innovative unionists got a boost from a related source, one of special consequence when the subject is Organized Labor, namely, the shopfloor, the warehouse, the checkout counter, the tool shed, and all the other worksites unions help keep sane, safe, and productive.

Union members began to experience the greatest overhaul in the way of doing work many had ever had to accommodate, and the example of how empowering certain uses of computers could be was not lost on them—with many wondering why their union wasn't adopting these new-fangled ways.

Consider the account below from an organizer for the Brotherhood of Maintenance of Way Employees:

> Historically, all we had to have was a strong back and a weak mind, and today that is not true at all. In the old days you didn't even have to have a high-school diploma . . . so long as you were of the bulk size to do manual labor. If you could do the work, you didn't have to know how to read or write. They were lookin' for people to work, not to think.
>
> All that has changed. Now, you have to have to be able to read and write proficiently, to understand instructions and writing, to qualify for a lot of procedures out there. Now, we have to qualify on all the electrical components of the equipment, this high-tech stuff, and know how to operate it, tear it apart, and go through it. Tests are given periodically. And there is a lot of training—much of it required by the federal government.
>
> We have multi-million-dollar machines which take the place of 50 to 60 men on the railroad. I'm talking about some of the machines we run on the tracks—you'd think you was inside an office building. With control panels. With computers. It reminds me of being in the cockpit of a jet airplane.
>
> When I first started, 25 years ago, I was on what they call a high-speed production gang. We used the latest technology equipment to find and repair uneven places in the track. If we did one mile a day it was a cause for celebration; we were really doing good! We were really kicking ass! We had about 37 men on that gang, and it was a helluva cause for celebration. Now, we have a machine that can go out there by itself with one man and do six, seven, eight, or nine miles in a day! And this has only been since 1975.
>
> By and large, most of the work on the railroad that now requires manual labor is done by machinery. We have crews of 20 men out there now doing work that used to take 150 men.

Over and again I heard comparable "war stories" from "veterans" of enormous change at work, change traceable to computerization, and change that left rank-and-filers wondering how long it would be for their unions to catch up.

Telling the Story

The better to understand where labor may yet go with computer uses, Part I is devoted to current computer utilization efforts. Chapter 1 looks at computer-aided services for dues-payers ("organizing the organized"), and Chapter 2 explores computer aids in organizing new members. As might be expected, the range of uses is considerable, and extends from prosaic to esoteric, from matter-of-fact to far out . . . with the scales tilted heavily in the unexceptional direction.

This cursory overview of current applications of computer potential is by no means an authoritative survey. I have had neither the research funds, the leeway, nor the expertise to tackle that far-reaching task . . . one someone else cannot attempt soon enough.

This notwithstanding, my overview suggests Organized Labor has considerable experience, and even some momentum here. The American Postal Workers Union (www.apwu.org) Web site, for example, registered over 134,000 hits since July of 1997, adding up to over 300 hits per day. The International Brotherhood of Electrical Workers (www.ibew.org), had over 90,000 hits in the same time period (Cantrell, 7). Yahoo alone displayed in 1998 over 370 union sites and 46 labor Internet connections (Yahoo).

The AFL-CIO estimated as far back as 1997 that nearly 2 million unionists of 14 million were already on line (Hart). Many more have come on-line since. The question of what they find when they look into union and local Web sites gets more important all the time.

Accordingly, I would have you understand, even as you read in Part I about current progress of which Labor is justifiably proud, that many activists I interviewed are eager to go further. They regard the content of Chapters 1 and 2 as the necessary but insufficient start of a scenario of transformational change barely under way. This exhilarating effort at the computer-added reinvention of Organized Labor makes the otherwise distant CyberUnion model (see Part IV) seem increasingly plausible and attainable.

1

Using Computers as a Servicing Aid

Obviously, most of the rejuvenation of the labor movement will begin in that movement itself.
—Robert Kuttner, *Dissent,* Winter 1986

Serving the membership is arguably the single most important thing locals and international unions accomplish. Members look to the business agent, local union officers, or international union representative to shield them (grievance process), aid them (bargaining), defend them (mediation and arbitration), lead them in battle (strike action), represent them (media relations), and occasionally remind them what it is all about (political action, alliances with do-gooders, community service, labor education, etc.).

Thanks to unions and locals busily making ever better use of computer options, the current rank-and-file is being better served . . . perhaps the single most decisive element in determining Labor's future. For only as current members believe, and let others know, that they are getting their dues' worth can locals hope to earn new membership (and ward off demoralization and decertification).

Service Highpoints

Today, for example, the LaborNet Web site of the AFL-CIO provides both official information and informal chat rooms for union activists. Many international union homepages, and others sponsored by especially forward-looking locals can be found on the Internet, along with specialized listserves, such as PubLabor, that enable unionists to engage in free-wheeling focused discussions.

Equally impressive are such innovations as a Web site the Hotel and Restaurant Union uses to warn unionists away from hotels it is picketing. The Flight Attendants Union created a site for collecting complaints from members about airplane equipment problems the union intended to address. Insurgents in the American Airline Pilots Union used faxes and e-mail to rally their troops. In 1997, cyberprotesters around the world bombarded Bridgestone-Firestone executives with e-mail protesting the company's treatment of its American work force, an electronic onslaught thought significant by proponents in helping to bring the bitter dispute to an end.

Certain local unionists report they cannot hold their own in arbitrations unless they are using a laptop. They cannot match the other side at the bargaining table unless they also employ a cellular phone and fax equipment. Indeed, it has reached a point in some labor circles that if your calling card does not have your e-mail address and your local's Web site URL, this is seen as a sign that you're some sort of Jurassic unionist.

(I recall being dazzled in 1998 by the amount of computer and fax equipment I observed being rolled into a downtown Philadelphia hotel when the Transit Workers local began bargaining there with management, an informatics arsenal the local had not felt the need of only three years earlier.)

Given this range of computer aids to serving members, it is not surprising that many union activists I interviewed were generous with relevant upbeat stories. Space constraints, however, permit discussion of only seven services below from a much longer list.

Outreach

Easily one of the major changes made possible by the use of computers concerns the networking endlessly going on as more and more unionists communicate with one another in ways the phone, mail, or fax just do not make practical. Many locals are troubled by their inability to stay in touch with far-flung members, so inadequate is "snail-mail" and so exasperating missed phone calls and telephone tag. Now, with e-mail, much of the problem is resolved.

Consider these thoughts from an activist whose locals span an entire state, one of the largest in the nation:

> I really see it as the glue. It is exciting to me, because that's going to be what holds it together daily. It's not going to be a thing like we run into

each other, have a neat idea, but don't see each other again for two or three years. It's going to keep ideas rolling. And we're not going to lose touch with people who disappear, or whatever. Traditionally, if we have three 24-hour shift groups (A, B, and C), if I was to leave A group and go on B shift, normally I would never or very rarely see my ex-compatriots again. But now, you can e-mail the postings every day and talk and communicate again.

As more and more members get home computers and modems, home fax equipment, and cellular phones, staying in touch should become less and less of a challenge.

An organizer, one of whose locals is especially active on a company-provided internal computer system, told me with pleasure of somewhat unusual outreach:

> This thing has evolved into a massive communication system, and any number of unofficial listserves have appeared. They touch on any number of subjects. It's gotten political. It's gotten religious. The bulletin boards do sell everything from products to you know what. We actually have a "Horrible Joke" list in the system. But you know what you are getting when you get into it, and you do not have to subscribe. Very, very crude—and many women subscribe to it. You are not automatically put on the list. And the company has not received any complaints.
>
> The employees even use the system to fire off letters to the CEO of the company, letters critical of the company. Members use it sometimes to criticize the local's leadership. But other people respond with e-mail that says, "Hey, you don't know all the facts. I think the union is doing a *good* job!" Democracy in the workplace!

While few locals I found had anything this extensive, I suspect this rollicking style foreshadows many more such computer-based settings as the possibilities get better known.

Keeping Members Informed

Especially in those cases where a company Intranet is made available to a local, a major gain in internal communications is possible. An appreciative field rep told me of a local he services that is doing especially well at this:

> The local uses the company Intranet all the time. To post notices of meetings. To conduct surveys of the membership. It is *very* interactive.

They use it to notify the company of grievances. The company uses it to notify the local of responses to grievances. I don't think the local prints a newsletter anymore. Rather than wait a week or two to have enough to fill up a newsletter, they use e-mail for short paragraphs, a short note from the president, short letters, and short news of the day. And frequently the local will send out an e-mail editorial.

A similar tale highlighted valuable savings, along with speed and ease of communication:

Most of the members of my union work for support contractors on a military base, and almost everyone has access to on-base e-mail. A newsletter is sent each month through the on-base Intranet to each member, and it is then posted on the public Web site. Since my local is very small, we probably couldn't afford the expense of a mailing a newsletter out each month, but this way it costs us nothing.

More and more uses of this type gain popularity, especially when use of an existing cyberspace system has been negotiated.

A related gain has a multi-site local use e-mail to knit together its far-flung officers at each of their locations. For example:

Five different locals scattered across four states use an Intranet. The presidents use it to communicate the latest safety issues, the latest company ads, the tragedy if someone got killed at one of the plants. Or a dialogue about what the union's role should be as far as drugs and the workplace. This has been a kind of solidarity builder, too. When these local union presidents get together in a meeting, they know each other a lot better.

Before computers, they might not have met once a year to share their concerns, like health and safety, and contractual issues. Now, they say they want a new agenda for that meeting, since they use the Intranet almost daily to iron out the bits and pieces we used to tackle in the annual meeting. It's made them smarter—and better trade unionists. The local is a lot more self-sufficient.

Over and again I was told of similar gains in solidarity, the teller often smiling with pride and satisfaction throughout the telling.

Tracking

Much time and effort are saved when computers are used to keep in close touch with relevant aspects of long and complex contracts.

One thing I keep up in my computer and on disks I have is all my contracts. So, whenever we get ready to negotiate I can get in there and pick out just the phrase or paragraph, or something like that, copy it over here, delete that, write what I want it to say. This makes negotiating a lot easier. Companies don't do that. "Here you are, here's a proposal" is what they say. And you think, "Well, I've got to get my contract and look that up." But if you've got it right there, in your laptop, you can just look it right up.

Similarly, computers are being used to help trace and type the decisions of various arbitrators, thereby enabling unionists to better prepare to argue a case before them:

> Our CDs have a new search engine on them. You could always look up cases covering a certain issue. But what you can do now is sort 17,000 cases back to 1994 by arbitration. By doing that, you can see an arbitrator's approach to a certain issue, such as overtime equability. There are real different schools of thought about the burden of proof the union has in such cases. And there is one arbitrator who does not buy this one particular argument. And if you don't know that, you'll go in there and follow that line of argument, and you're doomed. He does not accept that line of argument. The search engine now cues us in—thanks to our union.

While arbitration decisions have been tracked for many years, only lately have software search engines been sufficiently refined to permit very sophisticated typing by values, favorite rules of evidence, ill-advised language, and other telling cues to winning and losing cases.

A third form of tracking involves following and sorting members and non-members themselves, as explained by this organizer:

> Being able to sort, that's the best use I make of computers. I'll give you an example. We're gettin' ready to do negotiations at one of our shops. We've got, for the people in that shop, their shift, their departments, their union status—because Tennessee is a right-to-work state they don't have to join—so we can sort by department, shift, and membership. At that point, we can get the bargaining team a list which shows everybody in their department, and whether or not they are members.
>
> So whenever we start to gear up for a contract campaign, we can give that information out, and the stewards can start to try and sign up new members. Before computers, we would have had to rely on what-

ever kind of list the company gives to the union, which sometimes was different, and seemed like it was always the most difficult version. Sometimes they gave it in clock number sorts, which has no meaning at all to the union. Computers save us a lot of time and effort. I mean, a lot!

Systematic tracking showed up again and again as a favorite advance, a small step with a big payoff.

One final form of tracking warrants brief mention, both for its novelty (when one thinks of the stereotype of hard-boiled trade unionists) and its value, namely, the use being made to help rank-and-filers track their investments in the stock market. A fan reports:

> On my local's Web site, I made a point to create links to two major companies that a lot of our members have their 401K plan invested in, so they can just click on a Web site button and follow their investment—a *real* popular feature!

Exactly how this will play out when in a few years we have the option of wearing a tiny voice-driven computer/picture phone on our wrist (see Chapter 8) promises to be quite interesting—on and off the worksite.

Direct Access

Having spent years hearing dues-payers fume because this union bigshot or that one failed to return a call or answer a letter (a situation I know all too well myself), I empathized with many I interviewed who valued quite highly the ability of e-mail to put them through—almost regardless of whether or not it got them a reply. An activist much frustrated by pre–e-mail stonewall experiences explained:

> I think the value of the computer is that it puts many people who have to go through an information maze onto an equal playing field where they are able to—almost immediately—exchange ideas, and communicate without going up and down their various union bureaucracies, across union lines, and connect with public unions and other similarly situated unions that normally they would have no contact with. We're far too stratified. It's something we need to break away from.

Similarly, a local union president expects finer contact, but also related turmoil:

I think there is going to be a better ability than there has been to connect members to people at higher levels, so that they can know what they are *really* doing. So you are going to see a difference in the political landscape—and I don't know how higher-level officials are going to respond to that.

Much as users have had to invent "netiquette" to resolve new puzzles in Internet realities, so too will Labor have to work out norms to resolve the inevitable tensions between members willing to continue to use the traditional chain-of-command versus those who insist on their "right" to new computer-based access directly to the top.

Research

A little-known service has locals beginning to ask for computerized help from one another. Typical is this account:

> It's sort of become more accepted. Like, a bunch of locals got amalgamated into ours. And they're startin' to go into negotiations. And one of them is subsidiary of [name deleted] Corporation. And they had a suspicion the parent company was going to divest itself of it. So they asked us to look into it—and I went on the Internet to see if there was anything the financial analysts were talkin' about. And that move was suggested by the local itself, which heard we had Internet access. It wasn't somethin' I initiated. They don't know how to use the Internet, but they knew we did—and asked us to. People want the info. They are gettin' more aware of its capabilities.

Far more common is a local requesting research aid from a specialist at headquarters. One such staffer boasted:

> As a research tool, the computer is outstanding. It is rare that a week goes by when I am not required to perform research for the locals I serve.

Other unionists told me of e-mail requests for research data they had noticed on labor listserves, requests they had generously met, and of their enthusiasm for this new sort of exchange.

Less glamorous but no less valuable types of research are widely appreciated. Here is an example:

> We assign national organizers for two weeks to a specific metro area where they are required to visit several worksites. We ask each local to provide clear and concise directions to their worksites, but often get poor or no directions. Using Mapquest has become a regular part of the process. It allows the lead organizer to double-check all directions before deploying teams. This has saved countless hours of valuable time which used to be spent driving around in circles because of poor directions.

Housekeeping research-like tasks of this sort, while low-profile, profit considerably from the unique boost computer "smarts" can and do provide.

Naturally, legal research is a major resource, and it is painful to think back on how it was done before computers made it far more plausible:

> We are trade unionists, and we are not trained to be lawyers. After taking office, however, we find out quickly that we need to be. But with the Internet comes a ready-reference law library for free, with sites like Cornell Law School's Web page for on-line legal help. All the topics are listed in alphabetical order, and laws concerning everything from collective bargaining to pensions can quickly be found. Union officers can read the National Labor Relations Act, Family Leave, and other laws important to them or the members they represent. At Findlaw's Internet Web site, they can find legal precedents that may help them in their next arbitration case.

Though still reliant on trained legal staff for guidance, union activists have more valuable craft and confidence now—backed up by their computer legal research—than ever before.

Over and again I heard in the field of the pleasure activists had from computer research payoffs:

> Within my own local we've had people getting valuable information that had totally escaped the leadership, because it is still wedded to the stamp-and-envelope, and the telephone. It had to do with community charity work that we would have never known about otherwise.

As Internet search engines get easier to employ and better in feedback, more and more tales of research gains will buoy users and help win recruits over to this option.

Computer Education

Demand for learning how to operate and improve as a computer user grows stronger all the time. A steel union local president proudly explained:

> We've used money negotiated in the last industry-wide contract to pay for a huge computer training operation, an Institute for Career Development. We have an on-site computer lab, a 12-computer array in our meeting hall, and it is filled all the time with classes. We've opened it up to spouses and kids now, the demand for that was so strong. And we also have an internal training center within the plant to train anyone whose job requires using a computer. People are starting to get less scared of it. We're using computers a lot more all the time.

Especially promising is possibly the only site of its kind widely known in 1998, the OCAW Web site for shop steward training via distance learning:

> You'll see a thing there that says "Shop Steward Training and Education." It feels like "20 Questions." You click on True-False or Multiple Choice . . . click on, and bang, it takes you down to the Answer Page. Now, you see you are doing "Labor Law," under the *Weingarten* decision. "When do I have the right to a shop steward—under *Weingarten?*" Well, if you want to read the whole decision, just click here, and we will post you the whole decision of the Supreme Court. Or if you want to look under Section 29 . . . it will provide that.

This interactive approach is especially popular with computer users who recognize how it sets their tools apart from, and can make them far more engaging than, yesterday's printed-page material.

Similarly, unions are being prodded to take their apprentice schooling into cyberspace:

> The Painters Union now has a distance learning program with Marshall University. I've suggested they take their apprentice program and put it on-line. It may be the *first* access-to-all-materials on line for a labor union. . . . I told them the future is out there on the Web; you've got to get on the Web! And offer some access to people who can't get to your Training Center. Or who just want to upgrade their skills.

Still another kind of education has a local use its e-mail service to take and "teach" a position on a sensitive topic:

> A year ago we had a sexual harassment issue. The local used it as a platform to make very clear this was not just a company policy, that this kind of behavior would not be tolerated by the local. Members responded in every direction. Some sent everyone an e-mail that said, "I don't think the local has got no business doing this." And back and forth . . . an interesting exercise in democracy.

Surfacing different opinions, and drawing in more and more voices, e-mail exchanges of this type help a local remain vibrant and relevant, if also a bit contentious at times.

One final educational gain involves gaining access to distant experts when and how needed, as this anecdote from a union trainer illustrates:

> Five years ago, when I got a tough technical question in my safety class, I'd have had to say, "Well, I have to get back to you." I'd call back to the union office, hoping there's a person in the office and not out in the field somewhere working. I'd call in—"Run this down for me. Find out what you can find."
>
> Now, if I can't find it on the Net, I've got the e-mail addresses of [key] people, like our industrial hygienist. I'll simply e-mail him in Oregon. I'll call another one on his beeper: "I need information on such-and-such, asap. And if you have any questions, call me. Fax or e-mail me the answer." And then later I'll go check my e-mail. He knows. He can search it quicker than I can, because it's his business. He can get in and out of there while I'm still hunting around.
>
> I have the capability to combine my pager service with my computer, and then go back to the class the next day and say—"My researcher found this for me, and here are our results." Somebody will ask—"And where's is he at?" "He's in Seattle, Washington." "How did you get a hold of him?" "Used a computer!" "I didn't know you could do that." And then, after class, you've got to stay late because now they want to know how they can begin to do it.

Modeling the wide range of computer abilities, as in sharply reducing information-retrieval time, helps send the valuable message—Labor is where it is at!

Political Action

Reams of pages could and should be written about the remarkable difference computers have made in labor's electioneering, lobbying, and political efforts. Some insight is available from activist Carl Cantrell's account of recent efforts of his:

> On the IBEW Tenth District Web site (www.ibew10th.org) that I maintain in my spare time, I was able to add links to sites of all AFL-CIO–endorsed 1998 congressional candidates in Arkansas, North Carolina, South Carolina, and Tennessee (my home state).
>
> With e-mail, unions have the potential to be the most vocal, effective lobbying group in state and national politics. According to the AFL-CIO, there were 193,000 union members in Tennessee in 1997. Assuming that 25 percent of members are on-line, what if elected representatives received 48,250 e-mail messages from Tennessee union members on the morning of a vote in the Tennessee legislature? Would that have impact and change minds?
>
> The IBEW in Tennessee saw a need for a Tennessee Electricians Licensing Law during the last state legislative session. I remember getting a phone call on Thursday, asking me to contact as many of my members as possible before the following Tuesday. There was an important vote coming up in the house on the licensing bill, and it was felt that we badly needed to lobby for our bill.
>
> As anyone may guess, it can be very difficult to follow through on such a request. First, the local officer doesn't really have time to make that many phone calls because there are other "fires" to put out. Then, after making several tries and finally reaching a particular member by phone, that member has to be energized enough to actually follow through on the request.
>
> Getting members to write letters is even harder because that requires even more commitment of their time. However, with e-mail, a request like this becomes easily manageable, for one letter is written, and within five minutes is sent to all members who are on-line. Using my 25 percent membership estimate, in my local of 400 members, within five minutes I can send mail to 100 at no cost, and my letters will be in their e-mail boxes in less than two minutes.
>
> To make it even easier for my members to respond, I can even write a political action letter for them to forward. They simply "click," and what is now their letter is forwarded on to its destination with their return address on it. With a few strokes of a keypad, a union office

should be able to create a flood of e-mail letters to congressional representatives. No other group has the potential and membership numbers that we do.

Comparable tales were shared with me by other union activists, men and women who understand the indispensability of political clout.

Especially valued, then, is the ability of political action e-mail to galvanize a rapid response:

> Several times we been sent a "Rapid Response" e-mail message, asking us to phone the legislators and tell them somethin' about workman's comp, or something that is going on. I would get copies made, and I'd put them up around the plant so that people would see them. And I would then talk to the people . . . and more people would talk about it . . . more and more people have been complimentin' me on it. Before, it would have been a phone call. Or maybe I'd hear at a meetin'. This is much faster.

Faxes are also very helpful here, especially when a local is too small to have an office or computer.

Problems remain, and not simply the shortage of political action funds with which to do everything desirable. Consider this remark from a local union president:

> There is an entire area of legislative and political action where we are in the Dark Ages. We don't have our members identified regarding voter registration, legislative districts, or how active they have been in these efforts. We need to get on this issue quickly if we are to have half a chance of competing with the high-tech political operations that oppose us.

Others with whom I talked or exchanged e-mail agree the political front needs shoring up, though they were quick to also applaud progress already made.

On-line political initiatives over the Internet *can* be successful. More than 25 percent of all voters were on-line during the 1996 election, and about 10 percent made their voting decisions based upon information they received via the Internet. In both the Dole and Clinton campaigns, one-third of their volunteers got involved through the Web (Connell). Labor obviously has a great opportunity here!

Particularly progressive unions are already moving to empower members by directing them to *Vote Watch*, where they can click and check their representative's voting record. Or to *Thomas,* where they can read for themselves proposed laws currently before Congress. In many such creative ways, informatics, and especially its computer component, can help Labor win its fair share of (cyberspace-aided) political campaigns.

Case Study: Wining Big!

Especially valued are victories in political contests pundits thought Labor would lose. Thanks, however, in large part to ways computers help coordinate complex political "wars," the pundits, not Labor, lose.

Typical is the situation posed in 1998 by the challenge of California's Proposition 226, the so-called Payroll Protection Act. It was favored in polls by 70 to 30 percent at the outset, and Labor looked a sure loser.

Part of a nationally coordinated effort by anti-labor forces, the act would have required unions to collect written permission every year from every member before any part of their dues could be used for political action (a nightmarish task required of no other mass-membership organization). This would have drained time, effort, and resources in a very costly way, stigmatized Labor, and probably detracted from the quantity and quality of membership services (Corn).

Labor turned to the data-processing power of computers, the spread of fax equipment, the immediacy of cellular phone access, the persuasiveness of videos and TV "infomercials," and a great Web site.

Computers, in particular, helped in the coordination of 24,000 volunteers (20,000 of them new activists) who visited over 18,000 worksites. They walked more than 5,000 precincts. And they made 600,000 phone calls and sent out 4 million pieces of mail (Anon., *L.A. Times*).

After Labor rallied the troops and waged an extraordinary uphill struggle—one significantly aided by informatics—the act was defeated on June 2 by a 54 to 46 percent vote (with 67 percent of an aroused union electorate voting against it). While the campaign cost over $23 million, it succeeded in energizing California unionists as never before, and their vote (71 to 29 percent) proved the decisive factor in one of the most significant union political wins in years (M. Hall).

Reality Check

Naturally, the service-provision picture is not without tension and problems.

Typical is the impatience of some enthusiasts with those who exaggerate the difficulties entailed:

> Christ, the data base you should be able to build from laptops is what you need to win or lose your grievances! Right there—you have a little file—here are the ones we've won; here are the ones we've lost. Here are the key words from the ones we've won—here are the key words from the ones we've lost. Hello! This is *not* rocket science.

A local union president traces stress to a serious disconnect between eager rank-and-filers and top officers intent on staying in tight control:

> We have an institutional denial that we are "managers," and we also hate the detail of strategic planning. These habits work against us utilizing computers to the max. Those who do are also the activists who stress the top dogs the most. Therefore, they have a hard time being heard. The ranks, however, go on finding the best uses of computers without regard to the retarded practices of the upper officeholders, and they are making progress. The activists are way ahead of the bureaucracy already, and we will learn from those who push the envelope.

Tensions between enthusiasts and opponents promise to take a toll until computer use is far more commonplace. When, in a very few years, the equipment is voice-dictated/voice-responsive, and far more intelligence has been built into software, the situation should ease considerably.

Summary

Abe Raskin, the now-retired dean of labor journalism, believed that "reorganizing the organized must transcend all other union priorities if those inside, but divorced from any sense of genuine involvement, are to become bona fide trade unionists." Unless and until this was achieved, the movement would remain in severe jeopardy (Raskin, 13).

Now, with the timely aid of computers, Labor has a better chance than ever to reduce apathy, improve morale, and enliven unionism.

It can also foster the high quality of identity that can help weld the rank-and-file into an inspired and empowered social movement. No small matter this, for as a close student of union realities, Prof. Marick F. Masters, explains, "current members are often the most effective communicators with potential ones, and their systematic mobilization for this purpose is arguably the most powerful tool in Labor's organizing arsenal" (Masters, 161).

Recommended Resources

Exercise 1: Picture your union and/or local in 2005. What new services are being offered to members? How are they being paid for? How might computer uses help?

Exercise 2: Imagine non-union workers in 2005 that your union and/or local might want to unionize. What might be some of their service needs that, if provided by your Labor organization, might help in unionizing them? How might computer uses help?

AFL-CIO Community Services. *If You Think Unions Are Only Interested in Wages and Benefits, Think Again.* Washington, DC: AFL-CIO, 1997. An attractive, low-cost, and yet also thorough-going pamphlet that covers a wide array of services too few in Labor or in the general public know about or appreciate.

Shostak, Arthur B. *Robust Unionism: Innovations in the Labor Movement.* Ithaca, NY: ILR Press, 1991. Field research discussion of over 200 creative services, many of which are known only to those directly involved, while all warrant greater recognition. The voice of the skeptics is heard, and rebutted. Many informatics aids are highlighted, but computer uses per se receive little attention, reflecting the 1990 date of the research.

The Citizenship Project (VOTE!)—An immigrant labor/community–based organization, founded in 1994 in response to the passage of Prop. 187 in California. Now, a network of local organizing projects dedicated to expanded citizenship, including union organizing and cross-border Labor rights. Web site: www.newcitizen.com

Vote Watch can be accessed at pathfinder.com/ @RIdKD6LZig MAQKqCQ/index.html, and *Thomas* at thomas.loc.gov

See also the *Elections USA* site at http://www.geocities.com/ CapitolHill/6228/ Exceptionally comprehensive—reports from different states, all kinds of polls (including socioeconomic issues polls), links to selected newspaper articles covering politics and policy-related topics, and the early reporting and polls re the 2000 presidential race.

Labor's fix on candidates and issues can be had from *Voting Record,* an AFL-CIO service now on-line at www.aflcio.org/vrecord. You can access, download, and print out complete files on candidates and such topics as Fast Track, fair wages, education, health care, workplace safety, and workers' rights.

The Cornell Law School's web page can be found at www.law.cornell.edu.

Findlaw's Internet Web site is at www.findlaw.com

See also *Recent Developments in Labor and Employment Law,* a free service from Ross Runkel; available at labor-emp@willamette.edu

---

Reading 1

How a Personal Computer Can Enhance Union Political Action

Charles H. Laskonis
International Brotherhood of Electrical Workers,
IBEW, Local 364

Labor's political power is a key to Labor's prospects, a point well known to union activists, especially those "netizens" already busy using their computers to make a difference. The informal and engag-

ing essay below recounts how, after a full-time electrician got his children a home computer, he rapidly discovered it could help empower him as an unofficial labor lobbyist, increase his grasp of complex matters (MAI, etc.), bring him in touch with world-class activists (Noam Chomsky, etc.), and help him help others unionize their workplace. An unabashed enthusiast for union uses of computer power, Charles H. Laskonis is a model of the "Do it!" rank-and-filer on whom Labor's future hinges.

The day our computer came, I was very excited for my three kids. They now use it for hours on end, and continue to amaze me with what they learn on their own.

After a few weeks of fiddling around with it (with help from the kids), I felt comfortable enough to try to go on-line, and check out a couple of sites. There were some news sites, sports sites, and some political sites, and I was thrilled by all the information that was available by just using a couple of keystrokes and a mouse. It took a little time, but I soon became good enough to "surf the Web."

I knew from my union's magazine that the IBEW had a Web site, so I checked it out. It had a lot of information, including links to many IBEW locals around the country. Another link led me to the AFL-CIO Web site, with lots of great information to move our labor movement forward. Additionally, it had many ways unionists can mobilize together for good causes.

Now I felt I was on to something that could be very helpful and informative. The labor links could take unionists anywhere in the labor movement at the touch of a couple of keystrokes. I was beginning to imagine the possibilities.

A Democratic Party candidate for governor I had heard about in my home state of Illinois, Glenn Poshard, was a strong supporter of Labor and unionism. I accessed his Web page and found a speech deploring the North American Free Trade Agreement (NAFTA) and what it had done to working families across America. What a great candidate for Labor!

I asked one of the local's officers if they had heard of this guy. "No," was the answer I got. I asked another and got the same response. How could it be that a young 32-year-old apprentice like me was the only one who had heard of this guy and, in fact, knew of him fairly well, while no other members, including my local's leaders, had? I knew the answer to this question: The Internet!

Some time later, the Teamsters local in my hometown held a rally against "Fast Track" trade legislation, and Poshard was the keynote speaker. I was shocked to see only two other members of our thousand-member local. Only a small handful of other labor people came to hear him speak. As I was in line to get a beer (you've got to love those Teamsters), I mentioned the poor turnout to an operating engineer. I was not at all surprised to hear him say that he had first heard of Poshard and his strong union stance from the Internet.

While Clinton was busy pushing for Fast Track legislation, I was made aware on the Internet of a grass-roots campaign being waged against it. Unionists were urged over the Internet to contact their representatives in Congress and to strongly voice their displeasure with the proposed legislation. Many unionists, including myself, heeded the call, and Fast Track was beaten back.

Another key issue that I became involved with at the grass-roots level was the Multilateral Agreement on Investment (MAI). It would give corporations unlimited power to override labor legislation all over the world. Again, legislators *en masse* had to be contacted. Again, many unionists rose to the occasion and beat back the proposed legislation. Much credit for the legislation's defeat is now given to the Internet grass-roots campaign.

Democracy and the labor movement were finally working as intended! I could only wonder, if the Internet had been more widespread during the original NAFTA debate, might it have been defeated too?

Prior to my having a computer I had come across a book by Noam Chomsky called *Class War*. It is a marvelous book, telling historically and currently who the real power holders were and are, and the tactics they use to control people, and how they take democracy out of the hands of everyday working people. I was completely captivated by his insights, particularly relating to the American labor movement and the class war the powerful wealthy have waged on labor unions, the poor, and working people in general.

I feel this man is a genius and his observations could aid the labor movement greatly. The *New York Times* has called Chomsky "arguably the most important intellectual alive." Every unionist and working person should hear his ideas and observations on our society and government.

After subscribing to the Internet, I had to look for more information about Chomsky. I searched the Web, and of course there were many references. One is his official page at MIT, where he is a world-renowned professor of linguistics. I found a list of speaking dates, including one with an e-mail address for a nearby Central Labor Council (CLC).

A couple of my fellow IBEW local members and I went to hear the Chomsky lecture, which was very informative and inspiring. Afterward, we went to a reception at the Carpenters' Union hall, where we were able to talk to Chomsky personally for about an hour. His book, *Class War,* changed the way I look at the world. The help of the Internet and easy access to all his works have changed my beliefs and my life greatly. Without the Internet, I doubt this would have ever happened to this extent.

From the Chomsky site I found Z-net, whose "mission statement" is "A Community of People Concerned About Social Change." This is an interactive Web site that originates from *Z Magazine,* an alternative media source not captive to moneyed interests. Unionists can learn from "Economic Human Rights Watch," "Foreign Policy Watch," "Monopoly Politics," and "Corporate Watch," to name just a few.

Z also provides on-line college courses. They call it Learning On Line, or L.O.L. University. This helps socially concerned people and activists take courses via the Internet to learn or upgrade their skills so they can be more effective activists, teachers, or members for their specific causes to help reshape the world more positively.

There are also many Z forums where users can post comments or ask questions. Activists and people like Howard Zinn, Michael Albert, and Noam Chomsky have their own forum boards. They answer questions, give their reactions to events, and provide ideas on all kinds of political, economic, and other social subjects. I have e-mailed Chomsky via his Z forum many times and received e-mail replies in almost every instance.

Just think, great political thinkers such as these available to us at our fingertips on an almost daily, or sometimes hourly, basis. Think how long it would take to exchange ideas and comments if one had to write, mail, and wait for a response to the many questions I have had answered. It may have taken the better part of a year. Now ideas are exchanged almost instantly, with the only minor delay being the amount of time it takes to ponder a responsible reply or follow-up questions.

There is still another Z-net forum for discussion about labor unions that I partake of frequently. I have given advice to people trying to organize labor unions at their workplaces in areas all over the country, people whom I would have undoubtedly never even met had it not been for personal computers and the Internet.

One particular organizing campaign I have encouraged involves Cathy, a nurse I have never met, who solicited advice from Z-net's Labor Issues forum. She was trying to unionize 57 other nurses when we started our electronic dialog. Recently, after their organizing efforts had progressed, she e-mailed me before their NLRB election and wrote, "At times, I feel you are right there beside me pushing me on and helping. After all, you are available to me at about any time of the day through this e-mail!" Their campaign went extremely well, and they gained recognition rather easily.

Another great way to exchange ideas to move the labor movement forward is a number of union listserves that I receive e-mail from. Unionists who are part of these listserves interact with each other by sending articles and giving their ideas concerning topics that affect the labor movement. Through some of these, as mentioned, I have written my congressman and senators on all kinds of campaigns and issues and have received replies.

People that certainly would have never known each other even existed were it not for the Internet now exchange ideas and information and influence policy almost instantly. I have just recently initiated plans with my IBEW local to run a listserve for our local's members who have e-mail access.

It really boggles the mind to think how far we have come from a short time ago. Think of all the possibilities the labor movement could accomplish with the free exchange of ideas at this pace. With the Internet, and the subsequent "on-ramp to the information superhighway," there is almost no boundary to limit the exchange of dialog and ideas. Think of the possibilities the labor movement has in the future, provided we use the Internet to its fullest potential.

As Michael Moore, the creator of the award-winning documentaries *Roger and Me* and *The Big One,* urged in his book, *Downsize This!*, "If you abhor computers and/or the Internet, get over it. Corporate America has inadvertently given us an incredible tool to reach one another cheaply and quickly. Let's use it before they figure out a way to take it away from us!"

And don't think they are not trying to. In a recent interview, Bill Gates said that the two biggest problems with the Internet are the lack of more effective advertising and the ease with which anybody can post information.

I strongly urge every unionist who has the means to get on-line and participate in this new dimension of our labor movement. What a great communications and political tool unionists now have to use to change the world for the better!

Charles H. Laskonis is a rank-and-file member in good standing since 1992 of the International Brotherhood of Electrical Workers, Local 364. Charles lives in Rockford, Illinois, with his wife Laura, and their three children, Charles, Hillary, and Jacob. (He can be reached via e-mail at laskonis@xta.com).

2

Using Computers as an Organizing Aid

Most important, we must organize as we have never organized before. . . .
—John Sweeney, AFL-CIO President,
Fortune, September 28, 1998

Arguably, organizing is one of the most difficult jobs—if not *the* most difficult job—anyone can have in Labor's ranks, bar none! An organizer is at one and the same time "a secret agent, salesman, public relations expert, writer, human relations expert, and, above all, a charismatic leader" (Beeler and Kurshenbaum, 42). Holders of the role can make a good case that it belongs on a list of the 100 "Most Difficult Jobs" in the *U.S. Dictionary of Occupational Titles.*

Why bother, then? Because with natural attrition, plant shutdowns, the sending of American jobs offshore, and the loss of jobs to "smart" automation, Labor has no choice. Because research correlates union membership with economic and political power, shrinking rolls mean shrinking clout, which means shrinking gains.

There comes a point, one which Labor in America may be very close to, where union density "falls to such a low level that it seriously weakens a union's capacity to service current members, let alone organize new ones" (Masters, 7, 80). Greater and more use of computers may help change this rapidly for the better; it will certainly introduce new wrinkles.

Charting the Challenge

One of the nation's most admired organizers, John Wilhelm, president of the Hotel and Restaurant Employees Union, warns that "if we cannot organize more successfully in the private sector over the next several years . . . the labor movement in its present form will wither away" (Whitford, 180).

Labor's membership base has shrunk from more than 25 percent of the private-sector work force in the 1950s to less than 10 percent at the end of the 1990s (Whitford, 180). Exactly where its strength has lain, in the heavily unionized ranks of manufacturing employees, is where the cuts in payroll are deepest. From the 1960s to the 1990s the nation's semi-skilled operatives have slid from being 35 percent of the work force to less than 20 percent, and their numbers are falling still (Heckscher, 63).

Most recently, since 1990, factory productivity has been soaring at the fastest rate (3.6 percent annually) in the post–World War II era. Manufacturing industries that use computers heavily have increased their productivity growth from 3.2 percent annually in the 1980s to 5.7 percent in the 1990s (Mandel). A firm, for example, that used to take 12 hours now takes 3 to build a residential air conditioner: "Our work is up by 25% over a seven or eight year period, with one-third fewer workers. In 1991, we had 108,000 U.S. employees; today [1997] we have 72,000." (Smart, 4).

Not surprisingly, therefore, union density (union membership as a percentage of employed workers) fell from 35 percent in the 1950s to only 14 percent in 1998 (a 29 percent drop in the 1980s alone!) (Greenhouse, A-20). In the 1980s, Labor experienced its first absolute loss in membership since the 1920s (Masters, 1). More recently, between 1990 and 1995, Labor lost another 2 percent of its membership (Polman).

In 1997, organizing drives brought in some 400,000 new members, a very high number immediately cheered by labor boosters. Labor also won the highest percentage of NLRB elections in a decade (LRA September 1998). But this was offset by many layoffs, considerable outsourcing, a small number of workers voting to decertify their unions, and the inability of half of the new members to secure a first contract by December 31, 1997 (Burkins). There was a loss of 159,000 in union membership, though gains among public workers helped make it the first year in several decades with no net loss (public sector gains, however, are slowing) (Greenhouse, A-20).

If labor is just to stand still as a percentage of the work force, a net gain of about 300,000 new members a year is thought necessary. With a 50 percent win rate and average unit size of 75, that would require 11,000 NLRB elections—nearly four times the current level (LRA March 1998). A net gain of 1,250,000 new members is required to move Labor up just one percentage point (Trumka, 1996).

Instead, in 1998, the percentage of organized members slipped to 13.9 percent from 14.1 percent the previous year, and from a post–World War II high of 16,200,000 in 1983, the total membership has come down now to 16,110,000 members (Greenhouse, A-20). Unionization at the end of the twentieth century is close to the low point it was at 60 years ago when the 1935 Wagner Act first lent it government support.

Labor Fights Back

Despite, or perhaps because of, the threat of "death by a thousand cuts," in 1997 far more large international unions racked up a net gain, and far fewer, a net loss in membership, than at any time since the 1930s. Eight large unions had an unprecedented membership growth of 3 percent each. Unions held—and won—more representation elections in 1997 than in any other year in this decade (LRA July/August 1998). And, as AFL-CIO president John Sweeney likes to point out, several unions met his goal of devoting as much as 30 percent of their budget for the first time to organizing (Greenhouse).

In May of 1998, Rich Trumka, the AFL-CIO's secretary treasurer, proudly and loudly relayed these facts to me during an Albany airport coffeeshop encounter. He pointedly boasted: "We're on the move! We know we have no choice, and we're fighting for our lives! *Never* count us out!"

Informatics and Organizing

What may account for some of the new pizzazz is the growing use organizers are making of cellular phones, computers, faxes, videos, and the other empowering components of informatics.

In particular, more and more organizers appear to appreciate the computer's extraordinary capacity for data storage, analysis, and re-trievability. Carl Cantrell, a rank-and-filer who offers union workshops in computer uses (and who authored the wide-ranging essay after this chapter), outlines some of the many possibilities:

> In a hypothetical situation, employees of Company XYZ have come to me, a union organizer, and asked for help in organizing their workplace. They even bring me a list of employee names to help me get started.
>
> The company is a publicly traded company, so from Hoovers On-line (www.hoovers.com), an Internet site with hundreds of companies listed, I find the name of the CEO, the board of directors, last year's gross sales number, employee growth figures, and even the company's Web site address. I visit the company's Web site and find more information.
>
> I find enough that I now go to the Department of Labor's Web site (www.dol.gov) and request a copy of the 5500 report that all companies who have pension plans are required to file. Under the Freedom of Information Act, I can legally request and get the report; I just have to have enough information to identify the plan. This report gives me more financial information on the company.
>
> After researching Company XYZ and deciding that the company is a viable organizing target, and after getting my organizing committee set up, I go into action.
>
> First, since I already have the employee names, I again turn to my computer and go to People Search (www.cedar.buffalo.edu/AdServ/person-search.html), an on-line people locator, to find and download the addresses and phone numbers of all plant employees. Next, I access Mapquest (www.mapquest.com), an on-line map service, to download maps of those addresses. Each map not only shows the street where my organizing target lives, but a star is placed where his house should be. I divide my organizing committee up and hand each of them a list of names, complete with phone numbers, addresses, and even maps for house calls. I do all this without leaving my office and at no cost.
>
> Then, as the campaign progresses, my Web master is constantly updating our Web site with new, directed information aimed at perspective members within the plant. Leaflets with our Web site address are passed out, and our Web page becomes the primary place for the passing of information. With very little investment of money, we look professional and we are taken seriously.

While offered as a hypothetical example, Carl's scenario resembles a growing number of which I was told about over three years of interviewing.

Another activist, a woman who had helped organize her own workplace from inside, recalled with pleasure how helpful she had found using her computer:

> When we were still unorganized, I developed a database that I kept up every year. It contained names, addresses, departments of prospective members. And a minor profile, of whether or not they were leaning toward us or toward management. So we had everything already mapped out, and had a head start, when we were ready to unionize. This beat using index cards, because it made manipulating data easier. When things changed, when you got new information, it was easier to enter.

Others told similar tales of using computers to systematize matters and get beyond organizing on an ad hoc, expedient, and improvisational basis.

Even before a campaign is launched, computers can help with the underlying research. A local union president who has pioneered in this told me wistfully:

> Traditionally, if you've got companies in your area and you want to do research on them, we've got to get a helluva a lot more sophisticated about them before we touch them. Know who they are. Know what their history is. Know what's going on within that company . . . before we start moving around. Generally, we do some surface-like research, and see what develops. We've got to get a helluva lot better than that.

Overall, I heard much more about advances than about disinterest or disappointment, though everyone seemed to agree that the uses here were just getting under way.

Not surprisingly, some tension can emerge between pre-computer old-timers and computer enthusiasts, as witness this tale:

> When I'm organizing I've got my laptop in my car trunk. I carry all my stuff on it. I've compiled material on my computer from different newsletters that can be modified for each location. I'll frequently pull out my laptop, and say, "Here's what I'd like to put out. Do you have any suggestions?"
>
> Our lead organizer, within whom I work all the time, criticized the hell out of me the first time I did this: "It's absurd. You could do it later on. It was not necessary. You were showing off." I thought it would

impress this prospective member to see someone take out a $3,000 laptop and say, "I think I already have some work on here that I've been doing that can help you."

He knows that I'm right, as much as he has been criticizing me for it. And he now relies very heavily on this, on my ability here. In a subsequent meeting, the prospective members have asked me, "Do you have your laptop with you today? Can we work on an idea of ours?"

On the one day in negotiations that I didn't have it, one of my guys said to me, "Let's draft some new language, a new proposal during the next break." But I didn't have it with me . . . and I really missed it.

Even while meeting, then, with prospective members, a savvy organizer can use a laptop to have them design on the spot the kind of contract that directly appeals to them. It can be researched for legality, matched with relevant area terms, etc., and assessed in real time . . . while onlookers smile with appreciation and approval.

Saving Time

Organizers especially value the gains in time saved made possible by computers. Typical is this tale from a very pleased staffer:

In the first campaign that I did I didn't have a computer in the office. I was trying to do it all by hand, using the old forms, and there were almost 70 people in the unit. It started to overwhelm me. Because that was taking all my time, just trying to keep the record straight. Since I knew about database management, I said, "This is crazy!" So, I did it on my computer at home. Then I brought it in, and showed it at the local office. This is how much more time I would have to be out there organizing if I didn't have to do the paper stuff. And it would be more up-to-date. And so on. And now, we *all* have computers.

Similarly, the staffer for a major union in the public sector boasted:

Organizing has benefited by being able to use the text and graphics programs to generate organizing materials, such as flyers, announcements, and cartoons in literally a few minutes.

And a director of organizing noted with satisfaction:

> Several e-forms have been created by organizers to replace paper forms they had been using. Travel authorization and expense voucher forms have both been converted to an electronic format . . . this makes gathering the information for tax-filing much less challenging.

Time being among the scarcest of variables, especially for organizers fighting simultaneously on several fronts, gains here are very highly valued.

Coordination Challenges

Organizing campaigns get larger and more complicated all the time. An organizer with an upbeat point of view explains:

> I think database management will prove especially beneficial—with the increase in organizing now. As bigger drives are happening, and people are learning to stay in touch with the drive . . . by using database management, it makes things more at your fingertips. Like workers' names, and locations, and so on. Like people we haven't called in the last six months. Maybe we want to redo it. Like maybe we want to poke around in this campaign again. You can have this information at your fingertips, where you can query it. I think you might follow up on it—but if it is in a file drawer somewhere you don't see it, and one day you pull it out and now you've got to start all over again.

Undervalued by some unknowing outsiders, the ability of computers to hold together and make sense of a myriad of data means a lot to people charged with actually managing campaigns.

Organizing Using the Web

While it sounds far-fetched today, an especially creative organizer already envisions a time soon when unorganized workers will be invited to sign up by a message on a Web site designed especially for this purpose:

> If you want to organize, "click here." And you then offer all kinds of information. If they agree, you can download an authorization card: "Sign this card if you wish, in the privacy of your own home and away from your employer, and mail it in." I then print you up as a potential

union member on my daily information list. Not 10 pages, just one paragraph. Let's face it, going out to the factory gate and handing out leaflets doesn't work anymore. That's just a dead issue! Mass mediums don't work! Small mediums do!

Another variation here would emphasize the union wage advantage, as conveyed directly to a prospective member:

We have written a program that allows us to take information [about wages and benefits] from a non-union worker [whom we are trying to organize] and compare that with what they would receive from the area union contract. The program then prints out a comparison on one page that looks like two paychecks. We are putting this program on our Web site so individuals can do the comparison in the privacy of their own home.

An organizer might go into a non-union workplace via a cyberspace portal, and actually "talk" to prospective members at and during their work shift:

I'm trying now to organize [name deleted] company. The employees all have computer terminals on their own desk. There's nothing in the law that prevents me from sending e-mail from my office to theirs, unless their employer puts a firewall up. It's legal! So if I'm going to reach them, I'm going to flood them. As for getting e-mail addresses, that's easy: You get someone inside to provide them. It's usually their first initial and last name—at "com."

Similarly, a high-level staffer at a very savvy union expects to soon initiate what he is calling a "silent blitz":

First we will create a target program on our Web site to make our case. Then we will print up our cards with this site highlighted. When we go into the store to make some kind of small purchase, we will give a card to an employee and say there is something at this URL you will find interesting. Even before an employer knows what has hit him, we will have blitzed the entire store, or even a chain of these stores.

How far any of these Information Age innovations will go remains to be seen, as employers are likely to resist with shields of one kind or another. But the creative thinking is in the right direction, and some initial gains can be expected from a fresh initiative. At the very least, tongues will wag, heads will turn, and labor will gain valuable recognition for derring-do and commitment.

Reality Check

It is vital not to exaggerate the contribution computers can make in organizing. They are the "high tech" component of a formula that also calls for "high touch" if it is to reward as desired. A computer-savvy organizer urged me to understand that only as he earned and held the trust and friendship of prospective members did a drive have a chance—regardless of how much razzle-dazzle a computer might bring to the effort:

> The union is built in the street. In the alleys. In the easements. In the coffee shops. In the gin mills. It is not built because of me standing there with a leaflet, like an asshole. Or because of me issuing e-mail or press releases. That's not how we build unions. That's bureaucracy. Movement doesn't come from the top; only from the bottom up.

Similarly, another staffer warned that shadow, rather than substance, was often the situation in the front lines:

> In the organizing end of it, we're in the Neanderthal stage. We want to start using computers . . . like if you've got an organizing drive going on, instead of taking a piece of poster board and mapping your stuff out, and seeing what you have and don't have, you could throw that on a computer. And then you can analyze it a hell of a lot faster. We used to spend hours puttin' little stickers on poster boards, and this cannot change soon enough.

Far too small a proportion of union funds is currently being allocated to organizing, let alone organizing aided by new computer hardware and software. Unless and until this rapidly changes, the scene will host more wistful notions than actual efforts, and the decline will persist.

Summary

There is no doubt that the labor movement in this country is in grave peril. Andy Stern, president of one of most assertive organizing unions

(SEIU), maintains that "nonunion workers are ready to join unions. . . . The question is whether unions are ready to reach out to them" (Stern).

Should organizing make new gains, current members can profit from improved bargaining power, the unions from higher dues intake relative to servicing costs, and every level of the movement from greater political clout. Should organizing not improve, Labor's slide into insignificance seems assured. Informatics in general, and computer uses in particular, can help, and more creative, empowering uses might just prove the critical difference.

Recommended Resources

Exercise 1: Imagine your union or local's organizing effort in 2005: How might it differ from today? What different targets, tools, and strategies? What particular part might computers play? Why?

Exercise 2: If you were asked in 2005 to hire new organizers, what skills, attitudes, and abilities would you seek? How would the list differ, if at all, from the present? Would computers be part of your consideration? How? Why?

AFL-CIO. *Communities@Work: A Guide to Restoring Our Right to Organize.* Washington, DC: AFL-CIO, 1998. (Phone 202–637–5042). A new guide for unionists eager to enlist community groups in the fight for improvements in the right to organize. Emphasizes the message that well-paying union jobs are good for a community.

Aronowitz, Stanley. *From the Ashes of the Old: American Labor and America's Future.* New York: Houghton Mifflin, 1998. A vigorous and challenging assessment of past mistakes, current shortcomings, and promising directions for a new labor movement. Urges commitment of vastly larger resources to organizing, especially in the South, and in campaigns aimed at white-collar clericals and professionals and managers.

Bronfenbrenner, Kate et al., eds. *Organizing to Win: New Research on Union Strategies.* Ithaca, NY: Cornell University Press, 1998. Thirty-nine new essays examine the range and effectiveness of innovative organizing models and their potential contribution to a transformed labor movement.

Yates, Michael D. *Why Unions Matter*. New York: Monthly Review Press, 1998. Excellent analysis of the advantages of being unionized. Also includes advice for new approaches likely to help build a democratic, more independent, politically progressive, and tough-minded labor movement.

For more information about the AFL-CIO and organizing, contact the Organizing Institute at 815 16th Street NW, Washington, DC 20006; phone (202) 639–6200; fax (202) 639-6264. Or e-mail organizers @aol.com.

Reading 2

Sensing the Speed Picking Up

Carl D. Cantrell
International Brotherhood of Electrical Workers,
IBEW, Local 2113

Using a computer can substantially help an organizing drive—or so explains Carl D. Cantrell in the engaging essay below. He did not wait for a Royal Invitation before teaching himself how to prepare a Web site for his IBEW District; he just did it, and then won the district's grateful approval. Now, with its blessings, he shows others the many benefits of creating a labor presence in cyberspace, and he enjoys finding how excited they are to discover computer-based possibilities. Cantrell believes many like him are out there, available on a pro bono basis to help locals and union get on with it—especially as regards the organizing challenge—and for Labor's sake, this scenario cannot unfold soon enough.

Every year a "Progress Meeting" is held in each district of the IBEW, as required by our Constitution. This year [1998], since I had developed a Web site for the 10th District of the IBEW and had been maintaining it for the last several months, I was invited to present it.

I arrived early and set up a monitor and a laptop with the Web site on it in the hotel lobby, so people could come by and check out the Web site as they were registering. There were about 150 attendees at the Progress Meeting, made up of business managers and chief officers of IBEW locals in Arkansas, Tennessee, North Carolina, and South Carolina. I had several people stop by my table, and most seemed very interested.

I made a formal presentation to each of the workshops during the meeting. I used a monitor and a laptop with Microsoft's PowerPoint. I explained to a very attentive audience what the Internet is, how to access it, and then what would be found once they got on-line. I explained the value of using e-mail instead of postage for communication. The last part of my presentation was actually going through and demonstrating the 10th District's Web site.

A big part of my presentation was trying to show ways that the IBEW could and should be using the Internet. I explained how it could be a very useful tool for communicating with our members and educating them. We can use it for lobbying, and I used examples of how we can mobilize our members by e-mail, and how powerful a tool e-mail could be to their elected representatives.

I used examples of the Web in organizing. I had employees in a fictional company provide me a list of employee names and ask my help in organizing their workplace.

Since the company was a publicly traded company, I accessed Hoover's On-line to get the name of the CEO, board members, gross income of the company, and the company's Web site address.

From its Web site, I got enough information to go to the DOL Web site and request Form 5500, which every company with a pension plan is required to submit to the Department of Labor each year. From this, I decided that yes, this company was "ripe" for organizing.

Next, I used the Internet to assist my organizing committee. From the Internet, I got each employee's address and phone number. From another Web site, I downloaded a map of that address. I then armed my organizing committee with names, addresses, phone numbers, and even maps for house calls. All this without leaving my office.

And, of course, I would post an educational Web site for information during the campaign.

My audience at the Progress Meeting seemed especially interested in my links to law and the regs, such as the Medical Leave Act, the Americans with Disabilities Act, and the National Labor Relations Act, etc.

In the Q&A I got lots of questions. People made statements like, "We're fixin' to get on-line real soon, and this has helped!" "We didn't realize there was so much out there!" I gave out a feedback page, and later enjoyed reading comments like, "The IBEW should have been doing this a long time ago!" "Glad you are leading us into the Information Age!" There was not one negative voice, not at the meeting or in the anonymous feedback.

Since the presentation I've received several new e-mail addresses from attendees to add to the district's list. Another local within the district has gone on-line.

The district's Web page was launched in November of '97. We started out slow, but since the presentation we're getting up to 50 hits per day, with a total hit count approaching 6,000.

Several months before, I started my career in Web sites by doing one for our local. I had had an e-mail address and 5 megs of server space, but nothing to put there. I decided in June 1997 to use that space for my union, IBEW Local Union 2113 (www.ibew2113.org). After several months of "practice" on my "unofficial site," I asked my local for permission to make it official. They were glad to give it to me. For several months after that, I continued to pay for the Internet Service Provider. During that time, our Web site cost my union nothing.

On my local's Web site (http://www.cdc.net/ibew12th), I make a point to create links that will be of interest to our members. Since a large portion of our members work for two companies who each have 401k plans, I have placed links to their mutual funds' Web sites. They can click and check out their investments.

Getting on the Web and using it effectively does not have to be difficult. Every local out there has someone like me who would love to volunteer to do a Web site. And like me, they probably would donate their time.

The union Web site can be used to educate our members, but let's not forget to also use it for public education. Anything that we can think of that is respectable and appropriate is not above being considered for our Web site. If our Web site gets our members coming back to it again and again, we can get excited. But if we can also get the general public coming back again and again, we have a special bonus. We can educate them.

There are other uses of the Internet that perhaps we can make use of. In the construction trades, apprentices typically work during the day and then attend school at night, sometimes many miles away from their home or work. Wouldn't it be nice if our apprentices could receive some of their training on-line from their homes? Or, what if we set up our own Web sites for on-line continuing education and training of our workers in the skills that they need?

The George Meany National Labor College could be used as Labor's Mecca on the Web, helping us keep up with rapidly changing work dynamics. Why not offer some of the excellent labor courses that George Meany is noted for over the Internet so they could be more accessible to union local leaders and members?

Posting job announcements is another place where we can use the Internet to benefit members. Already, personal bulletin boards tell where construction jobs are, where overtime is this week, and where the halls with "walk-throughs" are found. At Joe Williams's Web site (home.earthlink.net/jw716/travelers.html) in Houston, Texas, IBEW members are encouraged to leave job postings or other messages for fellow members.

There are signs of change and we are moving. Our international officers, as well as our members, have to be educated to the possibilities. Most of our leaders came up through the ranks before the age of computers and cyberspace. They are from another age where one relied upon the telephone and the manual typewriter for communications.

We should not assume too much negative of our members. A few weeks ago I was in a local fast food restaurant when what looked to be a farmer walked in. He was an older gentleman, he was a little dirty, his clothes were a little worn, and he looked as if he had been in the fields all day. He joined a group at a nearby table and after some small talk told how he had made several hundred dollars that morning trading stocks over the Internet!

He could have been a union member or a factory worker or that laborer or someone else that we want to educate, assist, or target for union membership, but sometimes overlook when we think of using high-tech. In an age of dropping membership, we could just be dead wrong!

Overall, when I think about our direction within the labor movement in using this technology, I'm optimistic. I see us moving! I see more and more locals getting on the Web. It's inevitable! I sense the speed picking up.

Carl D. Cantrell is the Web master of both the IBEW 10th District and IBEW Local 2113, Tullahoma, Tennessee. He is also the legislative chair and insurance/pension chair of the Air Engineering Metal Trades Council. He graduated in 1999 with a B.A. degree in labor studies from the AFL-CIO National Labor College of the George Meany Center. (He can be reached via e-mail at cantrell@cafes.net or http://www.cafes.net/cantrell.)

Part II

VARIATIONS ON THE THEME

In the 1990s there is no status quo. The velocity of change in information technology has seen to that.
—Don Tapscott, *The Digital Economy,* 1996

Consider just four "gee whiz!" changes underway in computer uses, and ask yourself how the lives of rank-and-file unionists may be changed by them. The first could make everything electric appear "smart." The second vastly expands our capacity to store valuable data. The third shows the way to the end of carrying money. And the fourth promises to overhaul something as prosaic, but as vital in our everyday lives, as our grocery shopping experience.

In July of 1998 Sun Microsystems unveiled the first consumer version of a distributed computing fabric "which approaches science fiction." Known as "ubiquitous computing," it may enable every home, car, telephone, TV, kitchen appliance, and other electric part of the personal environment to become empowered by a universal network—that is, to gain intelligence from a connection, with or without wires, to a global computing network. Stuff will appear "smart," as it acts without our directing it, and nothing will be the same again. The usually restrained *New York Times* headlined its first-page story "Taking a Step Toward Converting the Home into a Supercomputer" (Markoff).

Similarly, late in 1998, the Hitachi Data Systems (DS) announced the release of a disk-based storage system with a maximum capacity of 3 terabits. That roughly translates to 1.5 billion pages of printed text, give or take a few million. At 400 words a page, a typist working at 100 words per minute, 24 hours a day, 365 days a year, would need about 11,416 years to type this volume of data (Feng, July 15, 1998).

Why develop such humongous storage capacity? Because between 1997 and 2000, the amount of data stored over the past 35 years may double, thanks largely to the rise of the Internet and electronic commerce (Feng, July 15, 1998). So, how big a deal is this? A specialist comments: "What an amazing development of a 'data storage tank'! Not so long ago, people were still buying gigantic 'data silos' which literally looked like a grain silo, but held only something like 500 gigabytes. Now, terabytes is nothing, and the 'tank' comes in a little box!" (Feng, July 16, 1998).

If the items above are a bit exotic, ponder the significance of something as otherwise prosaic as toll-collecting, a historic task being reinvented by computer applications.

New information-processing systems (Automatic Vehicle Identification systems) now enable drivers to pay in advance and zip through unmanned toll booths. An on-site computer "reads" the customer's account number off a transponder as a car approaches the toll booth, verifies sufficient funds, and flashes a green light . . . to the delight of impatient motorists everywhere (albeit at the cost of many toll collector jobs) (Feng, May 22, 1998).

Plainly, we may soon be able to pay in advance for nearly anything, thereby ushering in the long-promised era of a cashless society.

Finally, consider the humdrum matter of the weekly grocery shopping trip, itself also a candidate (like nearly everything else!) for informatics overhaul. New computer-aided shopping carts can scan the items you take off the shelf and put into the cart, offer a running tab, and make suggestions for complementarities and alternative products. As well, the cart will indicate the location of these items to speed the shopping process along. It will enable you to bag the items as you roll along, pausing only long enough at the store's exit for a transponder to record the total cost before you rush on by.

Once again, an appealing gain in convenience, ease, and time, albeit at a likely cost in many jobs for grocery checkout clerks (Brier).

Previously unimagined changes are taking place. What is Labor to do about any of this? How well prepared is Labor? What could it be doing? These are the sorts of questions that preoccupied me over the three years I researched material for this book.

Rank-and-filers need Labor's help in meeting the "continuous disequilibrium" of our times. For as labor educator Charley Richardson reminds us, "from barcode scanners in supermarkets to global positioning systems in over-the-road trucks; from CNC machine tools to robotic operators (voice recognition systems) . . . change has in fact become the only constant in the workplace" (Richardson, 104).

Historians later in the twenty-first century will note that Labor struggled hard in the 1990s to counter changes washing tsunami-like over working men and women. For example, while in 1977, only about 40 percent of businesses invested in computers, by 1998 the figure had risen to more than 80 percent. And while only 25 percent of workers in 1987 used computers, the 1998 estimate was 50 percent and rapidly rising (Madrick, 44). Little wonder that a usually restrained journal, the *Economist,* believes that computerization represents "a change even more far-reaching than the harnessing of electrical power a century ago" (Cairncross).

Labor's response to date has produced three major models, three very significant responses to computerization. The first has an organization do very little. The second would have it do first this, then that, and then the next thing—with little rhyme or reason. And the third model would have it do much, though, as I will argue later in Part III, nowhere as much as desirable.

In this second part of the book, Chapter 3 explores the first model, Cyber Naught Unionism, so-called because it represents a bare-minimum response to our changing times. Chapter 4 focuses on Cyber Drift Unionism, which combines aimlessness with thoughtlessness. In sharp contrast to these two hapless styles, the closing chapter highlights Cyber Gain Unionism, a proud model to aspire to, and one which sets the stage for the emergence soon (I hope) of its twenty-first-century successor, CyberUnionism.

3

Cyber Naught:
Paving Over the Cowpath

Today, inaction is the riskiest strategy.
        —Jerry Wind and Jeremy Main, *Driving Change,* 1998

Cyber Naught unions and locals seek to preserve and persist, rather than update or innovate. Where computers are concerned, they employ them only or primarily to satisfy traditional business needs, as in accounting and bookkeeping (dues and benefit records, payroll data, etc.). They are content to use data-processing systems to keep track of things and to codify standard business practices. Most are indifferent (the others, hostile) to what upgrades here might otherwise do to support people, plans, and progress.

The issue, then, is not as simple as whether or not a union or a local uses computers. Rather, the issue is why and how. Put starkly, Cyber Naught unions and locals use computers to get through the day, and do so in as flat and uninspired a way as is possible. A staffer with considerable computer skills contends as much in an e-mail to me:

> In occasional meetings with the staff of unions not using computers, I have noticed a culture of denial. They seem to be "shoveling sand against the tide while convincing themselves that the ocean will go away only if they shovel harder and faster."

Officials settle for inertia and quietism, forgetting that "anything that burns low and slow risks going out" (Packer, 72).

Much of the problem is rooted in conceptual inertia: Outdated habits of mind have far too many of these labor leaders preferring form to function, protocol to results, and rhetoric to risk-taking. This is not only about failings of intellect; it is also about failings of the spirit. For if, as Orwell warned, poverty annihilates the future, so also in its own way does poverty of vision (Orwell).

Cyber Naught power-holders want the future to be like the past, only more so. They treat unionism as if it can only be a passive institution, and they act as a deadening hand on change. In consequence, their unions and locals sleepwalk when they might stride, and they remain vulnerable in ways they hardly realize.

Indicators

How do you know you are dealing with a Cyber Naught unionist? Three clues are available: the first on first contact; the second via an indirect sign; and the third requiring a direct question. Taken in combination, they should make plain the presence of a Rip Van Winkle type, a befuddled and defensive time traveler from yesteryear.

At the outset, examine his or her business card. Naturally, it will have the mandatory union bug, a sign of solidarity. Odds are good, however, that it will not have an e-mail address, let alone a Web site URL. As well, the card-bearer may not be aware of or rue their absence. (A leading informatics guru insists, "These days, a business card without a Net address is seen as a sign that you're some kind of Jurassic manager" [Tapscott, 19].)

Second, ask how large is the union or local involved. The smaller the organization, the greater the likelihood of computerization lag.

To be sure, there are handsome exceptions, and some students of change expect more from small, out-of-sight, progressive locals than from high-profile, large operations. They maintain there are things you can do at the periphery, at the boundaries, that you cannot do as readily at the core. Perhaps . . . and certainly worth noting.

By and large, however, the adoption of computer uses seems to correlate positively with the amount of an organization's capital, creativity, and cautious risk-taking—all of which are more characteristic of large than of very small international unions or locals.

Cyber Naught unions appear more common among the 50 precariously small national affiliates of the AFL-CIO with 150,000 or fewer members. And, following their example, many of their smaller locals have not done much with computer possibilities.

Relevant here is this 1998 warning of the Labor Research Association: "One of the big structural problems with the labor movement today is in the dozens of small unions that are treading water and, while ultimately heading for the merger altar, are likely to do so too late—when it makes little difference to their members, their industry, or the labor movement as a whole" (LRA August 18, 1998, 1).

Finally, just plain out ask: "Is your union doing anything interesting with computers?" After some hemming and hawing, you are likely to learn that union attention goes everywhere but to that matter. If any further clues are needed as to the advisability of dropping the subject, they are likely to follow.

Untenable Price

I wince when I'm told of gaps and neglect. Typical is this response of the president of a large and progressive local of food workers who noted with dismay:

> Unions have generally not been on the cutting edge of new technology. Think about it. The retail industry has pioneered digitalized cash registers, computerized inventory control, and high-tech checkout stations. Meanwhile, union business representatives come to stores with pen and pad.

Large numbers of very small locals were still without computers of any type, or even a place to put them. An organizer with a large rural district explained to me:

> Only three out of 33 locals in my district has their own office. The rest have to be very creative. One meets at the local library. Another meets at the VFW hall. Another usually rents a room at Shoney's.

While inventive and brave, these bystanders along the road to the future are underachieving what they and Labor know is best for them.

A business agent from a midwestern building trades local spoke to me with visible regret:

> My local is really not into it. We're starting to do some courses, like word-processing, Basic, and spreadsheets, but it is really nothing. They

> say they intend to computerize some of the instruction in our apprentice classes, but nothing has happened. I think we should be learning everything about everything! The world is changing, and we should stay with it!

This plaintive note—"nothing is happening"—was struck over and again by those caught in a Cyber Naught vacuum.

Another organizer complained about the quality of representation his union tolerated on the Web:

> Our Web site is too "corporate." Old and stale. It is just sterile. It has a couple of links, as to the business agents, but you can't get down too far.

A very distressed staffer shared his exasperation:

> There is such a clamor out there for fresh information. And if you work with a computer, you're used to having your information almost in a millisecond. If it's up on the PR News Service, or the Bloomberg News Service, that information is almost in your folder in a millisecond. I'm getting this information daily.
>
> Every two months I'm getting the union magazine, and this stuff is two and a half months old! There's nothing in it that's worth my while.
>
> Why aren't we posting on an Internet site where I can click on to read it? And why aren't we at least having a listserve?

There is little reason to believe any of this has changed since the 1998 interviews.

Why Paralysis?

When I diplomatically asked why tolerate this situation, some unionists cited the sorry state of organizational finances, a barrier against buying newfangled expensive computer equipment. They noted high guesstimates of what additions or upgrades might cost, and maintained that upkeep, more so even than initial outlays, was simply prohibitive.

A second bloc pleaded ignorance. They claimed to know little or nothing about far more advanced uses other unions might be making of computers. They were seemingly comfortable retreating behind a "not-invented-here!" rejection of the idea of adapting bright ideas from elsewhere.

Rule by Tribal Elders

Not surprisingly, looming behind these prosaic weaknesses—seeming lack of funds, ignorance of appealing models, etc.—is a far more vexing (for being veiled) problem, namely, the covert opposition of precomputer decision-makers. These frightened power-holders, "the epoxy that greases the wheels of progress," are often threatened by computers, an esoteric matter they do not begin to fathom (Boren).

Preoccupied with keeping face in a brawny, profane world, many anxious leaders react with coolness, even mockery or hostility, to the notion that further use of computers might be worth their serious consideration. They defend against such thinking by employing "the process of dynamic inaction (doing nothing, but doing it with style)." Committees are established to study, to review, and to otherwise slyly suffocate innovation ("And we'll appoint incompatible co-chairs. Nothing is impossible until it is sent to a committee" [Boren]).

With vested interests to defend, many such power-holders have a private agenda focused anywhere but on planned change. Bill Fletcher, Director of Education for the AFL-CIO, suggests that we arc "facing a situation where too many of our leaders and staff are counting the days to retirement, hoping and praying that they can get out in time . . . hoping that they are not trapped in the empty room as the lights are turned off and the door is shut" (Fletcher).

Tired Message

Not surprisingly, jaded rank-and-filers expect only the "same old, same old" when these leaders take to the mike, use snail mail to spread their message, or in other ways pretend to have something to say. Typical are the videos produced before reformers took over the Teamsters Union: "The message: members are spectators in their own organization. Unions are officials in offices. Unions are technocratic bureaucracies. Unions are history" (Witt and Williams, 55–56).

Weary Response

Among those members and staffers who appreciate the computerization potential, frustration courses deep and wide, as witness this statement from an organizer:

Why is not my international doing things? And why is not my local union? I sent the IU a letter three months ago asking this. I brought up some issues . . . one of the more polite letters I've sent to them in a long time. . . . If we're gonna be dragged into the twenty-first century, at least we could be walkin' tall. They never responded.

Consequential change demands such a different view of things that relic-like leaders are often the last to be won over to it, if at all.

While these leaders may not know the difference between stability and paralysis, they can and do still make a difference, as in their ability to depress the use by their unions or locals of computers. Typical is this rueful report from an impatient enthusiast:

The president of my international is so old and set in his ways that he wants nothing to do with computers. Heck, they tell me some people around him actually put one on his desk, kind of hoping he might take to it. But he told them to take it away. We are just waiting for the new man to take over, as he is computer literate, and we expect good things.

This, at a time when about 50 percent of the nation's chief executives use the Internet an hour or two a week, and 25 percent use it an hour or two a day! (Quintanilla).

Tallying Up the Toll

Outdated leaders cost in ways that can go unrecognized. To cite one such way from a very long list, much is lost in the hiring process. Witness this account from a very talented and experienced unionist:

When I go in [for a union job interview] I make a visual survey of the office as soon as I'm in the door. And I ask—"If someone calls me, can they leave a voice mail message? Do you have e-mail to all your members? How often is your Web page updated? What do you use it for?"

The first thing I noticed was that there was nothing in high-technology. No computers, just a fax machine. And I immediately said to myself, "Do I want to work for a place that is this far behind the times?" I said to them—"Are you connected to the Internet? How do you connect to your members?" All these technological questions—and they said— "Well, we have a fax machine."

> I made up my mind immediately. I don't want to work for you folks . . . I mean, if you want to be a high-performance union, you need to attract people who are high-performance thinkers and workers, and this local was *not* going to get them.

As much of such decision-making remains private, too few Cyber Naught operations may even realize how much talent is passing them by.

A second overlooked cost stems from the rather astonishing exclusion of front-line service reps from the union's e-mail system, a sure way to lower morale and discourage computer use:

> I'm not hooked into their database. I think I'm not high enough on the ladder. Its just union managers and directors who are hooked into the New York system; it has not trickled down to the service rep level. I can get into the home page, and the services. But as far as gettin' into their e-mail service, I don't have the code.

Little wonder, accordingly, that some international reps are as discouraged as this one:

> I'm not optimistic. I think the same kind of politics that have always restrained the unions from doing the right thing in organizing, and in other issues of democracy in the union, will prevent them from using information technology.

Many such activists are basically waiting out the overdue retirement or demise of befuddled pre-computer overlords.

Finally, there is the matter of staying in the race. An activist with the Electrical Workers Union points out how far Cyber Naught organizations fall behind:

> I am a little worried about how we stack up compared to business interests. They have a much bigger headstart in the cyber world than we do. They have already integrated computers as their everyday tools to conduct business, so they are much more comfortable than the typical rank-and-file member of even the typical union. I only hope every attempt to educate and encourage members and leaders is made to further the cause.

Hope, while an indispensable start, needs much more in the way of resources if unionists are to soon change the Cyber Naught mess for the best.

On Talking Reform

On occasion I might ask unionists if they were settling for too little. I would warn against organizational anorexia. Change here need not be exorbitantly expensive or esoteric. It could be affordable and reasonable in character. The real calamity would not be that they changed course, but that they did not.

As for what to do next, I might cite this sort of advice from a staffer of a local of the Roofer's Union:

> Educate yourself! Take a class at a community college, and stay long enough to get the feel of the potential of computerization. Look at what other people and organizations are doing. Not just labor unions. Team up; working and learning alone is frustrating. Communicate with other people using computers, and you will be amazed what you can teach one another.

Along with this line of reasoning I sometimes added mention of potential cost-savings, sensing that this might resonate with key decision-makers.

Very helpful in this connection is the case for dollar savings made by activist Carl D. Cantrell, a contributor to this book:

> Because each international union maintains e-mail addresses of each member, they will be able to send out journals, newsletters, and legislative alerts to each member electronically. The savings in postage alone can save the internationals millions.
>
> Using my union as an example, we have around 750,000 members who receive the IBEW Journal for each of 10 months. Using a postage rate of seventeen cents, the cost adds up to $127,500 monthly. If we only send the journal electronically to the present estimated 25 percent of our members who are on-line, we will save $31,875 per month or approximately $318,750 per year. Add to that the savings of printing 187,500 fewer journals per month, and then start adding in postage savings for regular business mail that is transmitted each year to district offices, locals and members, and it doesn't take long to realize we can see substantial savings.
>
> Enough to pay for several people to maintain our Web site and to still find time for developing other ways of using this technology to

benefit our members. And, with the addition of other members on-line, the savings goes up each month, and let's not leave out the added benefit of being able to communicate directly and effortlessly with at least 25 percent of our members.

This argument never failed to elicit keen interest, and even some note-taking.

Indeed, most with whom I dared discuss the state of their union or local listened politely. Some cautiously asked how they might explore change options and strategies. Eager to help, I referred them to Cyber Gain unionists who had previously volunteered to guide others—Cyber Naught and Cyber Drift types—out of the desert.

Summary

A Cyber Naught union or local pretends all is as it has been, and as it will be. Its Web-fearing leaders, mesmerized by an eternal Groundhog Day fantasy of their own making, deny the need for transformation. So puzzled are they by the present, and so frightened are they by the future, that many desperately clutch the past like a talisman.

(The problem is by no means labor's alone. Futurist Alvin Toffler contends that "a new civilization is emerging in our times, and blind men everywhere are trying to suppress it" [Toffler, 25].)

Led by leaders in total denial, officers steering toward the Twilight Zone, Cyber Naught organizations sap energy and misdirect attention. These are not the worst of their failings—a distinction reserved for their pervasive fear of change. But they are the sort of thing that explains why so many such organizations stare only at "the blue screen of death."

A Cyber Naught union or local has two possible futures: a steady decline into oblivion, or a radical change into something far better for members and everybody else.

The slide into nothingness can happen at a snail's pace, in which case the chance of recovery is diminished by a false air of calm. Radical change, in contrast, can happen quite suddenly, as in the after-math of an unexpected election win by modernists (who worked "off-camera," using e-mail campaigning). Or it can follow the overhaul dictated by a union merger or the amalgamation of locals. For as

Canadian futurist Tom Walker explains, "Ordinarily, watching a glacier move is about as exciting as watching paint dry. Every once in a while, though, a chunk drops off the end and . . . WOW!!" (Walker).

Only this much seems certain: Doing little or even nothing is *not* an option, as it means falling farther behind. Given Labor's shrinking numbers and clout, it is clear that Cyber Naught unions and locals "do not compute" and must give way.

Recommended Resources

Exercise 1: If Cyber Naught unions are still with us in 2005, what might they resemble? Why might members remain members, if at all?

Exercise 2: If you were asked by a Cyber Naught union or local to help it advance beyond this stage, what concrete steps would you urge, in what order, and how would you measure success? How long would the process take? What would the outcome resemble?

Goldfield, Michael. *The Decline of Organized Labor in the United States.* Chicago: University of Chicago Press, 1987. Thoroughgoing analysis of reasons given for labor's decline, and a review of the conditions necessary for labor's recovery. Highlights the role of fierce employer opposition and public policy favoring such employers, both of which factors help explain much of the fear and defensiveness of Cyber Naught unions.

Lester, Richard. *As Unions Mature: An Analysis of the Evolution of American Unionism.* Princeton, NJ: Princeton University Press, 1958. A seminal exploration of the "hardening of the arteries" phase of organizational decline, and the uneven chances that unions can escape senility.

For a view the opposite of Cyber Naught fearfulness, see the Web site of the *Industrial Workers of the World* (IWW) at http://iww.org

See also the Web site of the *United Electrical Radio and Machine Workers* (UE) at http://ranknfile-ue.org/ The UE site contains a mission statement entitled "The Members Run Our Union" that Cyber Naught organizations might find quite challenging.

Reading 3

Social Change Prospects for Unionism

Kim Evon
Service Employees International Union,
SEIU, Hospital Workers' Union, Local 767

Although her life was threatened because of her advocacy of it, Kim Evon, the activist writing below, continues to believe whole-heartedly that union democracy is a key element, if not the key element, in union progress. She blames the Cyber Naught syndrome on union leadership that disdains democracy, clings to the past, fears the future, and misleads members into identifying Labor's power with some illusory ability to fend off change. Aware that everything is connected to everything else (an insight from futuristics), she adds to our reform agenda the need to win basic changes in the social infrastructure that bears on employability (job retraining programs, etc.).

If we would escape from the coma of Cyber Naught unionism, Evon urges us to promote democracy, secure job-aiding societal changes, celebrate our gains, and focus on winning a finer tomorrow, rather than whine over setbacks and wax nostalgic for a romanticized (and often mythological) past.

A firestorm of controversy erupted amongst the members when they were informed that the hospital's administration was considering a bi-weekly payroll system. "They can't do that to us," said one. "If our union doesn't do something to stop this, it's weak," said another. And much to my surprise, one commented, "They're trying to bust our union."

What the hell has happened here? How have things risen to such a level of mistrust between workers and their employers that an issue regarding a bi-weekly paycheck system has risen to the ranks of attempted union-busting?

Then I realized, after pondering these strange yet passionate cries of injustice, that this was much more than an issue of distrust. This was symbolic of something much more endemic to our labor unions. The bi-weekly paycheck controversy was on its face nothing more than minutia in the realm of workplace justice. However, it was just another example of workers' perceiving that they lacked any control over decisions that affected them.

I remember sitting behind my desk on Unit 5A at Rhode Island Hospital being virtually pushed to the point of a cerebral hemorrhage because a doctor would not remove himself from my computer station so that I could finish entering my orders and tests to get patients off to their exams. Consequently, I would espouse with great passion the maniacal attributes of those who sought to disrupt my work life and cause me to become a miserable shrew during the course of the day.

Now the question before you is this: Were these incidents of biblical proportion so as to rock the very foundation of my world? Did they so acutely affect my performance as to render me incompetent? No. They were irritating, frustrating, and commonplace.

But they served to propel my growing anger around more important issues like my pathetic wages, expensive health insurance, and diminishing importance as a viable contributor to the institution. Since I had no way of addressing or resolving these more important issues, I engulfed myself in minutia and waged a symbolic war around it.

It was at this juncture in my life that I began to hate myself. I was never one prone to whining or self-pity. But I slowly began to loathe the identity which I felt with these characteristics. I desired and needed some power, some sense of control. Witness my entry into the labor movement.

Like those hospital members, I could relate to their sense and perception of powerlessness even over a somewhat insignificant matter. The real test of my skills or any leader in the labor movement is to identify the root of the problem; to probe beyond the perceived surface of insignificance; and to find a solution to empowerment.

The phrase that I've learned is the First Law of Sociology, "things are seldom what they seem," is entirely appropriate in putting into context the problems of the labor movement. Our society is not static. We are in a constant state of flux which necessitates that we adapt and change. One of the biggest problems that both local and international unions face is this rapidly changing labor market and its consequences for members and workers across the country.

For labor unions, their leaders, union staff, and rank-and-file, changes brought on by downsizing, re-engineering, and job restructuring are wreaking havoc upon the membership and their perceptions of their union.

Unfortunately, members have come to equate a union's power base with its ability to maintain the status quo and fend off change. I feel that much of this perception has been encouraged by a complacent, uncreative, and domineering union leadership, one which has deterred the uses of labor union democracy for achieving real power in workplace decisions. I believe in nurturing union democracy and active rank-and-file participation over an irrational and false sense of loyalty to elected union officials.

My convictions surrounding this concept of union democracy are so strong that at one time my life was threatened by the very union leaders with whom I was working with to organize my workplace. I begrudge them nothing, but they have become the greatest learning tool for my endeavors in ensuring democratic processes. I would rather rise with the membership than rise above them.

The problems with such change in our industries does not solely rest in the laps of such union leaders. In this country, we lack a fundamental social infrastructure to deal with such changes. We have an archaic unemployment system which has no capability of offering displaced workers any ongoing or relative skills to the changing job market. This is exacerbated by an increasing trend toward temporary labor pools and a lack of investment by employers to increase the skills of their work force.

Workers are given a daunting task if they are to remain viable players in the job market. Not only must they immediately find work to support their families and other financial matters, but they must also find money, time, and resources to continue their education in the process. Add to this the shortcomings of our educational system, which is more consumed with quantity than quality, and you have the makings for a disaster.

One of the real problems facing our labor leaders is the ability to lead courageously. In order to do this, they must be able to present the rank-and-file with a real picture of the problems we face in this changing job market and our industries, while utilizing the most productive means to meet these challenges.

What does this mean? Union leaders must curtail their use of rhetoric which imposes a certainty that does not exist. Just as sociologists may make the mistake of forecasting future outcomes as "will" or "will not," union leaders fall into the same trap. It is this use of absolute certainties that gives the union rank-and-file a false sense of security: "Things will not change. You will not have to learn new skills. You will not have to adapt to technological changes. You will be forever cocooned in a parallel universe where nothing changes and everything stays the same."

When we send these types of messages, why are we surprised at our members' perception that the union is weak? Haven't we placed ourselves in lose-lose situations and encouraged our membership to see their union as failing them in attaining those standards which we set out to them?

Another important factor is the inability to focus on our gains rather than our losses. This is critical if we are to encourage workers to take perceived risks from the status quo. If we fail to identify the good things and praise them for their merits, we run the risk of creating more apathy, more criticism, and a greater fear of change among our members.

On all levels, in our locals and internationals, we must begin to focus our attention on the future rather than piteously lament the past. Our work force is changing, our industries are changing, and our needs as a society are changing. Therefore, the labor movement *must* change.

The "good old days" only serve us well when we extrapolate from them the lessons most appropriate in dealing with the future. The labor movement has great potential in rising above a minority status of power and effecting broad social changes for working women and men across the country.

The true test will lie in the substance of our goals, the realism of our intent, and the desire to adopt an agenda for American workers which will serve their interests far into the future.

Kim Evon is staff organizer and education coordinator for the Hospital Workers' Union, Local 767, SEIU. She entered the labor movement after helping to organize 1,800 workers at Rhode Island Hospital from 1993 to 1994. In the summer of 1994, she took a position with the Hospital Workers' Union in Cape Cod, Massachusetts, and has remained on staff to date. She expects to earn an undergraduate degree in labor studies shortly and looks forward to obtaining her master's degree. (She can be reached via e-mail at kim767@juno.com.)

4

Cyber Drift: Going Nowhere

I find the greatest thing in this world is not so much where we stand, as in what direction we are moving.
                                        —Oliver Wendell Holmes, Jr.

When I think of Cyber Drift, I think of a union or its locals moving aimlessly, like a cork bobbing on a turbulent sea, though with far less likelihood than a cork of staying afloat. I think of bewildered leaders, looking on as if in a daze, union officers to whom things happen rather than people who make new beginnings. Caught in this hapless course, labor's effort to use computers falls far short of its potential.

Computerization is persistently prolific, as it moves from stand-alone PCs to networks, and from computer-oriented humans to human-oriented computing. Its record affirms that we are in the midst of a revolution, not an evolution. But you would never know this from the inchoate and directionless plight of a Cyber Drift union.

I am reminded of my variant of the First Law of Sociology—Things are seldom what they seem to be. These unions and their locals are seldom the adequate and inspiring organizations they want to be thought of, much to the rue of all who really know them and understand how much more is possible.

Indicators

How do you know you are dealing with a Cyber Drift type? As in the case of the Cyber Naught unionist, three clues are available: the first on first contact, the second via an indirect sign, and the third requiring a direct question. Taken in combination, they should clarify the matter.

Examine his or her business card. Odds are fair it will have the union's e-mail address, though probably not a Web site URL. You will probably learn, however, that the e-mail does not come directly to the individual. The Web site remains under construction, or operates much like a static and stale billboard. The one really knowledgeable staff person has been reassigned. And for sundry other reasons, it would be best to move on to another subject.

Second, ask the size of the union or local involved. The smaller the organization, the greater the likelihood of informatics incoherence.

Finally, just ask: "Is your union doing anything interesting with computers?" After a diplomatic pause, you are likely to learn that the union's computer system is a low-performance one, as it relies on a traditional mainframe or minicomputer. It is probably not networked with computers in the locals, and it uses a command-and-control, or top-down noninteractive approach, an old-fashioned and chilling style.

Should you pursue the matter, and have the trust of the teller, you may then hear sad tales of the deaths of various seemingly worthy computer-based projects. Some lacked a powerful champion. Some lost their champion. Some were sabotaged. Some were launched, and never heard from again. Some may be still be in process, but this is uncertain. The picture, in short, is confused, to put the best possible light on it.

Why Aimlessness?

There are many reasons for this situation, prime among which is a costly division of the house. At the top you may have policy wonks open to testing new uses of informatics (e.g., mailing of shrink-wrapped VCR videos to prospective members). At the bottom, however, you may have staffers charged with a workload they already consider overbearing. Confronting "bright" new demands coming from distant headquarters types seemingly indifferent to frontline realities, the staffers may be less inclined to implement than to sabotage by neglect or misinterpretation. Drift, rather than delivery, is a common result.

Much of the problem can also be traced to the ill-advised absence of an MIS (Management of Information Systems) staffer or an Information Technology Officer (ITO), a specialist capable of grasping the big picture, seeing beyond the present, mediating among inside power-holders, and in other critical ways providing rewarding direction. Many unions claim they cannot afford to pay what a really good ITO can command. A staffer for a major union in the public sector complains:

> Essentially, we have a two-person MIS department with a need for at least twice that many. We do not have enough expertise in MIS personnel. We have no one who was an MIS-trained professional before coming to us. We need to recruit highly competent MIS professionals, which will require higher salaries. Because we are not doing this, our day-to-day work suffers as time is lost and goals are not achieved, due to software and hardware failures.

Cyber Drift unions and locals often try to go it alone, and the absence of a truly knowledgeable IT guru can take a heavy toll.

Various locals are left to reinvent the wheel in computer applications because their international union does not have a central office to help field-proven tools gain employ. No cross-fertilization occurs among the drifting unions and locals, except sporadically when a good listserve like PubLabor has a contributor highlight an informatics gain readily adapted elsewhere.

The Toll Being Paid

Among other things, going it alone often leads to a costly mismatch of equipment. Consider this complaint from a union staffer:

> I work with a MAC at home, but have to struggle with DOS equipment in the union office. I can bring home work that my MAC can handle, but it doesn't work in reverse. It is like going from the twenty-first century at home to the nineteenth century at the union office—and I don't enjoy it!

In other cases, a toll is taken by a gross underutilization of equipment:

> For all the power I have sitting in my desk, it should be used for a lot more. The 14 other regions all have e-mail addresses, but there is no way to communicate between each other yet. We're not on the net. Everything that is being done at our international office is being done

individually, on an ad hoc basis. On their own time, or in their space time at work. There are no one or two people on staff with the job of improving communications or resources with computers for the membership. Or the offices.

As well, there is often costly ignorance of available resources:

> One place I went to had one computer terminal, and there must have been about 12 people in the office. And I asked, "What do you use the computer for?" "Well, we get e-mail over it from different people." "Do you get grievances over the e-mail system?" "No." "Do you use your computer system to file and categorize your e-mail?" "No, there is no software for that." "Wrong," I said, "there is a unionized company in Boston that has all the software you need!"

Other unionists told me similar stories of software foulups, incompatible hardware, erratic purchases, lack of awareness, and other exasperating handicaps.

Comparably unwelcome, and very seldom discussed in public, are costly decisions to upgrade for no good reason, save for the absence of wiser heads:

> I think you have to be careful not to overdo it. I almost think that that's what we've done. I'm on my third computer in the office, because someone said, "Let's get rid of this one, and let's get a better one." Actually, probably even the first one, if I still had that one, would be powerful enough. If they look over how much money is being spent on unnecessary upgrades, it might be a little hard to justify. Whereas you don't have to have the top of the line.
>
> But once people started getting into computers, and they started seeing all the other things that it could do—the speakers, and all of that junk—you don't *really* need that! But once it started going, you say, "Well, give me that!"

Technolust, a motive that does no one proud, can blind unionists to cost-justification criteria and other sensible tests—and it threatens to take an ever-greater toll of Cyber Drift organizations.

Another major hindrance is rigid protocol, a set of unyielding rules that requires a daisy chain of officials to sign off before anything can be acted upon. A painful example follows:

A young woman wanted to know how to reach our organizing department. She went on the Internet, and went to the trouble of finding our Web site. She sent an e-mail out that said, "Help! I need a union at my company." It's a company that we'd been trying to make contacts with for years. On June 30 she sent her e-mail. On July 14, a piece of snail mail reached our organizer. It had gone through three organizing directors—our regional director and two others, all by snail mail.

I told my colleagues this is unacceptable! We need to get this straightened out. We have to return the call within 24 hours. If somebody calls, and you respond two weeks later, to something as important as organizing, you can imagine what they think you'll do when they have a grievance. So, the next time you get an e-mail like that—we understand the need for making sure that everyone knows what is going on, but just press "forward"—so we can make the contact. And go through the protocol thing that you have to do.

But the system *still* doesn't work that way. I was told we have protocol we have to follow.

Far more common than good for Organized Labor (or any like large-scale organization), old-fashioned "red tape" rules of this kind are malignant.

Going it alone can also mean another vexing type of paralysis in decision-making. A computer enthusiast told me of his frustration with being unable to get his buddies to resolve key decisions:

Some of the things we'd like to do we're not set up to do. I'd like to see us have programs so that we can identify every member by political district—congressional, Senate, House, and state (both houses)—so that we can target mailings on candidates. It would be far more effective . . . but the software, for a local of our size to do it, is still pretty expensive. And it's not so much the cost, as the constant updating.

So we're sittin' there tryin' to make a decision. Should we do it? Be out on the edge, and put so much funds unto it? Or, maybe it's not that important right now. And we should wait, and see whether it gets done on a broader district basis. Or if it gets done by the AFL-CIO.

An organizer in the South recalled a similar paralyzing situation:

We looked into getting a Web site, and setting it up through our office. But it seemed too expensive. About $20,000 to get it up and running and get it started. And then you would have to have someone designated to keep it up to date, and so on. We're hoping that down the road we may be able to do it.

Another organizer pinpointed the source of his Cyber Drift heartache:

> In the last six months two of us asked the international to send out a letter to all 155 reps who had an e-mail address, asking them to submit it back. We told them we'd even take care of the system. And what we would do is have a little mini-newsletter for reps coming out of head-quarters.
>
> The secretary-treasurer said, "I'm going to look into that. It's a great idea!" We didn't hear back for a month or two. Called back, and asked, "What's happening? It's a good idea. It's a good way for you to communicate with us. You'll find uses yourself for it."
>
> Their response was, "We can't do it, because not everyone has an e-mail address. We're not prepared to do it until we can get the same information to everyone at once." Our response was to tell everyone to get up off of their ass, and get access to the Internet.

Not surprisingly, this situation leaves enthusiasts like those above vulnerable to burnout, an occupational hazard made more likely and costly by a sense of isolation, a lack of ties to knowledgeable and supportive others who understand the toll Cyber Drift takes.

Consider these thoughts from a unionist who was once the *most* active dispenser of e-mail information by and for unions that I ever knew inside Organized Labor (then and now!). Today, as a burnout case inside a drifting local of a drifting international he has cut back very far:

> My time nowadays is mostly involved with contacts in the field and involves organizing, but also a large amount of B.A.-type work. I spend very little time with computers at work.
>
> When I first got into the "information peddling" aspects of computers and unionism, I had great hopes for what could be done on a networking basis. It seems that information overload may have caused a setback in this area. I consider myself to be a very active unionist, but probably delete 90 percent of the listserve e-mails due to lack of time or the varied nature of the topics.

Organized Labor has far too few computer aces to lose any, but a Cyber Drift culture does just that—and barely knows what it has lost.

What Can Be Done?

Gaining relief can be so difficult that some reformers pin their hopes only on the dying out of misleaders. They learned a long time ago that certain advances, certain changes in the Old Guard, come only "funeral by funeral" (Samuelson, in Wade). Others, however, contend any such wait is too long, and the reform job must be tackled *now*—a proposition so blasphemous to intimidated members that it must be correct.

Some help is possible from those with an oversight role, as is true of many executive boards. A rail union staffer offers this account of anti-drift pressures:

> Technology changes, and we have to constantly spend money to update, to stay competitive against the railroads, because they spare no expense, and spend a lot of money on computers. They've computerized everything! So, we have to keep up, or we'll be swamped over. And this is a big cost factor for unions. To have to pay to keep up with the Joneses.
>
> Our executive board is made up of, and is controlled by our members. You cannot be a staffer and be on the e-board. You must be a worker on the railroads. So we think we are pretty democratic. We have to convince the people on the e-board. They don't like to spend the union's money. We have to prove to them that computers are worth it, and, so far, we've been able to do just that.

Mechanisms of this sort help promote accountability, and that generally makes sloth impossible.

A second source of relief from drift can come from making cost-savings arguments, as these can lessen pressure to flounder. Carl D. Cantrell, a contributor to this book, offers sound advice:

> Web site development is inexpensive. Of course, you can go out and hire someone to design a professional Web site and spend as much money as you want. However, that isn't necessary. Web sites aren't really that hard to do if one has the right tools and a little training. With the purchase of a software application like Microsoft's FrontPage for around $100, a novice can be producing professional-looking Web pages in no time. In looking at many, many Web sites across the country, it is very difficult to tell any differences in overall quality between sites done by professionals or by "non-professionals."

Many activists eager to replace drift with direction will find their case strengthened by ease-of-accomplishment and low-cost demonstrations of theirs for power-holders.

Overall, I recommend that Cyber Drift unionists view their situation as solvable. I urge them to consult with their Cyber Gain counterparts, and recommend they link up to Web sites of Cyber Gain unions to seek transferable lessons (see www.unions.org).

I recommend these reformers clarify their goals, establish a timetable, and improve an overarching vision of what sort of labor organization they want five years out, five post-drift years ahead. Some issues will prove intractable, and a few questions will go unanswered. But they will have begun ... and they can strengthen their caucus via e-mail, and occasionally meet together to forge the kind of bonds that only personal contact can achieve.

Summary

Drift and Labor have a long and sorry history together. Sociologist C. Wright Mills wrote over 50 years ago that far too many labor leaders were "walking backwards into the future envisioned by sophisticated conservatives" (Mills, 233). As untenable as it was then, such behavior is even more costly in a "future shock" world like ours, one where previously hard-to-imagine changes are occurring at warp speed.

Having now studied Labor from within and without for about 45 years, and having worked myself in unionlike academic bureaucracies for nearly 40 years, I have no illusions about the ease of getting beyond drift and achieving bright and inspired change. But there is no choice: Bold and pointed risk-taking is *essential.*

Drift invites disaster. Aimless unions and locals find it hard to chose dynamism over paralysis, goal-guided change over goal-less wandering. Their situation is untenable. Much as in the related case of Cyber Naught organizations, those activists within who glimpse Cyber Gain possibilities must—and can—help their hapless organizations reinvent themselves.

Recommended Resources

Exercise 1: Imagine a union or local in 2005 that has a history of drifting, but has gotten beyond it: How do you imagine that happened?

What sort of covert and desperate opposition to ending drifting probably developed, and how was it countered? What part might computer use have played in the rescue?

Exercise 2: Think of a union or local you know now that seems adrift. Why has this occurred? Who profits? Who pays? What can be done?

Geoghegan, Thomas. *Which Side Are You On? Trying to Be for Labor When It's Flat on Its Back.* New York: Plume, 1991. A hard-hitting and revealing account of much that has been and remains wrong about union realities. An indispensable guide to life beyond drift.

Goldstein, Jeffrey. *The Unshackled Organization: Facing the Challenge of Unpredictability Through Spontaneous Reorganization.* Portland, OR: Productivity Press, 1994. Offers fresh and novel insights into organizational change, how to achieve it, and how to promote natural and lasting changes. Draws on very current theories, and makes them clear and useful.

Kelber, Harry. *My 60 Years as a Labor Activist: The Life Story of an Incorrigible Radical Who Never Stopped Fighting for Working People.* New York: A.G. Publishing, 1996. A memoir by a labor activist who tells it as it is, warts and all, and spins an instructive and thoroughly engaging tale of labor gains, weaknesses, and possibilities. Sheds valuable light on sources of paralysis. (At 82, Kelber authors a regular e-mail column on current labor events. See "Labor Talk" at hkeller @ige.org).

Activists will find a zesty mix of energizing ideas (and controversy) at a listserve primarily, but not exclusively, of interest to public service unions: See PUBLABOR; subscribe through Listserv@Relay .Doit.Wisc.Edu

Union Web Rings, or networks of autonomous sites, such as Eugene W. Plawiuk's Union Web Ring with over 300 union Web sites listed on it—www.geocities.com/CapitolHill/5202/unionring.html—allow one to "surf" for hours by following links from one labor Web site to another.

Reading 4

Searching for the Way

Bobby Brown
International Union of Operating Engineers,
IUOE, Local 450

As for excuses to drift, imagine that your union does not pay for computer equipment. And surgery unexpectedly keeps you from being able to drive to your union worksites. And many of your union brothers and sisters are suspicious that further use of computers may reduce the High Touch aspects of unionism they especially value.

You just might pack it all in—or, as explained by Bobby Brown, the activist below, you just might fight back, so convinced are you that drift is unacceptable and Labor's prospects hinge on ever more creative uses of computers.

Come meet a rare labor telecommuter (temporary basis), one who has much to teach us about the potential for Labor hiring people with disabilities, and for using CD-ROMs, along with the dollar-savings and teaching gains possible from expanded use of computers.

During the past two years, I have become increasingly involved in finding new ways to use computers in my labor union work. Unfortunately, my international union does not provide its field representatives with computer equipment. However, I consider computers important enough to fund my own increasing purchases of desktop and PowerBook (I am a Macintosh advocate) computer equipment for my personal, educational, and home use, and also for my union work assignments.

On the local union level, the new business manager of a local union that I have been assisting is a progressive individual who realizes that computers can offer solutions to his local union's administrative, representational, and organizing activities. One of his first initiatives was to completely upgrade and install state-of-the-art computer equipment in his main office and connecting computers in his outlying offices.

As a unionist my home computers have increased my capabilities to assist his local union through comparable computer technology (e-mail, spreadsheet, database, and presentation software, etc.). My physical presence at one of his offices or organizing sites is no longer an absolute requirement for productive interaction and union work with him and his staff.

For example, I am currently recuperating from spinal surgery and will be unable to travel for several months. The local's main office is approximately 570 miles from my home. Before entering the hospital, I was assisting it with an organizing campaign involving 700 employees. Although I am now unable to physically be with my local union associates, we have been communicating and sharing organizing information as they engage in a comprehensive NLRB election campaign. Our computers have given us opportunities to continue a limited, but productive involvement in the organizing activities. This could not be possible without our combined computer equipment and capabilities.

This also points out a secondary advantage. Computerization can allow for the participation and effective utilization of handicapped or disadvantaged individuals as productive members of any union staff. Disabilities should no longer be an impediment to disadvantaged individuals from contributing to unionization.

Also, as my final project in GMCLS/Antioch University's Comp 201 class, I used the excellent instructions of instructor John Griffin to work on my first multimedia presentation for union-related work. I prepared a simple presentation that could be used to support oral instructions in a preliminary organizing meeting with interested employees. Although the project is not ready for actual use (progressive comments and suggestions from Mr. Griffin have convinced me to make some alterations and improvements), I have now mastered the basic capabilities to prepare an efficient presentation that will be more interesting, comprehensive, and attention-grabbing for employees who usually have little or no concept of organizing laws, tactics, statistics, and procedures.

Such presentations can be stored on disk and updated as circumstances change. These presentations can also be shared with local union representatives who can modify and practice their oral presentations using the multimedia program at their own pace and discretion. This may ensure the continuity and consistency of information throughout the local union's organizing activities.

This is an important issue in organizing campaigns that are usually dominated by employer-generated misinformation, propaganda, and negative allegations. To counteract such tactics, union information must be accurate, consistent, and properly referenced.

Regarding the international's office, the education and training department recently modified and recorded the curriculums of the hoisting and portable (construction equipment) and stationary engineer (building operations and maintenance) training programs on CDs. These CDs are being made available to local union training directors and instructors to use in teaching the skills of the operating engineers' trade in apprenticeship and journeyperson upgrade programs.

Again, the obvious advantage should be the maintaining of consistency and the quality of the information and continuity of the teaching methods by using multimedia presentations as guidelines for instructors.

These computer resources can give local union and international union staffs abilities to compensate for any possible deficiencies in their teaching abilities, to be more professional, consistent, and effective in teaching workers, whether they be non-union employees interested in organizing or union apprentices and journeypersons seeking craft skills, knowledge, and training.

As for me as an international staff person, the obvious advantages of computers and computer skills are the abilities to be more productive and assist more local unions in geographical environments in which distances between local union offices, organizing sites, and my home office are between 200 and 700 miles. Computers can bridge the geographical gaps and bring distant representatives into relative cyberspace proximity.

I must admit that I am not satisfied with the level of use of computer technology in my union's labor relations work or with the pace at which such technology is evolving. However, I believe that these are temporary situations that will rapidly become a priority as logic and productive reasoning gradually influence the inner sanctum of traditional labor union administrations.

As these natural evolutions take place, I would hope to see an increase in the use of computers for communications between international union officials, international staff, local union officers, and members through e-mail, discussion groups, and strategic, comprehensive designed Web sites. Perhaps even computer-generated teleconferences (computer-based union meetings) for members separated by great distances could help dissolve the distances between union officers and their members. This would be a great improvement in increasing awareness and communications between union officials and their rank-and-file members.

Expected challenges to such activities may include the need for teaching discipline and procedures for the participants in such union communications. Members of my international are known for being provocative and sometimes confrontational at union meetings. They may object to the inability to physically confront, challenge, and resolve issues with union officers in face-to-face meetings, as they are accustomed to. However, members, like all employees, are gradually coming to realize and accept the necessity and cost-saving features of computerization.

Union members' scrutiny of treasury expenditures is a common denominator in most union memberships. The efficient use of their dues, when effectively explained, should give them the motivation to approve of such practices and accept and develop new methods and skills to participate in their applications.

For what it is worth, these are my comments on computerization and its evolution within my international union, its affiliated local unions, and their officers and staffs. We have a long way to go to reach productive computerized environments within our organization, but I am satisfied that the change is in progress and will ultimately succeed in becoming common practice. Years from now these upcoming computer systems may become the traditions future generations of union members will perhaps take for granted.

Bobby Brown is a 1998 graduate, B.A. in Labor Studies, Antioch University/George Meany Center for Labor Studies. International representative, International Union of Operating Engineers (IUOE), 1990–1998. Project organizer, IUOE Region 8/IUOE Local 450, 1986–1990. District 5 Officer, IUOE Local 450, San Antonio, Texas, 1980–1986. As a 25-year member of IUOE Local 450, Houston, Texas, he worked as a crane operator, mechanic, surveyor, job-site steward, and supervisor on commercial, industrial, marine, and cross-country pipeline projects in Texas, Colorado, Utah, and Wyoming, 1973–1986. (He can be reached via e-mail at b_brown@earthlink.net.)

5

Cyber Gain: Getting With It

What distinguishes society today is not only the pace of events, but also the nature of the tool kit for facing the future.
—David Brin, *The Transparent Society,* 1998

In contrast with Cyber Naught and Cyber Drift types, Cyber Gain unions and locals make much of computer possibilities. The good news is that their number appears larger with every passing year; the bad news, that their ranks remain far too small for Labor's good. Worse yet, they are actually often thought the end-all, when in fact they are way stations. Hopefully, they will succeed in becoming the CyberUnions discussed in Part III.

Cyber Gain unions employ computers to support people, plans, and progress, as well as to keep track of things (traditional business operations). They pour new wine into new bottles. Their use of computers can be creative (though, as I shall argue later, it still does not go far enough). Officers, staffers, and activists alike appreciate how much can be done, and they enjoy adapting gains made elsewhere in and outside of Labor.

Much success here can be traced to conceptual advances. Progressive habits of mind have Cyber Gain labor leaders, staffers, and rank-and-file activists preferring function to form, results to protocol, and risk-taking to rhetoric. In consequence, their unions and locals are dynamic operations, supple and original in ways in which they take justifiable pride.

Typical is this response from a local union president who has his own agenda for securing computer gains, and won't be discouraged:

We wanted to know who would use our Web site on a CD if we put the contract on it. We didn't get much of an answer back to the 3,000 surveys we attached to our newsletter. Since everyone has a copy of the contract already, maybe it wasn't a big issue for them. But we're going to pay one of our members to do this Web site anyhow, as we're intent on going ahead.

Activists of this stripe are not discouraged to discover shortcomings of computer professionals, but move instead to compensate:

We are writing our own programs. It has been our experience that computer program workers lack creativity. Unlike an architect, who takes your ideas and brings back more than you ever imagined, computer programmers couldn't grasp what we were trying to do, and often took too long and came up too short. By doing the writing ourselves, we can bring our ideas to life.

Many of the activists guiding Cyber Gain organizations perform computer tasks they never imagined tackling when starting their union careers.

Likewise, many activists intent on earning CyberUnion status set up computer schools to move their membership along:

We have a *huge* computer training operation. We have a 12-computer array in our trailer at our hall site, and it is filled all the time with classes. And we've included members' spouses and kids now. And we also have an internal training center within the plant to train anyone whose job requires using a computer. People are starting to get less scared of it.

We're using computers a lot more. And it is becoming harder to be ahead of the computers, because you can sit and talk with certain members, and realize quickly they are ahead of you on certain things they know about computers.

Others I interviewed were equally resolute about rapidly and firmly taking their union and their local with them into the Age of Information.

Indicators

How do you know you are dealing with a Cyber Gain type? As before, in the case of the Cyber Naught and Cyber Drift unionist, three clues are available, though only two are reliable. The first can come at first contact. The second requires a direct question. And the third, the matter of size—a useful guide in the Cyber Naught and Cyber Drift cases—is very "iffy." The first two, taken in combination, should clarify the matter.

Examine his or her business card. If it is the card of a Cyber Gain union member, the odds are good that it will boast an e-mail address, and possibly a Web site URL. At the very least these will refer you to the union that employs the brother or sister. Some aficionados actually add their own personal address and URL, so keen are they on inviting e-mail and Net communications from you and sundry.

(Unions per se are generally high on their Cyber Gain culture, and often want the world to know this:

> Our national union advertises the existence of our Web site at every opportunity—the stationery, business cards, press releases, flyers, and other promotional items all carry the Web address. We also ran a cover story about our Web page in our house organ.

Public relations efforts of this type send a strong signal of top-level support, and go far in generating more and more support.)

Second, you can ask "Is your union doing anything interesting with computers?" Be prepared with considerable time to spend listening, as Cyber Gain types love to brag, commonly have scores of anecdotes to share, and often want to play the "Johnny Appleseed" role in spreading word of transferable informatics gains they know at first-hand.

A fascinating variation here, by the way, has the Cyber Gain types outdoing their management counterparts:

> We're *ahead* of our management! No question! In PowerPoint presentation skills, we're way ahead! In the use of computer for surveying our membership, and a lot of other things. We have to push them to get us disks, and we're out there takin' digital photographs, and things like that. They tend to lag behind in our industry [steel], because it is considered among management that they've got to be careful not to be considered too flashy.

Similarly, boasting can be very specific:

> We have a really nice Web site. It's interactive. There are useful things on it. The local unions can get on it and get grievance reports. You

know, a lot of useful information. Direct e-mail line to the president. The OSHA guy. The recording secretary if you have a financial problem with your union records, or whatever. And a link to our organizing department.

It was quite a pleasure for me to share time with upbeat activists proud of the pioneering being done by their labor organizations.

Finally, you could ask how large their union or local is, but I am not convinced it is worth it. To be sure, prowess with computers generally requires capital, creativity, and cautious risk-taking—all of which are more characteristic of large than of very small international unions or locals.

At the same time, however, my three years of field research uncovered scores of small locals doing far more than I thought I had reason to expect.

Indeed, I met activists convinced that the innovative edge is in the farthest realms of the Kingdom, rather than back at the Castle. For example:

> You are going to find the *real* growth, just like in the labor movement in general, is at the bottom, at the locals and in some districts, and what have you. *They* get it!
>
> Most rank-and-file folks are more interested in what happens in the local. Why would any rank-and-filer go to an international Web site? They're going to go where they need information. If I want to find out what is going on in my local, I'm much more likely to go to that Web page.
>
> What information are they providing that I need? If it helps me with my certification for something, and they provide that course on-line, I'm going to go there. But if they're offering only a chance to see what the president looks like, I ain't going. Generally, the closer you are to the heart, the more likely you are to get participation.

Little wonder that some unionists contend, "There are more collective resources in the locals than in the international unions" (Rathke).

Over and again I heard disparaging remarks about high-level Web sites of no special aid, and a decided preference for those with immediate payoff. Only further research can establish whether units closest to the members are more or less disposed to give them what they really want—though headquarters staffers should pay this matter careful note.

Those Who Make the Difference

Several things explain why and how a union or local can go from the Cyber Drift state, a potential launching-pad, to Cyber Gain status.

Prime among the levers of change is the presence of one or more "true believers," or selfless visionaries with computer and promotional skills. A union staffer explains:

> They have a natural curiosity and a desire, frankly, to make their work a little bit easier. By and large (there are obvious exceptions) they are younger than their co-workers who have not taken the time to experiment with the equipment. They seem more inclined to take chances with new ideas and equipment, and they aren't afraid of making mistakes.

A rank-and-file activist put it in a similar way:

> Unionists who utilize computers, to generalize, are very intelligent. I don't know if "intelligent" is the correct word to use here or if there is a more politically correct way to say it, but that is the way it appears to me generally.

These change-agents know how to urge and win advances in computer uses. Savvy about the power game and how to play, they are patient, diplomatic, and dedicated.

Commonly early adopters themselves of computers, many of these activists enjoy reminiscing about the very primitive hardware they wrestled with in the Dark Ages (the 1970s or earlier), the esoteric computer languages they learned to write their own software, and the excitement they felt with their every computer-use success.

Several are sort of legendary in their own time, a special breed with little counterpart elsewhere in Organized Labor, as this activist explains:

> The people that are conveying the information, it's almost as if they come from a separate priesthood from the other unionists. They are trying to lead people into this world. They are on the computer, and are seen as some sort of mysterious beings.
>
> They say to the others, "It's not very hard! Anybody can get on. Anybody can talk. You don't have to be a prolific or talented writer to exchange information."

The people using computers, they're the spark plugs of today! They're ahead of the pack, ahead of the conventional leadership.

Still another account underlines the strategic value of a single inspiring person:

In 1984 we [staffers] still didn't have computers. But my general chairman, Jed Dodd, had one, and everybody thought it was something—because he could put the information into it. A few basic facts, like "John Smith was at a union meeting." Push a button, and it would spit out a time frame. Everybody was amazed!! It reminded me of people going around back in the old days, and showing people stuff they had never seen—because wherever he went with his computer, people were comin' out of the walls to see it.

He was a union officer, and he wanted to show that the union needs to come up into the twentieth century—with the technologies available that we didn't have. We were still doing everything by hand. We didn't have any computers to speak of . . . I don't think we had any. If we did, they were so hidden inside the union that the membership never heard tell of it.

Dodd had a college degree, and he had been using computers throughout his schooling. He had been a welder helper on a railroad train track, and after we see'd his computer stuff, we made him general chairman of a huge region of our union. Covers 14 states and more. From helper . . . to general chairman, wow! His computer use showed he was a sign of the times and could use technology. Could use information. Could develop it. Disseminate information; get it out.

So we undertook a program to introduce computer use in our homes. It was a huge step for us. Now, the first one I bought myself, out of my own money. I bought it specifically for union use, after seeing what Dodd could do with it. Even though we didn't have the money I saw at the time it could possibly help me, so I spent the money and bought the computer, and everything. We were able to do a lot of the work faster.

Jed Dodd sees the technology out there, as he correctly saw it in 1983. He saw the direction the union needed to take as far as computerization—and he still sees it now. Any resistance would come from people like me. And I'm not resistant to it, 'cause I see what has already been done.

Independent in being willing to take the first step, change-agents of the type saluted above are politically astute, and commonly take persuasive, nonthreatening steps to bring along many others they can influence.

"Star" change agents are often admired from afar, especially by those who wish they could replicate their success:

> Texas has a remarkable leader. Garry Mullins, who is a business agent in Texas, first pioneered computer use in our union. He spent untold thousands of dollars of his own money updating his own office. Now he is going to be a national officer, and hopefully spread the word. His region is better off for the classification, the filing, the retrieval and processing of information—right now, basically, the administration. He also can communicate with all his members throughout his region, which is Texas. He does computer bulletins, but he also does hard-copy mailings.

Many more such pioneers were cited, almost always with the utmost respect, and I was left hoping many lessons might be extracted from their example.

Not to be overlooked as a spur to change is the presence at home of still younger enthusiasts:

> My 14-year-old has launched three Web pages of his own, and is far ahead of me. I just share time on his computer—when he'll let me.

Similarly, activist Carl D. Cantrell shares this account from his own research:

> IBEW Local Union 1547, in Anchorage, Alaska, has a nice, professional-looking Web site (www.alaska.net/ibew1547/index.htm). Anne Hays, the local's communication director, gave the Web site creation to her 14-year-old son as a summer project. He earned $300 doing the page and is paid for time spent updating and improving the site.

Scores of like tales abound, and raise hopes that a happy byproduct of the entire computer movement in Labor may be the winning of recruits from the ranks of young computer tutors.

Competition with youngsters can also be a motivator, as recalled by a very talented computer instructor for a building trades union:

> Let me tell you—there's *nothing* that's more of a pleasure than having a red-neck carpenter from Georgia—who came ridin' in on his Harley—

stayin' in my class, because he wanted to know how to use that computer. And he goes back to school to show his kids! "Hey, Dad is just a carpenter, but he knows how to use that computer, too!"

We preach to them, "Use your kids' knowledge, too!" Tell your kids. This is what you wanna' do. *They'll* show you how to get there. Don't be embarrassed that your kids know more than you do, "cause you know more about building than they do. They just know more about the computer."

Again and again, interviews with computer enthusiasts eventually touched on the presence of a "propeller head" youngster as a motivating force.

Getting the Job Done

Working quietly behind the scenes can help take a drifting local into Cyber Gain status:

One shop, my largest with 500 members, decided to buy one. It grew to where everyone on the board said, "Hey, we need a computer here!" Most of the desire to get one for a local starts with a few people enjoying playing games. You know, a computer can be a fun thing!

They really didn't know how to set up anything. So I took a disk, and all the information I have concerning that local up there, and I put their membership data into it. So now, they have their own little thing, and they're doing a newsletter on it. And handouts, and stuff like that. I went up the other day, and when there was no one there I put in Office 97, and they were tickled to find it.

Others I interviewed had similar low-profile tales they had never told anyone else of what I regard as pro-computer/pro-labor "heroism," small acts that make a big difference.

Similarly, providing a clear example often wins converts. A woman organizer who works in the Deep South offered a fine example:

About three years ago nobody was using computers. We had only one big mainframe computer, an old Wang system, and we had our membership on it. I'm the one who got it started. I did it personally. I learned how to use it, and then started bringing it into the local's office. I got our local president interested. She saw me doing it, and then she bought a computer.

> And the next thing you know, everything started moving in the office. Real fast! The local then paid for all of us to go for training. Now, it's being used throughout the whole local. We're even producing our own newsletter.

A related characteristic is the willingness of activists to shoulder personal sacrifices, often financial in nature:

> I've bought my own laptop myself. And I've bought my computer in my office myself. And I've bought my computer at home myself. I knew that my chances of getting it from the union were next to none. But I also knew that it was enough of a benefit to me, that I wanted to make that investment. Its not been an outrageous cost. The benefits have far outweighed the cost. It has made my job so much more doable.

None of the many activists I interviewed expressed any regrets or second thoughts about their own outlay, whether in money or effort.

While I interviewed scores of different types of unionists over my three years of research, I got the biggest lift from meeting initiators of computer use, people very easy to admire and applaud.

Reality Check

Before too glowing an impression is given, it should be noted that Cyber Gain unions and locals have many telling weaknesses.

To begin with, most have little or no knowledge of the existence of one another. In keeping with the costly isolation of unions from other unions, they are busy reinventing the wheel instead of trading good ideas back and forth. Despite conferences the AFL-CIO has run to encourage cross-fertilization, workshops held regularly at the George Meany Center, and the efforts computers specialists of 12 or so major unions are making to stay in touch, it is as if the organizations were ships passing in the night.

Second, Cyber Gain unions and locals often try to do it on the cheap. Many are reluctant to pay the annual maintenance costs required to keep a complex, multi-machine system up and going, let alone to constantly upgrade it. In consequence, they often flounder trying to best computer problems they should not have had in the first place.

A third weakness is acceptance of long-standing gender biases, as made clear by this female activist:

The women take to computers much better. And I don't know if it is typing skills. I think that has something to do with it. But I also think it is the mentality in our particular office. The men in the office *never* did anything like *that.* Any filing, any kind of typing they wanted done, there were women in the office to do it for them. So now, we have to educate them—but they're still looking at it from that way. I mean, they'll stand back and ask someone else to turn it on and find them what they need, as opposed to doing it themselves.

Holdovers like this take a toll in morale, and send the wrong message.

Finally, and most telling of all, the Cyber Gain unions I studied had too little in the way of overarching vision. Many seemed to have lost sight of why they had started using computers to begin with. That is, they were not asking good questions about the desirability of this or that use with reference to the organization's well-being, with reference to what the rank-and-file might get from it (or lose to it). Instead, they were weighing computer uses in small-minded rather than grand ways, and they were missing transformational opportunities.

More specifically, where computer applications are concerned, Cyber Gain unions and locals often remain frozen in the first generation of Internet use. They are preoccupied with meeting straightforward informational needs. Their Web site typically offers their logo and basic facts, a static display critics dismiss as "brochure ware" or "billboards." They fail to understand or decline to value the fact that second-generation applications are quite different. Known as transactional, they emphasize the dynamic participation of the parties, rather than accept passivity, as at present in far too many Cyber Gain computer uses.

Summary

While the Cyber Gain model is clearly superior to the Cyber Naught and Cyber Drift options, it will not do. While it rebuilds, it does not adequately renew. Failing to take the full potential of computerization boldly into account, Cyber Gain organizations do not deal with the future as much as they streamline the past. Only a far more ambitious use of informatics in general, and computers in particular, will really do the job. I think this model will be adequate for only a few more years. The early twenty-first century requires far more.

Recommended Resources

Boyett, Joseph and Jimmie. *The Guru Guide: The Best Ideas of the Top Management Thinkers.* New York: Wiley, 1998. A far-ranging synthesis of current workplace changes, as explored by 79 top-flight consultants. Especially valuable are essays offering 33 reasons for resistance to change, 33 reasons for creating a learning organization, comparisons of traditional versus high-performance organizations, and the attributes of laudable leadership (continual learning, courage, curiosity, daring, discernment, farsightedness, humor, integrity, synergizing, and thinking win-win).

Cohen-Rosenthal, Edward, ed. *Unions, Management, and Quality: Opportunities for Innovation and Excellence.* Chicago: Irwin, 1995. Thirteen original essays, jointly authored by union and management "partners" in achieving outstanding workplace cooperation. Illustrates how a labor organization can break from old ways and construct a new and better reality.

Shostak, Arthur B. *Robust Unionism: Innovations in the Labor Movement.* Ithaca, NY: ILR Press, 1991. An exploration of the strengths and weaknesses of over 200 major ongoing reforms, paying special attention to their transferability. Features close-ups of remarkable change-agents and very varied projects. Many of the unions and locals cited warrant the honorific label of Cyber Gain operation.

The Communications Workers of America Web site is located at http://www.cwa-union.org. It contains a section on Union Labor and Information with links to the following: CWA Locals and Affiliates; Unions on the Web (North America); Unions on the Web (International); Other Labor-Related Sites; Labor and Industrial Relations E-mail Discussion Lists; and Related Areas on CWA's Web Site

In addition, the CWA site has on-line publications from the CWA research department, links to the CWA legislative and political Web site, links for members and the general public to participate in on-line activism, and a large section on industry information which includes Communications and Media Industry: Telephone, Cable TV, Broadcast Media, Newspaper Printing and Publishing, Public and Health Care Workers, Higher Education, Airline Passenger Service, and Internet Job Banks.

For a fine example of a site maintained by an enthusiast, see IBEW member *James Border's Web site* in Nashville, Tennessee (www .geocities.com/SouthBeach/Sands/1173/ibew.html). James, a member of IBEW Local Union 429, has developed his own unofficial IBEW Web site where he displays some labor links and basic information about the IBEW.

Indispensable is an independent Web site, *LabourStart,* edited by Eric Lee (author of *The Labour Movement and the Internet*). Updated early, it features labor news and numerous links to union sites around the world. It also offers a discussion forum, a directory of online labor conferences, a bookstore, and a labour channel that utilizes "push" technology to automatically bring users the labor information sought (see www.labourstart.org/).

Reading 5

Futuristics and Unions: The AFGE Experience

Sharon Pinnock
American Federation of Government Employees, AFGE

Below is perhaps the first-ever insider's account of what it takes to move a major union into Cyber Gain status—and what an excellent account it is! Threatened with major job losses, and serviced by a staff accustomed to reacting rather than to taking proactive efforts, the American Federation of Government Employees was fortunate to have at its helm a far-sighted president, (the late) John Sturdivant, intent on transforming, rather than merely tinkering with the organization.

Sharon Pinnock, AFGE's Director of Membership and Organization, helped the campaign from the outset, and shares with candor and enthusiasm the ongoing saga of a union still busy futurizing itself. She takes on many shibboleths along the way, including popular misunderstandings about what "changing to organize" means, and the real requirements if nonindustrial workers are soon to be organized.

Frank about how much unending work is required to earn and retain Cyber Gain status, Pinnock is convinced that the rewards outweigh the costs—and she makes a convincing case for this critical proposition.

Since America no longer has an industrial-based economy, the only way for unions to survive is to transform themselves, much the same way they did in the '30s and '40s when industrial unionism (which later came to be known as "business unionism") began to supplant craft unionism (Eisenscher 1998; Toffler and Toffler 1994; Heckscher 1988).

The basis for this theory is supported by a growing body of literature which purports that America has entered a third socioeconomic wave or cycle which is largely driven by "brain work," as opposed to "muscle work" (Dertouzos 1997; Pritchett 1996; Shostak 1997; Toffler 1980). Since the work has changed, so, too, must the unions seeking to represent this new work force. It is within this model that the concepts of futuristics and unionism can be linked.

I intend to examine attempts made over the last five years by the American Federation of Government Employees (AFGE) to "futurize" the union and make it more appealing to, and profitable for, workers of the twenty-first century.

My essay should add to the debate around what it will take to revitalize the labor movement. It will challenge the viability of current AFL-CIO strategies which continue to view the industrial unionism model as one which is sound, and only in need of shoring up by the reallocation of union resources and increased use of specific union tactics in organizing drives. AFL-CIO unions might be encouraged to transform, rather than only reform, their industrial-based organizations by my study of a union which employs information technology, strategic planning, and visioning in its futurizing efforts .

My findings will question long-standing theories about what "changing to organize" means. They will also offer an alternative, though unpopular, view about what it will take for the labor movement to attract workers who are increasingly engaged in nonindustrial work.

Making Our Future

AFGE set out to find a "future of preference" after the newly elected president of the United States announced in his 1993 inaugural address that he would reduce the size of the federal government by 250,000 and significantly "reinvent" government. After months of hand-wringing and meetings about what would become of federal-sector unions, AFGE's then-President, John Sturdivant, began to publicly share his view that AFGE had new opportunities as a result of the government reinvention process (DeWyngaert 1998).

Writing to his political supporters in October 1993, Sturdivant asked them to work with him to embrace the change on the horizon. "Change . . . however painful . . . wrenching . . . and difficult . . . is already taking place within the federal workforce. . . . There is overwhelming support across the country for cutting down the size of the federal government. . . . By adopting a bold and pro-active strategy, AFGE has strategically established ourselves as a credible organization . . . to move the federal government and its work practices to a high-value, high-performance workplace" (President's Report, October 1993).

As the leader of a union facing drastic downsizing and privatization efforts, Sturdivant knew that he had several choices: Do nothing and accept the probable future. Rely on AFGE's institutional knowledge and experience to try to prevent the change. Or do something to create a future that the union preferred.

That "something" came in the form of an aggressive futurization plan aimed at making sure that AFGE was in the room not only when decisions were made about how the federal work force would be downsized, but that it would still be present when the dust settled to play a policy-making role in determining what type of government twenty-first-century America could expect.

Strategic Planning

In December of 1993, Sturdivant began the first of what was to become an annual process of strategic planning by the common officers and senior staff at the union's headquarters office. This process involved analyzing the threats and opportunities the union was facing, as well as evaluating its strengths and weaknesses.

It was met with significant resistance from staff, many of whom were comfortable with their more familiar "crisis management" approach. Most of the officers and staff present at this first meeting were unaccustomed to developing long- and short-term objectives as part of the union's strategy development. However, outcome goals, timetables, and responsibilities were hammered out—and for the first time in recent memory, AFGE set its own agenda, instead of preparing to react to what the future might bring.

Computerization Improvements

Earlier that same year, the union began implementation of a computer systems modernization program under the guidance of the National Executive Council's (NEC) computer steering committee. Then National Secretary-Treasurer Bobby Harnage reported to the NEC in March 1993 that plans to set up the Local Area Network were being implemented and would soon allow everyone to share the same files/data base and give the district offices their research/access capability.

Plans to equip each member of the AFGE field staff with then-state-of-the-art 486 laptop computers—and train them in their use—had been 95 percent accomplished by November of the following year.

The system's modernization also included updating the system for billing locals. This had long been a sore point among locals and had been identified by the NEC as being a service issue that had to be corrected.

In August 1996, as part of an analysis of how infotech was affecting the "workplace culture" of AFGE, Sturdivant allowed a survey of approximately 50 percent of the headquarters staff regarding the impact of the Local Area Network (LAN) system. The survey results indicated that within two years of the LAN implementation, AFGE headquarters staff were working more efficiently, felt slightly more comfortable communicating with those outside their respective departments via the LAN, and enjoyed the flexibility of e-mail as a result of its availability.

If infotech could impact union staff in this manner, Sturdivant wondered, couldn't it also be used to advance the organizational vision of the union?

Internet Gains

In the fall of the same year, Sturdivant and Harnage convened an "Internet Taskforce" made up of key members of the NEC, department directors, and other key staff members. The committee was charged with the task of launching the union into cyberspace via the establishment of an AFGE Web site. After months of reviewing other union and corporate Web sites, interviewing Web-meisters and potential service providers, and considering a variety of cost factors, the AFGE Web site debuted at the union's 1997 Legislative Conference held the following February.

Not long afterward, a full-time position of "Web publisher" was created in the communications department to update and maintain the site. By January of 1998, the average number of "hits" per day (visitors to the site) on the site was up to 4,215. Just four months later (April 1998), that number had grown to 7,143 (AFGE Web Reports).

This type of information technology was a tool that AFGE's national union leadership believed could help spread the gospel of unionism to the world-at-large. However, there was still much concern that many of AFGE's locals had not yet gotten onto the information highway. Again, the union turned to survey research to help determine the degree to which AFGE locals and their leaders were using infotech.

Survey Research

Working closely with the Institute for Alternative Futures, the Drexel Center for Employment Futures, and the Wilson Center (directed by Phil Comstock), AFGE developed a survey instrument for use at its 34th Triennial National Convention. Results indicted 80 percent of the union offices had a fax machine; 78 percent, a phone-answering machine; and 61 percent had access to a VCR. A surprising 73 percent reported that the local office had at least one computer, and another 10 percent claimed access to one.

Seventy-nine percent of AFGE local unionists used word-processing and printing capabilities; 66 percent, the spreadsheet possibilities; 58 percent, e-mail and database features; and 57 percent said they utilized their computer's graphic package(s). Overall, AFGE locals appeared to have the basic hardware and software necessary to utilize these computer potentialities.

The news, however, was not all good. Only 44 percent could send faxes or access the Internet or AFGE's Web site. These two features were central to the union's goal of communicating its vision more effectively to local leaders and members. So this "technology lag" among nearly 60 percent of its locals made it difficult for AFGE to rely on this tool as its primary source of messaging.

A Strategic Victory

In October and December of 1995, the congressional architects of the "Contract With America" (a blueprint of the right-wing of Congress's preferred future) orchestrated two government-wide lockouts. AFGE believed the intent was to convince the American people that if they could live without 40 percent of the services provided by the federal government for three months, they wouldn't even notice if those services didn't return. For the unions impacted by the lockouts, this was not a future of preference.

On July 25, 1995, nearly three months before the first lockout took place, AFGE established a "Lockout Task Force Committee"—headed by Women's and Fair Practices Director Kitty Peddicord—to review the potential of a lockout, to establish goals for response, and to develop a plan to inform and mobilize the membership.

By August, AFGE had invited other impacted unions—SEIU, AFSCME, and NATCA—to join the Lockout Task Force, and had begun to build a list of activists to receive weekly fax broadcasts of the AFGE Lockout Task Alert. A telephone hotline number was established for incoming calls relating to the lockout. In early September, over 170,000 AFGE members were sent postcards alerting them to the impending budget crisis. The Lockout Task Force meetings were moved to weekly, as the specter of a government-wide shutdown loomed.

AFGE recognized that success in this effort depended on the union's ability to reframe the issue and effectively communicate its message not only to the workers impacted, but also to the public at large. The issue was not that nonessential government employees were being locked out of their jobs, but that friends and neighbors were unable to provide highly valued services because of an uncaring Congress.

As a result of careful planning and coordination, this message was delivered not at a Washington, D.C. press conference, but by AFGE members telling their stories to local newscasters and leaders around the country. This was a defining moment in the union's history in two respects: the union demonstrated the strategic importance of being able to effectively communicate its message, and it revealed its capacity to mobilize around a common vision and goal. As a result, the Congress backed down and returned federal employees to work—with full back pay.

The 1997 Vision Conference

In 1995, as part of their consensus-building efforts, the Sturdivant-Harnage team reached out to the AFGE field staff—who are represented by CWA—to establish a labor-management partnership. The goal was twofold: (1) for AFGE to practice what it was preaching (to the locals) in the area of labor-management partnerships; and (2) to find a balance between the traditional and the nontraditional approaches to problem-solving between the parties.

Precarious from its inception, the staff CWA/AFGE Partnership Committee struggled to ease the tension between various components of the union responsible for the overall organizing efforts. In the fall of 1996, the Partnership Committee recommended a meeting be held to bring together field staff and elected leaders to develop a shared goal for building the union. The idea was to work toward buy-in via input into the actual program, as opposed to the traditional approach of imposing organizing targets from the headquarters.

The union's National Executive Council approved the plan and in January 1997, the "Vision '97" Conference was held in San Diego, California. It featured a labor futurist to help participants explore some of the technological and socioeconomic changes taking place in the nation, a labor pollster to update participants on current organizing trends in both the private and federal sectors, and two organizational change consultants—one from Labor and one from corporate America—to teach new skills related to team-building and consensus decision making.

Asked as part of a vision exercise to describe what AFGE would look like in the year 2000, conference participants generally agreed that "In AFGE, we have a sense of community in which we celebrate our commitment to each other. AFGE is an organization where our diversity is a strength and our shared experiences give us a sense of family. People are the lifeblood of AFGE. We are committed to them and their quality of worklife" (Vision '97 Conference notes).

Without a doubt, the Vision Conference exceeded the goals of the Partnership Committee. Participants endorsed the goal of increasing

AFGE's membership from 178,000 to 200,000 by the year 2000; each district established its own organizing goal and developed a strategic plan.

Follow-Up Research

When conference participants were asked, over a year later, about the impact of the Vision Conference on their district or department, some 77 percent felt it had a "positive impact" on their views of AFGE's organizing program.

Most (63 percent) viewed the conference as the start of "work in progress." Thirty-five percent felt the commitment to inclusive strategic planning had increased significantly, while 31 percent felt the commitment had increased somewhat. There was widespread support for another Vision Conference in 1999, with the understanding that it would build on the commitment to inclusive strategic planning.

These results underline the value of inclusive strategic planning in the development of an organizing program. They build on research on organizational change which suggests people are more willing to buy into or support programs they have had a role in developing. Without a shared vision of what could be, various organizational components may suffer from the "disconnect syndrome" so many unions experience when attempting to "change to organize."

Follow-Up Work

One of the recommendations from the conference was to use a similar process to engage local union leaders and activists in developing a shared vision for the future of AFGE. Using a design modeled after the "search conference" structure pioneered by Fred and Merelyn Emery, AFGE held five "Future Forums" in different locations around the country involving over 200 local leaders and activists.

Future Forum participants evaluated the major trends and events facing Organized Labor. They discussed the new organizing initiatives by the AFL-CIO. And they developed scenarios for AFGE's preferable future. Their reports revealed a large consensus on key trends facing the union. The results were then integrated into a common vision for the union's future through a preferred future exercise.

The shared vision provided the basis for the program AFGE convention delegates were asked to support in August 1997. The NEC put forward four convention resolutions designed to help move the union toward its preferable future. Each resolution represented a major change to the AFGE Constitution. They were:

- Establish a funding formula to protect the union programs and services from inflation;
- Add more resources for union building and organizing programs;
- Implement direct affiliation of all AFGE locals with AFL-CIO state feds; and
- Establish a "Special Media Fund" and earmark new funding to educate the public about the services provided by government workers.

Since these issues had all come up repeatedly during the visioning exercises and analysis during the Future Forums, many delegates were familiar with the thinking behind each resolution.

Instead of having to "sell" delegates on the need to fund the union, AFGE found itself in the unique position of having had local leaders tell them, in advance, which programs they were willing to fund. As a result, delegates adopted the following resolution in support of the union's "preferred future": To provide for a $1.00 per capita tax increase to become effective on January 1, 1998, with 27 cents going to districts toward organizing, 35 cents toward inflation, and 38 cents toward affiliation of all AFGE locals with the AFL-CIO state labor councils.

The one program that did not receive any financial support was the creation of a dedicated media fund. The idea had not enjoyed floor debate in prior years, whereas the other three proposals had. In spite of its prominence in visioning sessions, establishing a "Special Media Fund" would also have required additional revenue well above the amount with which Future Forum participants had indicated they were willing to part.

Overall, AFGE had successfully used the futuristics tools of visioning and inclusive strategic planning to build consensus within the union for growth through organizing. Thanks to the convention action, by February 1998, every AFGE district had developed an organizing plan (an NEC criteria for accessing the 27 cents per member earmarked for organizing), and every AFGE local had been affiliated with the AFL-CIO state labor councils.

Summary

AFGE is still in the early stage of its change process. However, a number of lessons are already clear. The importance of top leadership commitment to change is crucial. It is the central theme running through the organizational change literature and has also been true at AFGE. Without the leadership team of John Sturdivant and Bobby Harnage, it is unlikely that the initiatives the union has undertaken over the last five years would have succeeded.

Another lesson is that staff and local activists must be included in planning the change effort if they are to buy into the organizing program. AFGE has added 11,000 new members to its rolls over the course of the five-year study period due in large part to its attempt to include everyone in the growth effort—not just a handful of skilled organizers.

This is no small feat considering the downsizing, contracting out, anti-government rhetoric, and massive reorganizations to which AFGE locals have been subjected. The survey research—while limited—tells us that AFGE's efforts to utilize visioning and inclusive strategic planning have been useful in changing staff attitudes about organizing and how the work of growing the union gets done.

Additionally, by equipping its leadership and field staff with the tools needed to work smarter and faster, AFGE has begun to embrace the changes occasioned by the infotech revolution—and use them to the union's advantage. For example, AFGE's successful use of electronic media, blast fax capabilities, telephone hotlines, and the LAN helped turn the tide in the union's favor during the crisis brought on by the government shutdowns of 1995–96.

Personal Thoughts

If the labor movement is to survive and grow, unions will have to make "systemic change" (Heckscher, 9). Various futuring techniques would be useful in helping unions reverse the current trend of decline. After all, as I learned in my course in futuristics, a trend is not a law, and based on the AFGE experience, I hope other unions might be more willing to include staff and local activists in their efforts to "change to organize."

I also hope unions will take to heart the many fine suggestions offered recently by the AFL-CIO ad hoc Committee on Labor and the

Web in their very timely report entitled "Why the Internet Matters to Organized Labor." This committee of nine union Web-managers suggests that the labor movement use the Internet to "create and project a dynamic, forward-looking image for all of our organizations" (Report, 7). As the ever-increasing number of visits to the AFGE Web site indicates, it is here that our current and potential members will seek us out in the twenty-first century.

I believe the AFL-CIO leadership should build on the experiences of AFGE and other affiliates (e.g., SEIU, AFT, and CWA) to transform its present "Committee on the Evolution of Work" into an independent labor think tank, one designed to advance the use of futuristics by unions. This group could study infotech and its impact on the American work force, as well as offer innovative alternatives to labor leaders.

If Herbert Hoover—campaigning seventy years ago on a platform of prosperity—could win the presidential bid by promising voters a "chicken in every pot" (www.groilier.com), why couldn't John Sweeney rebuild America's largest social movement by calling for a "computer in every home"? If the labor movement truly wants to reassert itself as a social movement, it must play a leading role in determining how the micro-computer chip will impact all workers—not just those who are currently in unions or those who can afford to buy a computer.

Listed as fourth among all AFL-CIO unions in a recent report charting percentage of growth among affiliates, AFGE's use of futuristics is worthy of continued study. Futuristics can give—and in the case of my union, is giving—forward-thinking unionists an opportunity to create a new unionism for the twenty-first century.

Note: My study is limited in that it looks only at one AFL-CIO union, AFGE, which happens to represent workers in an industry (government service) that has already started to respond to the changes occasioned by the third socioeconomic wave described above. (Gaulin 1998; Doeringer et al. 1996) In addition, close to 500,000 of the 600,000 federal workers represented by AFGE are white-collar employees. Since government as an industry is the single area in which union membership penetration has continued to grow, AFGE may be less likely than many of her sister unions to be locked into the industrial organizing approach out of fear of continued membership slippage. However, since no comparable data exist, it is not possible to correct any possible errors in this regard.

References

AFL-CIO Committee on the Evolution of Work. 1985. *The Changing Situation of Workers and Their Unions.* AFL-CIO Publication No. 165. Washington, DC: AFL-CIO. February.

AFL-CIO Executive Council Report, September 22–25, 1997.

Doeringer, P., A. Watson, L. Kaboolian, and M. Watkins. 1996. "Beyond the Merit Model: New Directions at the Federal Workplace." In *Public Sector Employment in a Time of Transition,* R. Bellman et al., eds. Madison, WI: Industrial Relations Research Association, p. 163.

DeWyngaert, B. 1998. Personal interview, February.

Dertouzos, M. 1997. What Will Be: How the New World of Information Will Change Our Lives. New York: HarperCollins.

Eisenscher, M. 1998. "Beyond Mobilization: How Labor Can Transform Itself." *Working USA* (March/April): 36.

Fletcher, B. 1998. Personal Interview, February.

———, and R. Hurd. 1998. "Beyond the Organizing Model: The Transformation Process in Local Unions." In *Organizing to Win,* Bronfenbrenner, Friedman, Hurd, Oswald, and Seeber, eds. Ithaca, NY: Cornell University Press, pp. 37–53.

Gaulin, J. 1998. "HUD Storefronts Show New Role." *Federal Times,* June 1, p. 4.

Heckscher, C.C. 1996. *The New Unionism: Employee Involvement in the Changing Corporation.* Ithaca, NY: IRL Press/Cornell Paperbacks.

Manning, G. et al. 1996. *Building Community: The Human Side of Work.* Cincinnati: Thompson Executive Press.

Minutes, AFGE NEC Meetings. November 1993, 1994.

Pritchett, P. 1996. *Mind Shift: The Employee Handbook for Understanding the Changing World.*

Shostak, A. Class lecture. 1997. "Futuristics." January 26.

Stack, H., and S. Pinnock. 1998. "Envisioning for the Future: Building Consensus and Capacity for Organizing." Paper presented at the UCLEA/AFL-CIO Education Conference, San Jose, CA, April.

Sturdivant, J. 1993. *President's Report.* October.

Toffler, A. 1980. *The Third Wave.* New York: William Morrow.

———, and H. Toffler. 1995. *Creating a New Civilization: The Politics of the Third Wave.* Atlanta: Turner.

Sharon Pinnock is a former federal employee (ca. 1974–80). Sharon worked as a staffer for the National Treasury Employees Union from 1980 to 1984, when she joined AFGE local 1923 as an organizer. In 1988 she took a position with AFSCME Council 20. In 1989 she began with AFGE as Director of Membership and Organization—her present post. She expects to earn an undergraduate degree in labor studies shortly at the AFL-CIO George Meany Center National Labor College. (Sharon can be reached via e-mail at PINNOS@AFGE.ORG.)

Part III

CYBERUNION:
INFORMATICS PLUS

A declining labour movement under attack everywhere cannot afford not to adopt these new tools.
—Eric Lee, *The Labour Movement and the Internet,* 1997

Cyber Gain unions are almost there, but not quite. Much as Dorothy, the Lion, the Scarecrow, and the Tin Man came to realize, so also do Cyber Gain organizations have it in them to achieve much, much more. They have proved that by passing many trials along the "Yellow Brick Road." But, as early in *The Wizard of Oz* movie, they still do not realize they can and *must* become something more, something I call a CyberUnion.

Chapter 6 explains what a union or local possesses when it achieves CyberUnion status, something exceedingly rare at present in this or any other postindustrial nation. Chapter 7 explores the first of four computer-based components (known by the acronym F-I-S-T) that set these unions and locals apart, or in this case, the practice of an art form known as futuristics. Chapter 8 highlights the value of innovations, and Chapter 9 calls for bolder services than presently available. Finally, Chapter 10 focuses attention on labor history, culture, and lore, all three vital sources of traditions without which Labor would lack a soul and unionism would not constitute a social movement.

Early in the twenty-first century CyberUnion activists will regard computers—newly formatted as wearables—as part of their routine equipment, and they will encourage members to follow suit. Everyone will have e-mail access to other members and to all the officers, anytime and all the time. Nothing or very little will be held back, and members will be able to learn almost whatever they choose whenever they choose, even as they will be expected to shoulder responsibility for helping to run the organization.

Specialized software programs known as intelligent agents (see Chapter 8) will seek ways to promote union-management cooperation, and especially ways to boost the competitiveness of unionized companies. Among other things, they could take the union job-referral effort of the late 1990s (UJC@unionjobs.com), and expand it into an international job mart of major proportions.

Modern and creative, new CyberUnions should attract millions of members excited by the notion that Organized Labor is finally out ahead of the curve, rather than only struggling to catch up. CyberUnions could join with progressive employers to outthink, outdare, and outperform the non-union and anti-union competition, much to the good of all.

Part III makes a case for you and me soon helping Cyber Gain unions and locals employ the F-I-S-T model, a transformational achievement which will enable them to become CyberUnions. As such, as reinvented instruments of employee power, they *could* substantially "compute," that is, they could make a valued difference in our new Cyberspace world.

A new type of unionism is necessary if labor is to soon meet the challenge that Richard Trumka, Secretary–Treasurer of the AFL—CIO, set the historic, first-ever 1996 AFL-CIO Conference on Information Technologies:

> We want our movement to be *the* model! We don't want people to look out at anybody else and say, "That's what we ought to be." We want them to look at the labor movement when it comes to technology, when it comes to communications, when it comes to any type of innovative program that deals with technology, and say, "That's what we ought to do! That's the model!" (Trumka)

CyberUnionism, a new type of unionism that takes the informatics potential to the max, and uses computer power as never before, stands out among candidates to meet the Trumka challenge. User-friendly and empowering, CyberUnionism beckons.

6

CyberUnion: Promoting Power

The strategic issue before labor unions is whether they are willing to break away from the status quo. Are they willing to depart from traditional practice . . . and make the commitment to a bold agenda of action?
—Marick F. Masters, *Unions at the Crossroads,* 1997

If Labor is to succeed early in the twenty-first century, it must invent new processes and forms, not merely rearrange familiar old ones. Labor's goal has to go beyond conventional modernization, the end state of the Cyber Gain model. It has to reach toward its own transformation, a thorough-going renewal that makes possible the craft and power it will need to hold its own.

While you would not know it from history learned in public schools or from the mass media, Labor has done this often before—as in the mid-nineteenth century, when workingmen and women unexpectedly created the National Labor Union (the first mass movement to include women and people of color). Or later, when an unprecedented coalition of working-class whites and blacks, males and females, briefly held together an elevating mystical organization called the Knights of Labor.

Or in the very late nineteenth century, when the craft unions finally succeeded in creating in the AFL a national alliance of skilled-worker unions (*sans* women and people of color). Or in the 1930s, when factory workers dramatically created CIO unions to organize the new mass industries (feisty unions that welcomed women and people of color back into membership).

Much to their credit, a small number of Cyber Gain organizations here and abroad are busy even now struggling to transform themselves into CyberUnions (see the essays in this volume by Breedlove, Giljum, and Pinnock), a term I am confident they have never heard of, albeit the contents of their experiments have much in common with my blueprint.

Why Change?

Reasons for seeking to become a CyberUnion—by whatever name—are many and varied. As an enthusiastic staffer in a large public-sector union notes:

> I may not plug the computer into my brain, but it is most certainly an extension of my brain. Microsoft programs actually anticipate your path, and the wizard (avatar) will automatically prompt you with suggestions. . . . I can retrieve my e-mail from any location, and I am in travel status sometimes three weeks each month. . . . E-mail allows me to say what I have to say, when I choose to, wherever I am.

An international representative of the Painters Union applauds unions establishing Web sites:

> Unions must have a presence on the Web in order to catch those who may stumble into them or may be seeking information directly. I often find myself using the Web as almost a combination phone book/encyclopedia, and anyone with workplace issues will find us when they are looking.

Scores of other "true believers" regaled me with reasons why their unions and/or locals are busy upgrading their uses of computers—even while also conceding there is still very far to go.

And that is where the CyberUnion blueprint comes in, as it offers detailed pointers, a rationale for attempting their securement, and a vision to help guide the way. What is even more, CyberUnions should be able to get Americans to think of Labor, and not just of business, when they think about future-making twenty-first-century organizations.

CyberUnion Outline

Whether of my design or independently discovered, a CyberUnion can be known by its distinctive uses of computer potentialities, uses that revolve around putting members rather than officers first, and putting democracy (rights *and* responsibilities) center stage.

Accordingly, a CyberUnion:

- employs computer-based tools to regularly survey members, both actual and potential, to learn in depth what are their needs and wants, their dreams and nightmares;
- employs computer-based tools to survey members to learn preferences and priorities among major questions confronting the organization. Every effort is made to improve member participation in union policy-making;
- employs computer-based tools to keep members abreast of relevant developments, and to learn of such from the rank-and-file. The union's or local's cyberspace homepage is updated weekly, and e-mail of real merit flows often between officers and the rank-and-file;
- makes officers and staffers accessible to members via e-mail, and promises personal responses within 72 hours of a message's receipt; and
- updates its infotech infrastructure regularly. It takes pride both in being at the cutting edge and in making a special effort to take the membership there with it.

These attributes go far beyond what Cyber Gain organizations regard as wise, and help Labor remember what it is ultimately about.

Making a F-I-S-T

Building on this foundation, a CyberUnion will also employ a F-I-S-T-ful of new tools, namely, *f*uturistics (a perspective), *i*nnovations (cutting-edge tools), *s*ervices (ties that matter), and *t*raditions (a vision and a commitment). Together they provide an eclectic mix of foresight, derring-do, riches, and heart (the essence of F-I-S-T) necessary if a Cyber Gain union is to consciously evolve into a CyberUnion.

Employing an art form known as *futuristics* (see Chapter 7), a CyberUnion can replace a "putting-out-fires" orientation with a far longer perspective, one that encompasses the here-and-now, but also extends five and ten years beyond it.

Employing *innovations* (see Chapter 8), a CyberUnion, for example, can replace lazy acceptance of shopworn communication tools (newsletters, mailings, etc.) with a "can do!" perspective, one that upgrades familiar tools (as in adding color to a local newsletter) even as it moves to the cutting edge of affordable communication tools (e-mail for all, listserves for many, etc.).

Employing *services* as never before (see Chapter 9), a CyberUnion can compete in the marketplace for the loyalty and appreciation of its members. It can open and run vocational schools, computer schools, and sundry other services—and expand their range, number, and enviable record.

Finally, employing *traditions* in fresh ways (see Chapter 10), a CyberUnion can replace hollow observances with whole-hearted celebration. This can help ensure that Labor's cyberspace (high-tech) gains are accompanied by comparable "high-touch" advances; e.g., a local's history and traditions could be "captured" in a memorable CD-ROM provided to all, or put on an extraordinary Web site available all the time to everyone on-line.

Attack and Rebuttal

Cynics will insist that the vast majority of union members are indifferent to computer uses, and that any CyberUnion prescription is therefore irrelevant.

Some will go further and dismiss futuristics as only for effete intellectuals. Innovation will be bad-mouthed as only for a techocentric elite. Services will be knocked as frills. And a CyberUnion's attention to tradition will be scorned as beside the point, given the drastic nature of Labor's situation. In all of this they are just plain wrong, and their negativism is a prescription for labor movement suicide.

In rebuttal, proponents point out that more and more unionized workers coexist with computers (a study in 1999 for the AFL-CIO found that 57 percent of working unionists had a home computer, [Hart]). Indeed, science-fiction writer Bruce Sterling has said "Web-surfing is a genuinely popular enterprise—it's like Monday Night Football or country line-dancing" (Chapman, 318).

Even if a unionist's living room does not yet contain a PC, his or her work station probably does. As well, advances in inexpensive devices to access the Internet without a PC (Webservers, etc.) promise to soon vastly expand the reach of the Net (a voice-activated/voice-responsive palmtop, or very small computer worn on the wrist, may be commonplace by 2003 or thereabouts).

In any case, the point is not that of hardware or access to it. Rather, the point is to rapidly and thoroughly link labor with all that a smart organization can draw out of computer uses, and to "bookend" such adaptation with futuristics, innovations, services, and traditions.

As for the attacks on the F-I-S-T components, a strong case is made for each in the four chapters that follow. Suffice it to say here that each is substantially aided by new computer applications. The availability of these Information Age wonders (such as computer modeling for futuristics, and virtual reality as a union service in apprentice training) is what sets all four components apart today from earlier versions of each. As often before, the cynics are attacking bygone targets.

Déjà Vu?

One set of doubts, however, stands out as especially worthy of further reflection. Certain skeptics (too wise to be cynics) startle CyberUnion fans by asking if their model isn't caught up in a fading dream. They ask if the Internet hasn't rapidly gone from being a "revolutionary" technology to just another communications medium, one that, for most people, simply supplements TV and the telephone.

These pundits wonder aloud if revolutionary zeal about the Digital Age seems, at best, two or three years out of date now—and at worst, laughable. In their view, the Internet, while still transforming the economy, is fading into the cultural background, merely a conventional staple of middle-class homes (Chapman).

In other words, if cyberspace is going to prove only a bland clone of the communications status quo, Labor can go as far into it as activists push, but in the end, Labor will be substantially unchanged, a conventional staple of no special consequence.

CyberUnion enthusiasts like myself agree that our mass culture has a genius for absorbing and taming nearly everything that comes its way. But we are not ready to concede that computerization and the Digital Age lack the "right stuff" to help activists reinvent organized

Labor. These tools have not yet been tested, and we persist in betting on the revolutionary possibilities of informatics.

In the Crystal Ball

One more matter remains to be explored before we go into F-I-S-T details, namely, the intriguing presence of pro-CyberUnion activists everywhere I looked.

Many activists I interviewed or got e-mail responses from have expectations congruent with CyberUnion possibilities, albeit the concept is not known by them. For example, a staffer shared his belief that only five years from now Labor would be very far along:

> Modernization by way of computers is inevitable, so efficiency will "soak in" even on the hardcore resisters. I see the more progressive unions going to a cyber-network in the next 5 to 10 years, one which will handle 90 percent of what is being done now by paper and mailings.

Looking ahead, another activist believes "unions could be communicating with their members with a speed and quality that could be very valuable." A third unionist is excited about the membership polling possibilities:

> Unions will be able to conduct e-mail surveys, efficiently and quickly, reaching all members at home. Information will be received timely.

An organizing director believes we will soon have two major breakthrough in services:

> Interactive games, which permit children to "experience" different periods of labor history in school, thereby gaining a more meaningful understanding of what the labor struggle in the United States has entailed. And "virtual reality" negotiations programs, which will help unionists sharpen their skills at the bargaining table.

Another activist expects to enjoy live video conferencing, interactive Web sites, and on-line union publications. And a West Coast activist sees the promise of computer technology in "the direct connection between workers worldwide to coordinate solidarity actions in the global economy."

All of which is to say that the ranks already host creative union men and women busy dreaming and working on behalf of a CyberUnion scenario—by whatever name.

Contrary to the misgivings of detractors, adoption of a CyberUnion model is not an implausible or impractical proposal. It builds on initiatives the AFL-CIO and key unions have already begun to take. Very much to the point is the fact that the Sweeney team renamed the *AFL-CIO News*, a bland and unexceptional house organ they inherited, *America@Work*, and transformed it into a bright, brassy, and "hip" publication, complete every issue with a "Homepage" devoted to cyberspace resources (see atwork@aflcio.org).

More so than any of the other models explored in this book, the CyberUnion honors the bottom-line thought of sociologist C. Wright Mills, who, in 1947, identified as *the* main reason for establishing unions—"to accumulate power and to exert it" (Mills, 7).

Summary

Organized Labor is on the move, gaining "smarts," and feeling cautiously hopeful. To keep up momentum, the AFL-CIO, its major affiliates, and their most progressive locals could now begin looking beyond their greatest achievement to date, the Cyber Gain union and local, and consider a novel twenty-first-century CyberUnion model.

Supporters like myself do not insist the CyberUnion is on the horizon, for we know that "the horizon is an imaginary line that recedes as you approach it" (D. Bell). Instead, we urge only a fair trial—convinced as we are that it offers more for less than any alternative labor now weighs.

Marked by even greater enthusiasm for the Age of Information than their Cyber Gain forerunner, CyberUnions are creative in making the most of what far too many unionists still find daunting. Activists are already dreaming of it, and experimenting with this and that aspect in prototype.

Mind-boggling advances in Information Age dynamics will continue to sow much confusion in and outside of the workplace. Organized Labor, thanks to its CyberUnion use of a new F-I-S-T combination, could settle much of the confusion to Labor's advantage, and prove that a powerful new stripe of unionism *does* "compute" in the early twenty-first century.

Recommended Resources

Martin, James. *Cybercorp: The New Business Revolution.* New York: American Management Association (AMACOM), 1996. Promoted as a game plan for corporate survival, for the next major corporate overhaul, this pioneering book focuses on informatics and organizational transformation rather than mere reform. Derisive of excuses for resisting wired changes, it champions an agile, virtual, and exceedingly creative business, the kind Organized Labor will increasingly sit across the table from, and must match in vital ways.

Shostak, Arthur B., ed. *For Labor's Sake: Gains and Pains as Told by 28 Creative Inside Reformers.* Lanham, MD: University Press of America, 1995. First-person accounts of the trials and tribulations of activists seeking to create Cyber Gain organizations, the better someday soon to help move them along to CyberUnion status. While most of the reforms championed are of the high-touch rather than high-tech variety, the lessons learned are widely applicable to Labor's transformation in all guises.

MEME: A four-year-old source for exploring the possibility that when people look back at the 1990s, the Internet will be seen as *the* defining characteristics of our century at its end. Available at listserv@ maelstrom.stjohns.edu (send a message that reads subscribe meme your first name your last name).

UnionRing: A network of labor/union/worker-related Web sites around the world. Available at http://www.geocities.com/CapitolHill/ 5202/unionring.html

URCOT (Union Research Centre on Organisation and Technology): Undertakes workplace research which would assist union and management representatives involved in major projects involving organisational and technological change. Available at http://minyos.its.rmit .edu.au/zkaren/

Reading 6

The World of Tomorrow

Carol Rodgers
Office and Professional Employees International Union,
OPEIU, Local 2

Written in a chipper and engaging style, the essay below by activist Carol Rodgers is actually an alarm bell going off, a "heads-up" call of the most serious nature. A "technology train" is roaring down the tracks, she warns, and it may run over millions of unionists (and even more non-unionists) unprepared for turmoil in the work world. Robots of every conceivable (and some hard-to-conceive) variety are coming, and they may take out millions of conventional (pattern-able and repeatable) jobs. Only major changes in retraining may help, though the threat may overwhelm even that old resource. Will we need to think for ourselves, Rodgers dares to wonder, and if not, what goes next? Very little time may be left to climb aboard the technology train, one whose conductors, Rodgers wryly suggests, we will know full well.

Brothers and Sisters: Ten years from now, computers will probably be at home in our pockets, inside our televisions, coffee makers, and almost everything else. Scientists could pack vastly more computing power into tinier, lighter packages. If the most optimistic scientists are correct, tomorrow's shirt-pocket computers could hold a billion bytes (equivalent to 2,000 books) in their memory, and run at 50 million times the speed of today's fastest personal computers.

All of the above I can believe. I know that when rumors started 100 years ago about something taking off and flying through the air unassisted like a bird, people thought it was a crazy idea and it would never happen.

As time travels ever closer to the new millennium, we may enter an era where grocery shopping and the mall become passé. Do you hate to cook? Chances are good automated cooking may take care of this.

What about working on your computer? Have trouble searching the Internet? No problem, just ask your personal knowbot [Information Agent].

This all sounds very exciting. However, there could be a downside. It's highly probable that unless you are currently in a career position where technology is kept up to date, you won't have a career. We all need to climb aboard the technology train. If not, some of us may be stranded at the station.

It is highly probable that in the next 30 years machines may not only take over manual labor, but also intellectual labor. Millions of bluecollar workers and middle managers could lose their jobs by the early 2000s. Unless these workers are computer literate, they could be stuck in low-skill, low-wage service positions.

There are many jobs where automation could take over. Since machines can do undesirable and risky jobs, if properly applied, robots and automation could reduce manual labor and increase productivity. Artificial intelligence could push up the amount of tasks that a machine could do, which, in essence, could challenge people to higher levels of thinking.

I'm afraid it has already started happening. Whole rows of assembly line workers have been and are still being replaced by robots. Many, many telephone operators have been displaced by computers. These days, whole labs full of highly skilled lab technicians are being replaced by robotic minilabs. Mining jobs are being taken over by robots. And, as robots have started to become mobile, security personnel and hospital food servers have been replaced.

Unemployment rates edged up after the introduction of commercial computers, about 40 years ago. However, the real impact may be on wages. The incomes of bluecollar, clerical, and now many whitecollar workers have stagnated.

As machines get smarter, people have to get smarter too. As late as the 1960s, a man could drop out of high school and get a well-paying assembly line job with union benefits and make enough money to buy a little house. If a person does this now a days, he/she will find themselves serving fast-food at minimum wage until retirement.

Better-educated people are in greater control of their lives, but educating the workforce can go only so far. Not everyone is a potential college graduate. Not everyone will be able to run intelligent machines. Many people are naturally talented to do skilled craft labor that does not require deep thinking, but does require manual dexterity. Just the kind of work that robots may soon fill.

As robots become as smart and dexterous as reptiles, then mammals, then kids, and finally adults, as they multiply, they will no longer just suppress wages. Fewer and fewer jobs will be safe. The assembly line worker is already on the way out, and although ambulatory jobs have been fairly safe, that will change as robots become as agile as, and then more agile than, people.

In a couple of decades, jobs such as garbage collection, gardening, janitorial, and household work could be done more cheaply and efficiently, thanks to our friendly robots. Robots will probably be cheaper than human domestic helpers and more efficient.

Migrant farm workers can soon forget their jobs. They probably will lose out to robotic pickers that gently pick fruit and vegetables 24 hours a day, and they won't care a bit about pesticides. Gas station attendants and mechanics—Robotic! Delivery services and postal employees—Robotic! Robocops! Robocabs! Robofiremen! Robodoctors!

We need to think of a way where people and machines think together inside and outside of the workplace. The way things are now, let's say, on an assembly line, technology is already laying off workers right and left. These workers may go to their unions for help with the technology fight against their employers, but let's face it, technology will win.

Ordinary workers need to be highly computer literate, understand systems science, possess statistical quality-control skills, and most important, quickly learn to use new technologies. Education and training are the keys to staying on top of the changing workplace. We must all bargain for a technology and education clause in our contracts. If there is a way to ward off the possibility of a mass downsizing, we must find a way.

An educated, skilled work force that can operate complex machines and systems favors automation that challenges workers to continuous improvement through education, experimentation, and feedback. Workers and computers need to interact to optimize production. However, where educated and skilled labor is not readily available, then automating people out of jobs could be more attractive.

Let's now take a look at the future of manufacturing.

By the year 2025, there is likely to be a decline in manufacturing's percentage of Gross Domestic Product to 20 percent from a peak of 30 percent in 1953. Manufacturing employment will probably free fall from 30 percent of nonfarm jobs in 1960, to 17 percent in 1990, to less than 8 percent by 2025. The gap between the value of manufactured goods, and the knowledge and service industries is likely to close steadily. In 1925, manufacturing produced 20 times the volume of service exports. By 2025, the two should be roughly equal.

Retraining programs will probably not save the jobs of many less-skilled workers. Training needs to be done on a continual basis, not all at once when a position is in fear of being downsized. New jobs could require more skills and abilities than a three- or six-month retraining program could provide. These jobs will probably go to multi-skilled candidates with undergraduate or graduate degrees.

Education, education, education! In 1983, my senior year of high school, we received the first computer at our school. In 1988, when my son was in preschool, there was an Apple computer in every classroom. Only five years had passed before preschoolers were being taught that computers were a part of everyday life.

By 1998 we should all have an idea how the world could change in 30 years. Those toddlers from 1988 could end up replacing us before we're ready to retire. While we wait for new technological equipment, and then struggle to learn new programs, to those toddlers, the jobs will be second nature.

Do you want to know more about cooking and shopping in the future? You'll have to read next month's article. Personally, I can't wait for something to cook and do my grocery shopping for me.

And what about the knowbot [Information Agent]? A little piece of technology depicting a person inside our computers, able to answer any question asked. Alas, will we need to think for ourselves anymore?

So don't forget to be prepared for that technology train. When it rolls into the station, it probably won't stop: You'd better grab a handle and jump aboard. The conductors? Our kids.

Carol R. Rodgers is a secretary at the AFL-CIO headquarters, who is currently working on a grant project for the Railway Workers Hazardous Materials Training Program at the National Labor College of the George Meany Center for Labor Studies. She is a union member with OPEIU Local 2. Carol expects to soon earn her undergraduate degree in safety and health at the National Labor College of the George Meany Center. (Carol can be reached via e-mail at railway@erols.com.)

7

Futuristics: Promoting Alternatives

We must seek to make what happens, in substantial part, a logical *result of our having planned that it should happen.*
—Simon Ramo, *Century of Mismatch,* 1976

While hardly any of them would recognize the title, many union activists are actually amateur *futurists.* They endlessly scan the horizon, looking for clues of consequence. Will the employer remain competitive? Will "smart" automation cost more jobs? Will a corporate raider take over? Will overseas competition intensify? Should a contract reopener be exercised? Should the local buy high-powered computer equipment?

Men and women with decision-shaping power in Labor operate with a finger in the air and an inner sense attuned to signs of possible, probable, preventable, and preferable matters. These worldly-wise activists never arbitrate, bargain, collaborate with other groups, endorse a candidate, evaluate their political opposition, grant an interview, or organize, without first carefully weighing the prospects, the consequences tomorrow of actions taken or not.

In over 40 years of studying unionism and learning from unionists, I have not yet met one formally schooled in the methods, theories, and jargon of *futuristics,* a serious discipline with practitioners who can make a good and honest living at it. Indeed, outside of the course I created in 1986, and have taught since at the National Labor College, I know of no opportunity in the world of labor education for a unionist to study futuristics (an omission that cries out for reform).

Nevertheless, union activists are often damn good at making forecasts. They can and do imagine alternative futures. They trace links among future-shaping matters. They look ahead, as does a training director at an IBEW School who boasts that his students do things like "study zoning applications and other government documents, searching for clues to what kinds of work might be coming down the pike" (Holcomb, D-3). In 1,001 other ways, these amateur futurists use foresight to make things happen, rather than merely react to change. Many of them know they can get better at all of this, and as CyberUnionists, they will do so.

Futuristics

According to sociologist Wendell Bell, one of the subject's most able proponents, futuristics is "a new field of inquiry that involves systematic and explicit thinking about alternative futures. . . . It aims to demystify the future, to make possibilities for the future more known to us, and to increase human control over the future" (Bell, 2).

Futurists are risk-takers who "analyze the limitless possibilities of tomorrow with some practical aim in view . . . as, for instance, the slim yet admirable hope that our children may inherit a world more influenced by imagination and foresight than our own" (Brunner).

Their tools can be esoteric, and may require sophistication in computer use, interviewing, statistics, and like matters: A few, listed alphabetically, include Cross-Impact Analysis, Cyclic Pattern Analysis, Delphi, Environmental Scanning, Global Modeling, Judgmental Forecasting (genius/intuitive/expert), Models/Simulation/Gaming, Risk Assessment, Scenarios, Social Change Assessment, Technology Assessment, Technological Forecasting, Trend Analysis, and Visioning—the last of which many unions have recently used successfully (see the Pinnock essay).

Unions and Futuristics

Labor is no stranger to forecasting. You find traces of forecasting throughout labor history, as when leaders like Powell (Knights), Gompers (AFL), Debs (ALU), Murray (CIO), and others offer empowering and energizing visions of a preferable future. No strike has ever been called and directed without considerable forecasting at its core. And no merger has been initiated without an end in sight.

More recently, as I explain in my 1991 book, *Robust Unionism,* several major international unions have set committees the valuable task of preparing a blueprint for consideration at a change-oriented convention.

Typical was such an initiative taken by AFL-CIO President John Sweeney while president of SEIU. Like his counterparts in Steel, the Postal Service, and elsewhere, he appointed a "Committee on the Future" made up of local union activists throughout the country. It ultimately made recommendations to the SEIU convention which changed the organizing focus of the union. In 1996, the SEIU Committee on the Future suggested, among other things, that SEIU "shift resources to industry organizing as opposed to 'hot shop' organizing" (Fletcher). This is exactly the course current SEIU president Andy Stern is pursuing today, and one he credits for bringing in more hospital workers in 1998 than in the previous five years combined (Burkins).

Futurizing Process

Progressive unions like the SEIU generally create a blue-ribbon "Committee on the Future" to put the thinking of leading futurists at their disposal. Many such committees, after carefully reviewing the literature and interviewing relevant forecasters (Alvin Toffler, John Naisbitt, etc.), draft alternative forecasts for the next 10 or 15 years, complete with the pros and cons of future-shaping policy options the union should consider as early as possible, e.g., cooperation with or opposition to "virtual" organization advances.

Material of this sort enables labor organizations to improve their image and vision of a successful twenty-first-century union, including long-term goals, strategic options, and priorities needed to come closer to matching that profile.

Known as "applied futuristics," this approach helps a quality union plan ahead, offer clear statements of its priorities, make difficult trade-off decisions, and substantially improve its strategic information base.

Neither an artificial exercise nor a cover for rubber-stamping a set of predrawn conclusions, applied futuristics sets quality unions firmly on an empowering path that the public and media associate only with cutting-edge business organizations . . . not bad company for progressive unions to keep.

Case Studies: Applied Futuristics

An especially smart example of how to use futuristics is offered by the Steelworkers Union (USW), which has embarked on a three-year process of asking, "Where is our union? Where does it want to be? And how do we want to get there?"

Education Director Melana Barkman (an enthusiastic student in my futuristics class some years ago) explains that in the 1980s their convention eliminated the union's organizing department, and from that point on membership started to decline. It was not until the early 1990s that the USW slowly started to build again: "We are resolved not to let this happen again. Now, we have money in the bank, our credit is good, and we are growing!"

To keep up momentum, the USW is busy holding Town Hall–like small planning meetings, called Future Forums, as regional-level precursors to its convention. Rank-and-filers are invited to come and participate, as opposed to being lectured to:

> We start by showing a 14-minute video on computers and stuff in 2019. We talk about the importance of making the future now! Of considering today what we want to be tomorrow, and beyond. And we determine how we are going to get there.
>
> We lay out some of the things we know about our existing environment, and we grapple a bit with futuring. We want people to understand that you *can* change the future! We give them a history time-line of the union, which shows how increases in revenue have resulted in increases in membership, and decreases in revenue have resulted in decreases in membership and services.
>
> We break people out into smaller groups. We break them out of their comfort zones so their locals don't all cling together. And then we work them through a number of exercises which are designed to have them think about their own local, the union in general, and where we need to be going. At the end of that process we survey them about their future goals for our union.
>
> So, what we're working with as a union now is a kind of combination of some of this visioning, and this futuring—but also with a strategic planning element. And an organizational development element.

Field-tested and proven, this model empowers and invigorates, much as its proponents promise.

What Is There to Puzzle Over?

Typical of the major issues futuristics might help CyberUnions wrestle with is the puzzle concerning baby boomers and retirement. The question asks, "Will they or won't they leave the work force in 2011 when they begin to reach the traditional retirement age of their parents?"

If the boomers do retire "on schedule," millions of jobs they vacate can go to younger folk, to say nothing of the millions of new jobs created by the leisure-time expectations of 76 million new retirees. If they chose not to retire at 65, however, but to continue on as "consultants" or holders of part-time jobs, as some 80 percent now say they intend to, everything will be different (Vitez).

Not surprisingly, as with much else that matters, the experts disagree. One authority dismisses as a myth the idea of an endless work life, the idea that boomers are going to want to continue working full-time until they drop (R. Lewis). Another, however, insists they "are going to be working their buns off trying to make up for past retirement savings sins" (R.A. Lee). With a lot of jobs at stake, Labor will want to follow the research and forecasts here closely and *very* carefully.

Similarly, no consensus yet exists about such labor-relevant items as domestic robots or direct brain-computer interfaces (Aronowitz and DiFazio). At least one major forecaster publicly dismisses them as unworkable or undesirable (Dertouzos), while others forecast their imminent and welcome arrival (Rifkin). CyberUnions will monitor the debate, seeking to safeguard labor's best interests.

A third and final example notes that in July, 1998, the *Wall Street Journal* advised readers about a new computing "environment" that could put very sophisticated computers "in charge of themselves, seeking their own connections in solving problems. Networks could develop a life of their own, creating unimagined new structures and processes." Its developer calmly explained, "It sounds so lifelike. We're creating a system fully capable of self-reflection." The newspaper's columnist concluded that it was "impossible to overhype such a world" (Petzinger).

Rank-and-filers should be able to look to CyberUnions to research radical changes like these and still wilder ones on the horizon. Accordingly, CyberUnion researchers will boast the kind of open mind modeled by the White Queen in *Through the Looking-Glass,* a pragmatic and worldly-wise sort who practiced believing "as many as six impossible things before breakfast."

Where Next?

How will CyberUnions capitalize on futuristics, on the sort of mental exercise traced in very sketchy fashion above?

They will establish a subcommittee of their executive board devoted to scanning the futures literature and reporting to board meetings the forecasts of greatest relevance (as in the case of boomer retirement signs). Some will commission a prominent futurist to contribute a guest essay to every issue of the union's magazine (and place it prominently on its Web site). Many will subsidize the attendance of staffers and regular members at the annual meeting of the World Future Society, the major organization of forecasters in the world. A leading few will hire one or more researchers skilled in the use of futuristics tools. And CyberUnions will promote futures-skills workshops at every major function. Members can and must improve their own ability as long-range forecasters—a goal that helps transform and empower any organization smart enough to pursue it.

Attitude will be the key here. Unlike Cyber Gain types, who take a defensive position regarding the future, CyberUnionists will be excited by its possibilities. They know some rank-and-filers fear an onslaught of "Frankenstein-like" computer monsters, the loss of control to artificial intelligence, and the disappearance of jobs lost to robots. They will not flinch when the director of the AT&T labs forecasts that "eventually, sometime after the year 2000, yesterday's science fiction will become our reality with virtual reality transporting us to distant places (and times) and intelligent offices (and home/cars) responding to our commands" (Weber, 84). Instead, CyberUnionists ask, How do we make the best of this?

Earning Future-Shaping Respect

Few in the general public, and few in the ranks of unionists, seem to equate Organized Labor with future-shaping activities, either of the forecasting or enabling variety. This cannot change soon enough, for it is a very costly negative impression. Only an institution viewed as a future-shaper can hope to command respect and allegiance in a period of "continuous disequilibrium."

Struggling to understand the downward slide of the democratic Left, a troubled partisan notes ruefully that "It's been the right that seemed to own the future: Microsoft, biotechnology, the stock market, these things all seem to belong to conservative ideology" (Packer, 68). In like manner, the public must sense the significance of the 86 percent increase in business spending on computers from 1994 to 1998, far outpacing all other types of investment (Mandel, 63). No comparable figure exists for Organized Labor, and its unavailability speaks volumes.

Not surprisingly, the vision of the future promoted by the Right invites humbling servility (Shades of the revealing old slogan— "What's good for GM is good for America!"). It calls to mind the "rhetoric of the 1939 Futurama, which offered consumers a whale of the ride if they'd only let General Motors do the driving. Promised automatic highways, kitchens of the future, and hotels on the moon, we actually got the Interstate system, nuclear power, and unsustainable suburban sprawl" (Prelinger).

Labor *must* champion an alternative design, one that would put citizens, especially unionists, in the driver's seat. And Labor must be seen doing much to secure its democratic vision.

Activist Paul Johnston puts the challenge quite well, noting the importance of a vision that can energize and inspire:

> The first question is not how to organize but what to organize—what kinds of unions do we want? How will they make the world a different place? How, through them, will unionism recapture our imaginations with a credible fight for a future that is more than marginally different? . . . We need . . . visions of unionism that re-capture our imagination as agendas for social change that are both profoundly radical and 'as American as apple pie' " (Johnston).

Accountability, collective responsibility for the vulnerable, consensus building and dialogue, promotion of equality, solidarity . . . all this and more.

Encouraging are "blips" on the screen raising hope that Labor *is* upgrading its claim as a future-maker. Typical is the welcome presence of a unionist (Linda Chavez-Thompson, AFL-CIO Vice-President) on a well-publicized list of 20 prominent women mentioned as capable of being president of the nation (Glover). Another encouraging sign was the invitation extended in 1998 to AFL-CIO president Sweeney to address the World Economic Forum, the first time any labor leader had done so. Perhaps best of all, more and more rank-and-filers seem to be participating in the Labor Party, the New Party, and other fresh efforts to shape a vision that makes a difference.

The question, however, remains: Can Labor's use of informatics in general, and computers in particular, be grounded in so compelling a vision as to help it soon "reclaim" the future? This is imperative if labor is to command respect for future-shaping prowess.

Summary

Just when you think you're ready for twenty-first-century America, it changes on you yet again," or so contends journalist Michael Lind (*New York Times Magazine,* August 16, 1998, 38). Union activists, especially power-holders over 50, would have no argument, albeit many who surf the Net might smile, while others who have never been on-line would probably only sigh.

Much as immigrants fresh off the boat at Ellis Island looked to labor unions in the 1800s to help them make sense of a new world, so should twenty-first-century Americans look to Organized Labor for clues with which to explore their future, "that foreign country whither we are all willy-nilly being deported . . ." (Brunner).

Asked by Larry King on national television about Labor's stereo-type as only reactive and endlessly behind the curve, Richard Trumka, Secretary-Treasurer, AFL-CIO, vigorously rejected the characterization: "I don't think you'll see us lag by five, ten, fifteen years behind the event that necessitates change because we didn't see the change happen" (Trumka, in King). If this forecast is to prove accurate, Labor must make far more creative use of (formal) futuristics than true at present, and CyberUnions can help show the way.

Recommended Resources

Bell, Wendell. *Foundations of Futures Studies: Human Science for a New Era.* Volume 1: *History, Purposes, and Knowledge.* New Brunswick, NJ: Transaction Press, 1997. A unique, engaging, and seminal exploration of the subject, complete with strong views, fresh material, and useful tools. Weak only in its confinement to mainstream thinkers and topics, but adaptable to far more colorful forecasters and matters.

Ogden, Frank. *Navigating in Cyberspace: A Guide to the Next Millennium.* Toronto: Macfarlane, Walter, and Ross, 1995. A sparkling, brash, and highly informative personal exploration of the future. Vexing in its total dismissal of the survival possibilities of Big Labor, but useful nevertheless for those committed to disproving this particular forecast.

Rifkin, Jeremy. *The End of Work: The Decline of the Global Labor Force and the Dawn of the Post-Market Era.* New York: G.P. Putnam's Sons, 1995. Easily one of the most challenging of recent explorations of the possible massive loss of payroll posts to "smart" equipment. Offers a unique sets of solutions that organized labor must take into account.

Schiller, Dan. *Digital Capitalism: Networking the Global Market System.* Boston: MIT Press, 1999. A fresh attempt at a systematic explication and critique of the political-economic development of computer networks, including the Internet. The book first tries to set the development of computer-communications networks in the context of transnational corporations' demands for greater proprietary control over these strategic systems, and it then goes on to consider the development of the Web as a new consumer marketing medium.

The Hawaii Research Center for Futures Studies of the University of Hawaii offers information about the future, including the future of work and unions, with links to other future-oriented sites: Its Web site is at http://www.soc.hawaii.edu/future/

FUTUREWORK is an international e-mail forum for discussion of how to deal with the new realities created by economic globalization and technological change: "Our objective in creating this list is to involve as many people as possible in redesigning for the new realities. We hope that this list will help to move these issues to a prominent place on public and political agendas worldwide. The FUTUREWORK lists are hosted by the Faculty of Environmental Studies at the University of Waterloo. To subscribe to FUTUREWORK (unmoderated) and/or FW-L (moderated) send a message to Majordomo@scribe.uwaterloo.ca saying subscribe futurework Your E-Mail Address. "

FW-L, the moderated list, cited above, serves as a bulletin-board to post notices about recommended books, articles, other documents, other Net sites, conferences, even job openings, etc., relevant to the future of work and to the roles of education, community, and other factors in that future. There are also some useful links to other Web sites on the FW homepage.

Outstanding as a resource is the World Future Society, the oldest and largest global organization of its kind (1-800-989-8274; www.wfs.org). See especially its 1,000 quotes for the millenium (www.wfs.org/Q-intro.htm).

Reading 7

Teaching Futuristics

Arthur B. Shostak
Communications Workers of America,
CWA, Local 189

Having learned at first hand as a teacher of futuristics how well unionists do when they elect to take my course for credit, I am convinced we cannot expand the number of such courses soon enough. Accordingly, I offer below some reflections about how I do it, hoping that you will campaign for such courses wherever you can help influence the labor education curriculum. It is not enough that unionists employ forecasting with experience-honed intuitive skills: It is vital that many soon also employ formal tools and models best secured from classroom work. Only in this way can Labor keep up with the skills already part of the schooling of business majors and M.B.A. students; only in this way can Labor hold its own, and then some!

Negative stereotypes about working-class Americans abound, thanks in large part to TV figures like "Archie Bunker." When you add the media's preoccupation with certain notorious bluecollar union leaders (the Teamsters' Jimmy Hoffa, etc.), it would seem that working-class unionists would not be a promising group for a college-credit course in futuristics.

In 1974 the AFL-CIO opened the nation's only labor-directed residential college–degree program for unionists. Housed at the George Meany Center for Labor Studies on a 240-bed campus in Silver Spring, Maryland, the National Labor College offers a bachelor's degree in labor studies. Unionists are resident for two weeks a year, most of them twice a year, and they do considerable course work on a correspondence basis in the interim.

Despite working full-time with their unions, and trying to maintain a decent family life, the vast majority (average age, 35) successfully complete the program in three or so years, an accomplishment many previously thought not a likely part of their lives this time around. To the great pride of their immediate families and their union, over 300 Meany Center alumni are now "making a difference."

One year after the Center's college-degree program began, I was invited to teach a basic sociology course and another in industrial sociology, an honor I have enjoyed ever since. Impressed by my working-class co-learners (a term I prefer to "students"), I sought and received permission in 1988 to introduce a third elective, a college-credit course in futuristics.

Having first taught the subject to college students at my primary employer, Drexel University, back in 1980, I thought I could merely tweak it a bit, and adapt the syllabus and readings with little or no problem. How wrong I was! The challenge here proved formidable.

To begin with, like far too many of my Drexel undergraduates, my union adult co-learners had little or no formal background: Few had read Alvin Toffler's best-seller, *Future Shock*. Few had much familiarity with classic anti-utopian works like Aldous Huxley's *Brave New World* or George Orwell's *1984*.

Even fewer knew any of the utopian literature, even that of the Church, albeit most dimly sensed that much of the ideological conflict that had animated the 1960s and 1970s entailed profound disagreements about the preferable future(s) and how to get there from here.

To compound this problem, my union co-learners—unlike my Drexel undergrads (who were 15 to 20 years younger on average)—were initially very resistant to the sort of venturesome thinking required in a futuristics course. Accustomed as are most union activists to a world of harsh realities, frequent disappointments, daily heartache, and defensive skepticism, many were initially reluctant to engage in the "willing suspension of disbelief" that William James identified as a requisite for fresh learning.

Every year since 1988 I have learned from course evaluations a little bit more about how to do the course better. I now approach the challenge with seven major tools, all of which in combination help me come closer to my aims.

First, I encourage hope by highlighting historical matters of which the unionists have little or no prior knowledge. To counter the bleak view with which many begin the course, I review the extraordinary progress we have made as a species in extending our life span, raising the level of well-being, and strengthening the infrastructure of governance and civility.

Taking care not to ignore painful gaps in equity and the atrocities that mar the front page daily, I help my co-learners process their many grievances with runaway capitalism and other mortal threats to the world's well-being. I go on, however, to emphasize my belief that more has been gained than lost in recent centuries, a trendline that I think we have it in our power to extend for time indefinite—provided we find the willpower, creativity, and capacity to care enough about one another.

Second, I review recent well-known successes of major unions in this or that organizing drive or political campaign. I emphasize the long-range planning entailed in such campaigns, and identify such planning as a key component of futuristics. I also discuss how Fortune 500 companies and all major branches of federal, state, and local government make extensive use of futuristics. This whets their appetite for bringing this new tool—long-range planning—back to their union sponsor.

(I mention here my success over the years in bringing top union leaders in as panelists at the annual meeting of the World Future Society. These power-holders generally earn strong applause from initially skeptical, if not hostile, attendees, once the unionists review the uses being made of forecasting in guiding the labor movement. I also talk about my occasional consulting with unions eager to explore ideas with a professional forecaster.)

Third, I refer over and again to the democratic dimension in futuristics, emphasizing thereby their responsibility for becoming major players in helping to decide our future(s). I reject the notion that there is any one future to be predicted, as in the absurdity of the paper's daily horoscope column.

Instead, I work closely with them in explicating probable, possible, preferable, and preventable futures. We assess the strengths and weaknesses of each, but only after first uncovering and weighing the major values underlying each. I get them to tell of their own voter-registration efforts, their local union meetings to debate policy issues, and many of such labor efforts to make a difference—and I link all of this to futuristics.

We make the future in the present, I maintain, either through acts of commission or omission, but the responsibility—especially in one of the most advanced democracies the world has ever known—is fundamentally ours.

Fourth, I put special emphasis on mind-boggling matters, the better to get unionists to reassess their unexamined assumptions and struggle to take an open-minded approach. I highlight developments almost as fantastic as those dreamt up by science-fiction writers. We explore biotech "miracles," the prospects where nanotechnology is concerned, the possible impact of wearable computers and personal Intelligent Agents on our lives, and so forth and so on.

Fifth, I explain the tools we have in futuristics for gathering data (Delphi Polls, Expert-Genius Interviews, large-scale polling projects, computer processing of massive data banks, etc.). I also discuss the tools we have for assessing impacts of developments; e.g., technology assessment techniques, social indicators research, computer simulations, etc. Special attention is paid to tools for evaluating forecasts, and learning from their fate. Above all, I focus on the values inherent in reliance on a tool, and on the transferability of a tool to the special forecasting needs of Organized Labor.

Sixth, I rely on books that are engaging, clear, short, and relevant. From the outset I have used a great 1975 utopian novel, *Ecotopia,* by Ernest Callenbach. It offers a plausible upbeat scenario for America's thorough-going overhaul, a blueprint my co-learners find fresh and challenging. I also require *Beyond Humanity,* a 1997 paperback by Gregory S. Paul and Earl D. Cox, easily the most mind-stretching book in futuristics I have come across in years. Their forecast of the securement soon of artificial life (far beyond artificial intelligence), very advanced robotics, and nanotechnology, takes forecasting far beyond any place familiar to my union co-learners.

I prepare my own chapter-by-chapter true-false open-book take-home quizzes to accompany my texts. Co-learners thank me for this in course evaluations, as it helps me highlight what I want them to focus on, and they take pleasure in getting high scores week after week. Each quiz features two write-in questions that ask what surprised, or pleased, or dismayed, or puzzled you the most in the assigned reading.

Finally, I make a point in closing the course of connecting it to one overarching possibility that could just make Labor's renewal a better-than-ever prospect. I call this scenario the CyberUnion Prospect, and use it to pull together many strands of the semester's work.

Naturally, I have each class do an anonymous course evaluation of every aspect of the course, especially the books and the essay assignments that guide their learning over the six-month interval between the week-long start of the course and the one wrap-up session.

An elective course, futuristics generally gets a full enrollment, and in the hallway scuttlebutt apparently ranks very high.

The danger to it has come from other quarters. For example, two straitlaced faculty colleagues, without any prior discussion with me, recommended to the dean a few years ago that the course be canceled and squeezed instead into an hour of my Intro to Sociology course (so as to free up elective time for other course offerings). Both alumni and then current students circulated a "keep-the-course!" petition, and a delegation went into the dean's office to rail against this advice. The course was continued.

Overall, I believe that trade unionists are organic "futurists," devoted as they are to grievance resolution, collective bargaining, and political influence, each a profound exercise in making the future in the present. All the more important is their matriculation in a college-level course that surfaces much that they need to know if they are to strengthen their record as future-shapers.

I am very pleased to pioneer here, and hope to soon learn of many more such efforts wherever free trade unionism is struggling to help create a world closer to our heart's desire.

Note: A much longer version of this essay appeared in the *American Behavioral Scientist,* November–December, 1998, pp. 539–42.

8

Innovations: Promoting Risk-Taking

The challenge facing unions is not to stop the unavoidable forces of change, but rather to exploit or capitalize on them. . . . Perhaps more than present memory can recall, unions need to think "outside-of-the-box."

—Marick F. Masters, *Unions at the Crossroads,* 1997

CyberUnions will be rich sources of bright new projects well worth creative adaptation by the AFL-CIO, international unions, city central councils, and local unions alike. Driving this will be the need to stay current, so rapid will the world be changing. What will separate CyberUnions from Cyber Gain organizations will be their respective attitudes: CyberUnions will enjoy the challenge, and respond with zest, while Cyber Gain unions may find the need to endlessly innovate exasperating, and respond with testiness.

Learning Cultures

All of which is tied to the single greatest difference between the two types of labor union where innovations are concerned: CyberUnions will be learning cultures, while Cyber Gain unions may or may not be.

A "learning culture" places a high value on agility, creativity, and seamless schooling (the quest to learn from anything and everything). It addresses the need talented staffers have for learning continuously, for believing that their employer (in this case, a CyberUnion) values intellectual challenge. As a strong proponent, former Secretary of

Labor Robert Reich, contends, "talented people join up in order to learn" (Reich).

CyberUnions as learning cultures will be free of fear, the number-one impediment to innovation in organizations. Risk-takers will not fear embarrassment or even punishment if and when their ideas occasionally disappoint (as some always must). Instead, setbacks will be valued for the lessons that can be wrung from them, and innovators will build creatively on past mistakes.

CyberUnions as learning cultures will nurture creativity, the number-one source of innovation in organizations. Risk-takers will get schooling in lateral thinking, brainstorming, visioning, and many other field-proven methods of "thinking out of the box" and breaking through. Financial and status rewards will be linked to clear evidence of applied creativity, and prize-winning ideas will be celebrated in all the media outlets of the organization.

Finally, CyberUnions as learning cultures will disavow conventional barriers to change. They will scorn the "not-invented-here" bias against adopting good ideas from outside. They will scorn the notion that "if it isn't broken, we need not fix it." They will recognize instead that everything is always wearing down, and is in never-ending need of repair. And they will scorn the prejudice against borrowing innovations from the management side of the table, recognizing that "only by using the same tools as the employers can unions hope to survive and prosper in the years ahead" (Lee 1997, 47).

Payoff for the learning culture organization will come in many ways, not the least of which will be the inclination of staffers to persist, rather than be easily deterred. Listen, for example, to an activist who refused to let a shortage of software hurt her performance, when she knew she could dare to create her own:

> There's not much software out there for unions. We hired a company, and ours is customized software. For our union records. For our regular organizing, I did my own, using a Microsoft program. I got all the stuff from the union-focused companies, and we tried it, because that is what we wanted to do. They even had a grievance procedure module, and that sort of stuff. Our system, what we now have (I worked with the computer programmer when we had our old Wang system), our system blows theirs away! It's fantastic.

Learning cultures, in short, send a strategic talent-recruiting and talent-holding message: Innovation valued here!

Stages in Computer Uses

CyberUnion learning cultures will be invigorated by incredible changes tumbling after one another in the computer sciences and in related applications of computer potentialities, all of which promise to substantially improve the innovation process.

We are leaving behind the first two stages of computer use. Mainframes dominated at the outset, and we mastered the science of amassing, sorting, and using massive amounts of data with unprecedented speed. In the second stage (one we are only now leaving) we owned a relatively few computer files, and used e-mail and the Internet gingerly. Memory and computing power were expensive, and crashes and disappointments were all too common.

In the third stage all sorts of electronic devices should be able to pool their efforts and "talk" among themselves, without worrying about compatibility or formal introductions. One possibility would have software and hardware able to turn existing telephone wiring into an inexpensive network that connects information appliances to one another—freeing us of reliance any longer on the PC on our desktop (Wildstrom).

We should be able to stop storing files on a particular computer, and float files instead in cyberspace. A CyberUnion activist should be able to access them from any network-connected machine, at home, in the union office, at a worksite, or from a phone booth. All that will be necessary is to tell the system (not type!) what you want, and it will do your bidding.

CyberZones

One of many gains from the Third Stage described above will have CyberUnions capable of "engineering" spaces, say, a union office, hiring hall, or headquarters, within which specialized information floats in cyberspace for your use.

An activist entering the physical space will be able to immediately use his or her cell phone, or old-fashioned laptop, or trendy new "wearable" computer, to access and learn from custom-tailored information floating invisibly around in a CyberZone, a neat gain for all in the speed of information transfer and focus (Gelernter).

Available around 2002, CyberZone details should be so easy to operate that we will master the controls with no strain in just a few minutes. The same set of controls will command our phone, TV (HDTV), video library, and other high-tech communication aids (Gelernter).

Internet Centrality

Key here is the role of the Internet. While only 50 percent of American households in 1999 had a PC (and only half of those a modem), specialists expect this to go over 80 percent as soon as 2003. Web-TV will help, and many households will gain access to the Internet without ever getting a PC. No wonder that futurist Frank Ogden considers the Internet the "fastest growing community in history, and the most extensive communications system on Earth" (Ogden, 17).

Accordingly, millions of working-class families are likely to join Net-User ranks in the years immediately ahead. Half of all goods may be sold through Net information services by the year 2018. Pundits, like John Doerr, a Silicon Valley financier, optimistically maintain "it is possible the Internet has been *under*-hyped. It's like the Big Bang— it's like creation of a whole new universe. It's going to go a long, long time. And it's going to affect every part of society" (Lewis, 62).

As the Net gains sway, various informatics tools—computers, cellular phones, fax, TVs, etc.—are likely to become voice-activated and voice-responsive. This control-and-command mechanism will replace the old-fashioned keyboard and make computer equipment accessible to millions who lack typing skills. It will recognize one's voice-print and handwriting, thereby adding security and privacy. Overnight, members of CyberUnions quick to employ this software will become full-fledged "Netizens."

Shortly after the millennium year the PC at home or in the office may be able to learn how its various users prefer to learn, work, play, and communicate. It should be able to anticipate the needs of the humans with whom it interacts, and actually do work *before* being asked ("Look, Ma, no hands!" gives way to "Look, Ma, I didn't even have to ask!"). Once again, CyberUnions should be the first in Labor's ranks to employ and gain from such equipment.

Wearables

Still more astonishing is the likelihood that by 2003, 2004, or even 2005, unionists may begin wearing their computers on their persons. These new wonders may take the form of a watch-like item worn on the wrist. Or a keycase-like item carried in one's purse or pants pocket.

Whatever the format, the "wearables" should help integrate CyberUnionists into the Age of Information with an intimacy and immediacy greater than anything they have previously known. For better and for worse, they will have "closed the loop," so to speak, and made themselves accessible, endlessly on-line, a new part of the largest information machine ever built, the Internet, 24 hours a day, seven days a week, every week of the year.

Intelligent Agents

When computers become as integral as wristwatches, CyberUnionists may be among the first to experiment with the use of powerful personal "servants" accessed through computer wearables. Called "Intelligent Agents" (or "Information Agents"), these ingenious pieces of software will be "housed" in the wearables, the "voice" of which will be transmitted from them.

Built from, and composed of, the answers provided by the unionist to a never-ending stream of questions asked by the Agents (questions like "What do you like? Fear? Hope for? Dream of? Run from? etc., etc."), Intelligent Agents may change human existence more fundamentally than almost any other aspect of informatics on the horizon.

Intelligent Agents should be able to compress time and space by letting CyberUnionists do many things at once, some in this reality, and others in cyberspace. They could be able to do research better than ever done before. They could shop *the* best buys, both on behalf of the CyberUnion and on behalf of each and every member. They could free everyone from mundane tasks, like office supplies management, thereby substantially increasing leisure (or work) time. And, most exotic of all, Intelligent Agents should be able to form useful-to-us alliances in cyberspace with the agents created by other humans (Hill, 1994).

Case Study: Checking on Investments

Keeping in mind our need to expect "continuous disequilibrium," to think loose, and to expect innovations from CyberUnions, what, if anything, could computer wearables and Intelligent Agents mean for unionists as such?

Consider just one example, the case of a growing need by rank-and-filers to know more about their 401-K investments (their pension plans). Simply by asking their Intelligent Agent to "check out" the record of a mutual fund or single stock or bond, a rank-and-filer will rapidly and painlessly know much more than is common or even possible today.

Second, local union members and allied employers will be able to compare and contrast the pension and health fund particulars of various unions and companies in "Net time," meaning in very short order.

Third, rank-and-filers and/or employers will be in a position to share information with one another, and compare and contrast findings using the Internet—a process that could involve many in a wide-ranging and unending discovery process (the sort learning cultures nurture).

Fourth, local union members and allied employers could ask their Intelligent Agents to uncover, evaluate, and improve alternative investment strategies—such as socially screened investing—and help build alliances with non-union progressives to promote change in current corporate strategies and actions.

Intelligent Agents, in short, could revolutionize attitudes and behavior in ways CyberUnions will be the first in Labor to explore . . . the better to make the most of this awesome prospect.

Reality Check

All of the "wild ideas" above will probably take more time to gain wide use than the promoters concede: "A fundamental lesson is that even revolutionary technologies take time to cause a revolution. No matter how great the tail wind of hype and venture capital, the Next Big Thing takes time to change the practices and habits of companies [and unions] and people" (Lohr). As well, none of the ideas will succeed unless and until they become more mainstream—"easier, more reliable, and more useful for the workaday chores of the economy" (Lohr).

Refurbishing

Naturally, even while CyberUnion innovators explore stuff as glittering and novel as the mind-boggling innovations above, many will also seek gains for Labor in fresh variations on old ideas, variations impossible without the newfound power of computers.

Typical are projects CyberUnions could mount to offer members an overdue "report card" of sorts on the union. Drawing on the social indicators literature, activists could create a computer-based system for gathering a very large amount of very current data on how the union is doing (e.g., size over time, grievance record, arbitration record, organizing-drive results, attendance at functions, number and character of "letters to the editor," number of visits to the Web site, etc.). These separate indices could be combined in a high-powered, complicated statistical format (one that computers handle with ease) designed to yield one or more cumulative measures of the union's performance, much as does a grade at the end of a course.

Sharing this sort of accountability "report card" with the rank-and-file would go far in assuring the best possible performance by elected officers. It could head off false rumors possibly spread by opponents of the incumbents. It could boost morale among satisfied dues-payers. It could stir critics to take action, intrigue prospective members, and lend some solid numbers to a controversial topic—"How are we doing, *really* doing?"—that otherwise often lacks valid measures.

A second type of historic innovation worth revisiting is the idea of ownership of workplaces. Activist Jeff Gates offers a very thoughtful plan for using ownership solutions, including Employee Stock Ownership Plans (ESOPs), for "putting some movement back in the labor movement . . . another way to save members' jobs and, just possibly, the union movement" (Gates, 98). This will require CyberUnionists to use computers to finesse details that can otherwise overwhelm ownership efforts.

Related here is an opportunity "to refocus Labor's varied competencies on the rebuilding of social solidarity, Labor's original purpose" (Gates, 108). At issue is the idea of bartering worktime rather than only or primarily selling it. Colorful efforts are being made nowadays to create neighborhood or even city-wide exchange-trading systems in place of reliance on money and the marketplace. More than 500 such schemes are up and going in Australia, Britain, and the United States, as Web sites help community activists in locales print their own "money"—in effect, create an organized barter system (with all the laborious record-keeping done painlessly by high-powered computers and dedicated software).

Among other things, these "new economies" provide a way of jump-starting job creation without waiting for or relying on government funds. In Ithaca, New York, for example, citizens can trade odd-jobs for other services, using an alternative currency called "Ithaca Hours" (Coyle). In certain locales people are helping to meet needs that otherwise might go unmet (coaching, environmental restoration, mentoring, scouting, tutoring, etc.). CyberUnions would research, assess, and improve on this innovation.

A list of other "refurbished" innovations might include taking a fresh approach to the union's running a resort like the ILGWU's Unity House. A CyberUnion might offer a computer "summer camp" for members (adults and their offspring alike) at a leased resort. This would allow an emphasis on celebrating traditions (labor culture and lore) even while boosting the cyberspace craft of attendees.

Similarly, when innovating for the English-language storefront schools run by a progressive union like UNITE, a CyberUnion might add a bevy of proactive courses in dynamic citizenship roles (how to use the ballot, the referendum, etc. [Johnston, 1998]). This would help promote a zesty reformist role for new citizens, rather than the supine and grateful, or begrudging, role of the past.

Where unions of communication workers (CWA), pilots (ALPA), steelworkers (USW), and others have used teleconferences for major events (conventions, strikes, etc.), CyberUnions will innovate their use for ordinary once-a-month dialogues with dues-payers reached in their living rooms.

Where labor educators have used TV for some few distance-learning courses, CyberUnions will take the curricula into cyberspace, and offer on a union-based network many innovative degree programs in labor studies. Guided in part by Canada's pioneering project (Athabasca University, the Canadian Union of Public Employees, and the Solidarity Network), the CyberUnion computer system will offer high-quality material unconstrained by time and physical space, material that will feature dialogue via extensive conference exchanges. This system will "serve rather than drive the educational needs of adult labour studies students" (Taylor, 36).

Summary

M.I.T. professor Alex P. Pentland recently explained to *Business Week*: "People have always had a fascination with making themselves personally more powerful. We used to associate that with magic. Now, we're getting close to working that magic into fully realized designs" (Pentland).

CyberUnions will celebrate the innovative possibilities of informatics, especially its computer-based options, with the sort of eagerness and creativity that learning cultures uniquely nurture. Their social (high-touch) and technological (high-tech) breakthroughs will help Organized Labor show the way to a finer twenty-first century.

Recommended Resources

Gates, Jeff. *The Ownership Solution: Toward a Shared Capitalism for the 21st Century*. Reading, MA: Addison-Wesley, 1998. Offers some of the most creative *ideas* for transforming Labor available anywhere. Explains how unions could profit from taking a broad-based capital-ownership role, possibly *the* key to achieving a more just and equitable economic system.

National Writers Union. *Authors in the New Information Age: A Working Paper on Electronic Publishing Issues*. New York: NWU, 1995 ed. (212-254-0279; or nwu@nwu.org). A unique, engaging, and informative pamphlet guide to constructive responses by a union to radical innovations in the industry (". . . before we ask to be heard, we have to know what we want to say." p. 5).

Waterman, Robert H., Jr. *The Renewal Factor: How the Best Get and Keep the Competitive Edge*. New York: Bantam, 1987. Engaging and rewarding ideas about how the best organizations nurture innovations, especially the reinventing of themselves. For organizations intent on not ending up as fossils.

A zesty and trendy magazine, *FAST COMPANY*, is an excellent resource for anyone interested in organizational change and Third Wave workplaces. (See especially May 1999, p. 70.) It can be had in hard-copy or at www.fastcompany.com

Labour's Online Bookstore offers a large selection of books (some substantially discounted) on the labor movement, carefully chosen and often with brief reviews attached. Available at http://www.labourst-art.org/labour10.html

LaborNet supports human rights and economic justice for workers by providing labor news and information, comprehensive Internet services, training and Web site design for union and labor organizations—United States. Available at http://www.igc.apc.org/labornet/.

LabourNet offers computer communications and news for the labour movement. Available at http://www.labournet.org.uk/

———

Reading 8

What Must You Know to Be Employed in the Year 2025?

Joseph Breedlove
International Brotherhood of Electrical Workers,
IBEW, Local 481

Why bother getting ready for workplace changes hard to conceive, like those related to exotic new energy systems? In part, because arbitrators today are increasingly awarding work to the union that appears most current, the union whose members seem most well trained to handle change. Activist Joseph Breedlove offers below an encouraging account of a local intent on staying a (computer-aided) winner. He writes knowingly of the challenge posed by the rapid arrival of "smart" equipment, and he does not flinch. Instead, he offers a guide to union progress here, taking care in closing to urge like attention by Labor to nonworkplace puzzles (possibly the "key" to labor's continued existence). Upbeat and quietly confident, the essay reassures and inspires, even as it makes clear the hard work entailed in staying twenty-first-century competitive.

If we are to be prosperous in the year 2025, the world of technology will probably be the easiest to prepare for because we can train and educate ourselves.

Our first assignment is to educate our members in order to remain employed in our industry. Unlike 30 years ago, when you received an education from an apprenticeship program and received a journeyman's card, that knowledge was enough to assure you a career until you retired. Today we must continually educate and reeducate our membership to the advancements in our industry.

Local 481 has taken several steps to encourage this practice in its most recent collective-bargaining agreement. We continually include incentives that encourage our membership to participate in journeymen improvement classes at the JATC. Courses such as welding or knot tying and rigging are being replaced with courses in fiber optics, instrumentation, and Introduction to Windows 95, I and II. With the newly implemented incentive plan we have seen a growth from 15 percent to nearly 45 percent of total membership participation per year.

Local 481 has also taken an aggressive approach in training its leadership. Currently, we have three business agents with B.A. degrees from the Meany Center, and should have three more individuals by the year 2000.

Through education we have also realized and come to understand the importance of the information system. We have equipped our office with a newly installed computer system and provided all our business representatives with laptop computers. We have also installed a Web page for our LMCC (Quality Connection) located at http://www.qualityconnectionindy.com.

We are currently in the process of developing a Web site for Local 481 that will keep our members and potential members better informed. We recognize that this is just the tip of the iceberg in terms of changes for the future.

At a recent constitutional conference, we were awarded jurisdiction for solar shingles that are beginning to become popular in the Southwest. The IBEW was the recipient in the jurisdiction because we were the best trained for that type of installation. Undoubtedly this is an indication of how all work will be awarded in the future. The international with the best-trained people will be granted the work.

As an international organization, we must prepare our locals for growth in areas such as smart houses, space travel, and solar and nuclear energy. We must stop thinking in terms of tomorrow, but in terms of years, because tomorrow is too late to prepare for change.

We must also be prepared to find our place in the working world with "smart" machines. They are not like anything we relate to today. With today's equipment, an individual relays to the machine what is needed. He then assigns the task to the equipment, and programs the machine to complete the process. The "smart" machine will be able to receive information, analyze the problem, determine the best way to do the process, learn from any mistakes it makes along the way, and correct them without any intervention from a human being.

In the world of automation and infotech, the amount of growth is unimaginable. We will see a worldwide network of communications through fiber optics and other techniques that will virtually keep us in contact with any person, at any time, anywhere in the world. This may intimidate those members with a "Big Brother" phobia, but at the same time it might benefit the business representative–to–member relationship.

These are just a few of the items that must be dealt with by our locals and their membership in the not-too-distant future.

Some of the more perplexing nonwork issues will be those of government structure, religion, and social issues. They must be closely monitored if we want to retain our membership. How we educate our membership to handle such things as genetic cloning, economic policy making, or Intelligent Agents may be the very key to our unions' existence.

Joseph D. Breedlove completed the apprenticeship program and became a journeyman wireman in 1980. In September, 1990, he was appointed business agent for Local 481 in Indianapolis. Joe began his studies at the Meany Center in 1995 and graduated in the summer of 1999. (Joe can be reached via e-mail at jbreed@on-net.net.)

9

Services: Promoting Ties

. . . the labor movement cannot be content with defending the status quo, or reliving past glories. We must constantly look to the future, develop new leadership, [and] adapt policies to changing conditions and new technologies . . .

—AFL-CIO President George Meany,
Convention Proceedings, 1979

CyberUnions will offer innovative services likely to enhance Labor's use of modern computers, help rank-and-filers feel themselves members of a caring "community" (actual and in cyberspace), and uniquely appeal to prospective members. These services will go far beyond what Cyber Gain unions may regard as advisable or possible.

Seven appealing services beckon: Members can be helped to purchase or lease union-assembled equipment at great savings. They can be offered the advantages of a prepaid plan. They can be lent informatics equipment at key union functions. They can be invited to use a "high-tech/high-touch" learning center. They can have access to their own skills upgrade center. They can get help in meeting large-scale coordination challenges, as in political campaigns and creating sound mergers. And they can be offered greater-than-ever aids to staying in touch with union affairs and one another.

Computer Deals

Many unionists I have spoken with wonder why the AFL-CIO or its major unions have not "cut a deal" with providers of computer systems to offer rank-and-filers a very good price and service contract. They note, for example, that the AFL-CIO Union Privilege Program available through their internationals offers a break on travel costs, insurance costs, mortgage rates, legal advice, prescription drugs, and other attractive items—why not on computers?

When I asked AFL-CIO spokepersons about this, they sighed, and explained that much time and effort had gone into trying to arrange this. Two obstacles, however, were proving especially difficult. First, computer assembly plants in the States are non-union, as are many of the relevant retail chains, and the AFL-CIO declines to deal with them. Second, computerization is moving so fast that one runs a serious risk of disappointing members who may condemn their Labor-endorsed purchase as "obsolete" soon after getting it home.

CyberUnions might try to organize a stateside assembly plant of a parent company eager to get a chance at selling to millions of unionists, a sizable potential market. If that company promised neutrality, and would accept a card count, the plant might soon be unionized, thereby qualifying it for Labor's business.

Alternatively, Labor could help to arrange the considerable financing necessary to upscale the one or two very small unionized computer manufacturers now available. These companies have a history of pro-Labor actions, and merit the boost possible from a massive order for union-made equipment.

As for worrying about members judging their union-backed equipment out-of-date shortly after purchase, this is an educational challenge. At issue is the need to help members appreciate the longevity of computer systems unfairly labeled "obsolete" by crafty marketers eager to push glitzy newer goods.

Labor could explain that bare-bottom low-price (ca. $500) systems, or old computers with low specs, are still very useful, and can rival high-end models with frivolous "bells-and-whistles" in their ability to get the job done. ("Today's $1,000 PC does a better job at core functions than a $2,500 machine did two years ago" [Mossberg].) With the help of mass purchasing via a CyberUnion program, "Newbies" can save a lot of money purchasing such equipment.

Prepaid Plans

CyberUnions will talk via e-mail with unionists in Europe about a money-saving computer-based idea that has taken the continent by storm, and then help import the four-year-old idea back to the States.

Unionists overseas are turning increasingly to prepaid cards to "democratize a product and service long confined to the well-heeled." These cards are programmed to represent a certain amount of money the owner has given to the card seller. Mobile phone subscribers, in particular, like the cards because they then have no 12-month contracts or monthly fees to contend with. Phones are activated by dialing a phone number and a personal identification number printed on the card. When the money runs out, you simply replenish the card by making a fresh payment (Naik).

CyberUnions could use this service to help members wary of contracting for Internet access services in the 12-month-contract format. Instead, they would pay only when actually using the service, and then by using their prepaid card. Savings could be considerable.

Lending Laptops

CyberUnions could take advantage of a relatively new and little-known business service. A host of small companies now offer to rent powerbooks, notebooks, and laptops at reasonable rates by the day or week. Scores could be made available to delegates at a wide array of union functions, especially the all-important national constitutional conventions.

Why bother? Because this service would send a hard-to-miss message about the union's priorities ("We want you to 'get with it,' and we intend to help!"). It would establish a valuable new institutional norm, i.e., when we meet, we naturally employ the best computer hardware and software available ("We are the *best,* after all!").

Second, it would introduce non-users to various types of computers in a real-time demonstration of ease of use and utility. Carefully chosen and prepared mentors could provide tutoring on the spot for novices just getting into union-aiding uses of informatics. The mentors could emphasize the fun possible from increasing ease of use, and demonstrate the many different rewards possible from creative use.

Third, use of rented high-quality equipment would help heighten the return on the union's investment in the event itself. Attendees could retrieve, store, and otherwise manipulate valuable information. They could also caucus electronically, consult with far-flung brothers and sisters, take home on disk their own version of the proceedings, and otherwise upgrade their participation.

"High-Touch" Learning Centers

CyberUnions recognize the importance of balance, as cited by futurist John Naisbitt in his 1982 classic, *Megatrends:* "We are moving in the dual directions of high tech/high touch, matching each new technology with a compensatory human response" (Naisbitt, xxii). Accordingly, many will offer a special setting for learning new informatics skills (high-tech) in the company of attentive and caring others (high-touch).

Designed to create a socially rich environment, CyberUnion learning centers might feature a coffee bar, a children's corner, VCR viewing equipment, Internet access, and books and magazines (as would be expected of a well-equipped public library). Cozy, warm, and exceedingly user-friendly, they will have all types of day, night, and weekend courses in any and nearly every aspect of informatics.

Located possibly in part of the existing union hall, or in rented quarters nearby, these attractive learning centers will take advantage of many sound lessons Labor has garnered from over a century of adult education done by and for unionists.

Naturally, special attention will be paid to computer instruction, as so many users have gotten their start in such Labor-geared courses:

> In February of 1997 I came to a three-day Meany Center workshop on the Internet and Organizing. We had about 12 people in the class. It was the first, and I think they've taught it once more since then. It was *good!* It was very interesting! Hands-on. Everybody had a computer. We went over researching a company, and they picked some companies they had researched already . . . and we then did the research. They sent us all home with a lot of good information. It was good.

Instruction will be offered in cutting-edge matters, such as how to produce still images and streaming video for your union Web site or your own PowerPoint presentation ("If you're not using video now, you are already behind, your audiences can be bored, and your competition will be delighted" [Brock]).

Particular attention will be paid to getting elected officers comfortable using informatics, especially the use of the Internet. A 1998 survey found that 50 percent of the nation's chief executives use the Net an hour or two a week, while another 25 percent use it an hour or two every day! (Quintanilla). Until the same or better is true of

Labor leaders the CyberUnion learning centers will keep after them.

Rank-and-filers eager to go on with their formal education will be able to take brush-up (computer-aided) courses, prep for the SATs or Graduate Record Exam, and examine on-line the course offerings of higher ed here and abroad. Special attention will be paid via a search of the Internet and the Web to the many scholarships, fellowships, grants, and loans that can otherwise escape notice. As 60 percent of the jobs created through 2005 are expected to require some post-secondary education, this could prove a major service of CyberUnion learning centers (Gleckman).

At the other end of the spectrum, very diplomatic courses will be offered to help members get past a fear of appearing dumb in sharing e-mails less well expressed than one might have wished. This handicap can hurt many rank-and-filers, especially those whose K-12 schooling was far less than it should have been. Intent on making it possible for all to enjoy full membership in the new "electronic community," CyberUnions will custom-tailor onsite and on-line courses in adult literacy and writing skills.

Similarly, ESL (English as a Second Language) courses will be computer-aided and made relevant to life, citizenship, and union realities. CyberUnion officials will know that by 2006, immigrants will probably account for half of all new U.S. workers, and only 63 percent of recent new arrivals have finished high school. Learning centers run by Organized Labor can play the same vital role as back in the Ellis Island days, with a similar payoff for Labor and America alike (Gleckman).

Naturally, various computer user clubs will be hosted, and a special hand will be held out to the retiree/computer user club. Taking a leaf from the few cyber cafes that have remained in business, the centers will have many affable human assistants (of all ages!), and will change interior color schemes often to keep the environment perky.

Overall, these centers will not be satisfied until union members and their families come to regard them as a post-millennium social center of preference.

Skills Upgrading Center

Many union members confront job skill obsolescence, even as college grads who choose a career in the field of technology are being told to expect 20 percent of their skills to become obsolete every 12 to 18 months (Bailey). Typical are the changes recounted by an organizer for the Brotherhood of Maintenance of Way Employees:

> Historically, all we had to have was a strong back and a weak mind, and today, that is not true at all. In the old days you didn't even have to have a high-school diploma—so long as you were of the bulk size to do manual labor. If you could do the work, you didn't have to know how to read or write. They were lookin' for people to work, not to think.
>
> All that has changed. Now, you have to have to be able to read and write proficiently, to understand instructions and writing, to qualify for a lot of procedures out there. Now, we have to qualify on all the electrical components of the equipment, this high-tech stuff, and know how to operate it, tear it apart, and go through it. Tests are given periodically. And there is a lot of training—much of it required by the federal government.

Less than 3 percent of employers are now providing formal training, and, sadly enough, research suggests that they are investing less in skill training than a decade ago (Baugh and Pines, 40).

Instead of relying on uneven and expensive proprietary job-training schools, or a company's (self-serving) training operation, a CyberUnion could run its own program of vocational instruction geared to the present and possible interests of members. The Communications Workers of America (CWA) has been exploring this idea for a few years now, and can serve as a resource for all.

Classrooms will be loaded with up-to-date computers, instruments, and equipment. Courses will cover high-tech subjects like algebra, applied physics, computer-assisted design, and engineered work standards, along with the intricacies of industry standards and government regulations (Lund). Course members will do things like "study zoning applications and other government documents, searching for clues to what kinds of work might be coming down the pike" (Holcomb).

These CyberUnion skills centers would stand out from the competition. For one thing, they would salute union traditions by making extensive use of pro-Labor art, literature, etc., as part of the decor and curriculum (their courses would accredited in the Labor studies curricula at post-secondary institutions). They might adopt a peer-oriented system, built around the theme of "each one teach one." And all of the courses would be user-friendly; none would require a total-immersion course to figure out what is going on.

A (unionized) staff will be computer literate, receive ongoing in-service training, and be cross-trained (Lund). And, along with a bevy of job-linked courses, the skills centers will offer short-term, assisted computer-training in a comfortable space complete with Internet access, teleconferences, virtual-reality simulations, and other informatics options (Rosen).

Coordination Assistance

Typical of the coordination challenges computers can help Labor meet was the situation posed by the 1998 midterm elections. Union strategists knew better than to spend primarily on ads, as they had in 1996 ($25 million on broadcast spots), a strategy with little payoff.

Instead, unions focused on a good, old-fashioned, time-honored approach that emphasized grass-roots mobilization. Nearly 400 coordinators were paid to work full-time for more than a month in congressional districts nationwide (Greenhouse, November 6). Thousands of volunteers used computer-created address lists and maps to go door-to-door, and they succeeded in registering over 500,000 new voters. They prepared computer-generated labels for nearly 10 million mailings. And they used computer-processed lists to make nearly 6 million phone calls.

When all was said and done, Organized Labor celebrated very strong results. Exit polls showed that voters from union households increased to 24 percent of the electorate, up from 14 percent in the 1994 midterm election. Even though the number of voters was down 2.5 million from 1994, the number of votes from union households jumped by 6.7 million (Greenhouse, November 6).

John Sweeney, AFL-CIO President, boasted that "in the last 20 years, there has never been a union-led effort like this one for working families" (Harwood and Calmes, A-11). He might have added: And in the last 20 years we would not have been able to do it. Only our steadily improving use of computers made a mammoth coordination effort like this possible.

Similarly, steady gains are being made arranging for the merger in 2001 of the Auto Union, the Steel Union, and the Machinists Union. On completion, the new Metal Trades Union will be the largest (nearly 2 million members), wealthiest (with net assets in excess of $1.4 billion, and a combined strike fund in excess of $1 billion), and most powerful union in American history (Masters, 180). Given many plausible incentives, other mega-mergers to create comparable superunions are in the making. Some onlookers expect the 74 unions in the AFL-CIO today to be down to 40 or so by 2005.

Reaching Out

CyberUnions will take meetings into the living rooms of members, and provide a free-wheeling forum between meetings—all in the service of ever-finer communications.

The problem with socialism, according to Oscar Wilde, was too many meetings. Unionism suffers from the same infirmity, many unionists would argue, and most just don't bother attending. The norm is actually nonattendance, and union officers are startled and often upset by a large turnout.

While many of us know that the first message in 1844 over the telegraph, the forerunner of the Internet, was "What hath God wrought?" few may know that the second asked, "Have you any news?" (Standage, 3).

Over and again in my interviews, unionists expressed a desire to get the news, to have computers help meet their need to get and stay in touch:

> I would like to see all the locals be able to communicate with each other. [Tell about] things like a program I've worked on. Or stuff I have gathered. Or just notes that I've gathered. Some of that could be sent electronically. We do conference calls now, and it could be cheaper to use a chat room and bulletin boards.

CyberUnions will offer members the service of an internal computer network, either a mailing list or bulletin board. It will be uncensored, free-wheeling, and the host for suggestions, passions, hopes, frustrations, and rants.

These forums will permit a higher level of candor than ever before associated with union exchanges. Mechanisms will permit even anonymous postings, though this does not mean that any and all commentary is acceptable. Harassment ("flaming") will not be tolerated, and unionists will be guided by the same policies as when they talk face to face (Richtel, Sept. 7).

CyberUnion officers will pay close attention, especially to candid criticisms, in large part to take the pulse of the organization. They will participate, and give as good as they get—though they will consciously model constructive dialogue (and keep in mind three questions helpful to consider before posting anything: Is it true? Is it necessary? And is it kind? [Covey]).

Over and above this e-mail–based service, CyberUnions will also offer a new improved version of the large-scale, difficult-to-schedule, and expensive conference call.

This new-style electronic forum will simulcast union events over the Internet using technology that lets rank-and-filers both listen in and talk back. Instead of having to wait for a written account, the unionists will get to hear the words being bandied about, and the vocal tics and inflections that go with them, direct from the source, and without delays. They can phone in questions directly to event participants, and have everyone hear both their questions and the answers they get back. As well, they will be able to replay archived records of the union meeting, convention, or whatnot. All in all, this interactive option could give quite a boost to union democracy (Mount).

Reality Check

Skeptics will ask, Where can the funds come from to pay for these new services? Who has time to provide them, given how full a plate most union staffers maintain they already have? And why bother?

Expenses entailed in operationalizing these services may require a dues increase, always a hard sell where union members are concerned. But if the services are as helpful as they appear, resistance inside CyberUnions may prove less formidable than Labor history would forecast.

Staffers in CyberUnions will find time to offer these new services in the form of time saved, thanks to their creative uses of computers. A delighted staffer explains:

> Our use of computers . . . it's freed up the staff's time . . . we now do a newsletter. We didn't do it before. But now, because a lot of those tasks that took so much time before, to report to the international, for instance, that would take so much time . . . three or four days . . . now they just push a button, and that is it! The rest is ready to go, so that

person's time is freed up for something else. . . .

We haven't reduced any staff in the office, but everyone is getting different kinds of duties, because they have more time now. And it's things that we've always wanted to do. . . . It was, "Do we want to hire another person to do that?" And so, we've been freed up for other things.

Others told me similar stories of their surprise and pleasure with discovering ways in which computer use freed up time for still better purposes.

Finally, as for the question "Why bother?" CyberUnions will answer that these services meet high-priority needs in a fresh, sensitive, and caring way, and that is reason enough. That they also help "organize the organized," and appeal to the unorganized is just so much more.

Summary

CyberUnion services will combine high-tech with high-touch in an innovative and empowering way, one that will send a message members and prospective members alike will appreciate: "This union exists to serve you and your vision of the Good Life. Thanks to its reinvention as a CyberUnion, it can now do that with aplomb. Satisfaction (damn near) Guaranteed."

Recommended Resources

Kriesky, Jill, ed. *Working Together to Revitalize Labor in Our Communities.* Orono, Maine: UCLEA, University of Maine, 1998.

Mogensen, Vernon L. *Office Politics: Computers, Labor, and the Fight for Safety and Health.* New Brunswick, NJ: Rutgers University Press, 1996.Revealing exposé of the failure of Labor, business, and government to help those who work with video display terminals (VDTs) to gain protection against new occupational health and safety problems. Prescribes how Labor might render far better service in the "office of the future."

Union Privilege. Web site, maintained by the AFL-CIO, is *the* key resource of its kind: www.unionprivilege.org

Guide to Labour Oriented Internet Resources. Maintained by the Institute of Industrial Relations, University of California, Berkeley. Available at http://www.lib.berkeley.edu/IIRL/iirlnet.html

LaborLink is a worker-specific list that can be searched by subject, such as government, law, or politics. Available at http://www.igc.org./laborlink/

Labour Left Briefing Links. A comprehensive directory, organized by categories. Available at http://www.llb.labournet.org.uk/links/

URN: Union Resource Network. Wide-ranging material maintained by the Communication Workers of America (CWA-AFL-CIO). Available at http://www.unions.org/

WebActive has an extensive directory with a searchable listing of more than 1,400 sites maintained by activist organizations. Available at http://www.webactive.com

Workindex. Your link to workplace Web sites, by the School of Industrial and Labor Relations at Cornell University. Available at http://www.workindex.com/

Reading 9

A Virtual Office for Operating Engineers
IUOE Local 148

Donald J. Giljum

How do we get there from here? Coming down from the clouds, exactly what is entailed in moving a modern local into the twenty-first-century mode of operation known as a "virtual office?" What are the strengths and weaknesses of this option? What sort of ser-

vices are likely to profit from the move, and why? How important is it to first study the entire matter? And why should we bother, to begin with? Don Giljum offers some down-to-earth advice and clear-headed thinking below, a blueprint for moving up and out.

The rapid advance in computer and communications technology, especially technology that allows people to network from various off-site locations, is changing the way people do business. The traditional scenario—where employees of an organization travel to a centralized workplace—is being challenged.

It is becoming ever more feasible for organizations to do away with their centralized workplaces and instead allow their employees to work from their homes, temporary locations, even from their cars. The term for this revolutionary concept is "virtual office."

In this paper, I will explore how a virtual office might be implemented for my local union and discuss the pros and cons.

Reasons for Considering a Virtual Office

There are three main reasons why Local 148 may want to consider switching to a virtual office: remoteness of existing office; expense of maintaining the existing office; and potential need to reduce costs/raise capital.

Remoteness of Existing Office

Local 148 represents members in a rather large geographic area that includes eastern and central Missouri, southern Illinois, and southeastern Iowa. Our office is located in Maryville, Illinois, about 15 minutes east of St. Louis. Our members and staff live within a 200-mile radius of the office. The business manager and most of the business reps face a two-hour round-trip commute to the office, wasting many valuable hours in the course of a year.

Largely because of its remoteness, our office is underutilized. Few members attend meetings or other functions at the office. In fact, the union conducts 12 off-site meetings throughout the various jurisdictions each month.

Expense of Maintaining the Existing Office

Our union members have paid off the office building and land. Even so, we still incur significant operational expenses. This includes insurance, maintenance and repairs, and utilities. Additionally, a large part of our auto expenses are a result of the long commute to the office. These expenses would be easier to justify if we had better utilization of our facilities. However, that is not likely to change.

Potential Need to Reduce Costs/Raise Capital

Most of our members work in the electric utility industry. This industry is being deregulated, and the security of our members' jobs may be in question. Should our union begin to lose membership, we may be forced to reduce costs and find ways to raise capital for our operations. One obvious possibility is to sell the union office and grounds. Should this become necessary, we will need to reinvent how we operate.

For all the reasons listed above, it makes sense to at least consider adopting a virtual office concept.

The Virtual Office Defined

It is not easy to define exactly what a virtual office is, simply because it is an evolving concept. For purposes of this paper, I shall define it as follows: A virtual office is the use of computers and communications technology to link members of an organization together, in place of a centralized physical location.

What makes a virtual office possible are these technologies: desktop and laptop computers, cellular and digital phones, voice mail, electronic mail, modems, faxes scanners, pagers, teleconferencing, the Internet and Intranets, and specialized virtual office services.

My Vision of a Virtual Office

Following is my vision of how a virtual office might work for Local 148.

Intranets and Internets

The core of our virtual office would consist of an Intranet, which we might think of as a private Internet for Local 148.Our Intranet would contain all information essential to our organization: software, member records, contracts, grievance records, and variety of other documents and information. Even our union newspaper could be converted to a digital format.

The business manager, other officers, business reps, and union committees would use the Intranet regularly to review information, update union files, and collaborate on projects like grievances, contract negotiations, and organizing. The business manager and each business representative would be home-based. Our Intranet would be the regular meeting place for the business manager and his staff and for the executive board.

Members would also have access to the Intranet and could read the newspaper on-line, check on the status of a grievance, or submit questions to the staff members.

By tying into the Internet, we could also create an "Extranet" that would give us the ability to allow those outside our organization, such as consultants, vendors, and other unions, to get access to our Intranet on a limited basis.

I do not have the technical background to understand exactly how the Intranets and Extranets work. However, I am aware that many companies across the country are already using them. From what I understand, the users of these Intranets see screens and Web pages that are very similar to what you see on the Internet. The only difference is that everything pertains to your own organization.

Desktop and Laptop Computers

I envision that the business manager and business reps would all have desktop and laptop computers. Working out of our homes, we would be able to tie into the Intranet 24 hours a day to download our e-mail, conduct group meetings, leave messages, do research, and a variety of other tasks.

On the road, we would take our laptops with us. This would be a great benefit, especially at arbitrations and contract negotiations, because we could access tremendous amounts of information on past grievances or past contracts or past correspondence with the employers. This surely would give us a tactical advantage, since the employers we deal with do not yet have such capabilities.

It would also be beneficial for other union officers, stewards, and the general membership to have their own computers, so they, too, could benefit from regular use of the Intranet. Some already have their own personal computers which they could use for this purpose. Others might be motivated to buy a computer to take advantage of the Intranet. Prices of personal computers are dropping all the time, and a group purchase could probably be arranged that would enable our members to buy computers at significant discounts.

Teleconferencing

Teleconferencing technology would enable our union to conduct regular meetings from scattered locations. We could conduct our union meetings, e-board meetings, and special meetings without leaving our homes. Again, this technology would be tied into our Intranet.

Using Other Technology

Other technology would be essential if we are to make our virtual office work. We would need a scanning system to digitize all of our existing paper files. They would have to be indexed to make searches quick and easy. It would also be important for our full-time staff, who are often on the road, to be equipped with cellular or digital phones and pagers. This would make us available to our members as well as to our families.

Specialized Virtual Office Services

New companies have been created recently that offer special services for organizations that do not have a centralized office. These companies will answer your phones and direct your calls to your home, your cellular or digital phone, your pager, or your fax machine. They can even forward your calls to any number you choose. These companies also offer temporary office space, complete with fully equipped TV and video equipment for important meetings.

Benefits of a Virtual Office

I believe there are many potential advantages to a virtual office, including the following:

Flexibility

A virtual office would allow full-time staff members to work from home. They would avoid daily commutes, saving time and aggravation. This would probably contribute to a better home life, since we would be more accessible to our families and would be more likely to be home for special occasions or in the event of an emergency. Additionally, we would have more and better access to all of the information we need through our Intranet. We would also have better access to each other.

Cost Savings

By selling our central office, we could raise a significant amount of money to use for other activities, such as organizing, training, and legal fees. We would also eliminate the regular expenses of building maintenance and repairs, utilities, and insurance. Our transportation costs—gas, oil, maintenance—would also be reduced.

Efficiency

A virtual office would give us more time to do our work. In most cases, our full-time staff would eliminate two hours of commuting time each day. There would likely be less stress, too, from fighting traffic. We would also spend much less time searching for paper files, because all of that information would be located on our Intranet. We could use key-word searches to quickly locate the information we need and print it out if necessary. It would also be practical for us to put training programs on our Intranet so each of us could become better able to operate the software we use.

Enhanced Image

Organizations which adopt new technology are seen as progressive leaders in their industries. Converting to a virtual office would surely place Local 148 in that category. Also, with the specialized virtual office services referred to earlier, our union could have a mailing address and physical presence at a prestigious office location, which would enhance the public's perception of us and be a benefit during organizing drives.

Challenges of a Virtual Office

Just as there are many advantages to a virtual office, there are also many challenges.

Administration

How do you manage people who work from their homes? And how do you manage a union that is connected by an Intranet? These are questions that can only be answered by trial and error. Certainly it would require an adjustment in the way we all think and act. There will be many questions as to the physical administration of the hardware and software. Where will it be located? Who will be responsible for maintaining it? What happens if there is a hardware or software problem?

Training Requirements

Changing to a virtual office will radically change the way we operate as a union. It will require new skills. We will have to become educated and trained in the concepts of the new technology. We will have to develop expertise in using an Intranet, scanning, and operating computers more effectively. Undoubtedly, we will have to learn how to use new software systems.

Isolation

The staff will have a lot less face-to-face time with each other. Working from home may make us feel more isolated. And although our members and retirees seldom come to the union office, they may still feel as if they lost their home base. Often the union office or hall provides a psychological anchor.

Adaptation

Adapting to the virtual office will take time and effort. The business manager and business reps would have to take the lead and sell the concept to the rest of the union. It is likely that many members would resist such a change, preferring the status quo.

Dependency on Technology

Making a virtual office work requires a dependency on technology. This is scary, because our union has no in-house expertise in computer technology. We would have to rely on outside contractors to design our system, set it up, train us, and be on hand to maintain the system.

Also, the future development of technology is uncertain. Things change so rapidly that what we invest in today could be obsolete in a year or two.

Security Issues

There are also security issues. We would want to make sure that sensitive information was safeguarded and could not be read or distributed by those who are not authorized. And what happens if the system crashes or telephone lines go down? Would that bring our operations to a complete halt?

Conclusions

The concept of a virtual office is both exciting and frightening. Certainly there are many potential advantages: flexibility, cost savings, efficiency, image enhancement. But there are also many challenges: administration, training, isolation, adaptation, dependency on technology, and security issues.

Before we would initiate a switchover to a virtual office, we would have to become much more educated about the concept. We would need to talk with other organizations that have made the jump. We might want to publish a White Paper for our members, so they could become educated as to the benefits and potential problems. We might want to try some kind of pilot program to test the concept.

When I first came into office in 1984, we were without a computer system. We purchased a minicomputer that was a great help in handling our financial accounting needs and storing our grievance records and membership files. We upgraded in the early 1990s with a PC network that is much faster and offers us greater word processing, spreadsheet, database, and presentation software capabilities. In addition, we hired a contractor to create a membership system just for us.

We have taken advantage of advances in computer technology in the past, and it has helped us do our jobs better. Of course, not everything has gone smoothly, and we have faced our share of problems and aggravation.

I believe that to do nothing, to let technology pass us by, is a recipe for disaster. Other organizations will surely take advantage of the new tools and capabilities computer systems now provide, giving them greater control over information. My union must at least investigate and evaluate the concept of a virtual office if we are to survive and prosper.

Donald Giljum is a 28-year member of the International Union of Operating Engineers, Local 148. He has served as Local 148's business manager since 1984.Prior to becoming business manager, Don served the local union as a shop steward, chief shop steward, trustee, and business representative. Don currently serves on the executive boards of the IUOE-North/Central States Conference, the Missouri and Illinois Operating Engineers State councils, the Missouri AFL-CIO, and the Missouri State Utility Workers Conference. He is also president of the St. Louis Gateway chapter of the Industrial Relations Research Association. In addition to his responsibilities as a union official, Don has taught labor relations at Bellville Area College in Illinois since 1989, and he currently serves on the advisory board of the University of Missouri Labor Education Program. (Don can be reached via e-mail at dgiljum@oe148.org.)

10

Traditions: Promoting Roots

We must never forget that the human heart is at the center of the technological maze.
—Stephen Barnes, *The Transparent Society,* 1998

When I think of what immersion in traditions makes possible, I think of a response a distinguished 78-year-old film critic, Pauline Kael, gave to a young interviewer who wanly explained,"When I am at the movies, I feel like I'm swept up, lost." To which Kael gently responded, "I feel like I'm found" (Goodman).

Labor movement traditions help us find ourselves, enable us to render meaning to the flux of events. For here is where we tackle the most important questions of all—questions of purpose, of the right and wrong ways to act, and of the common good . . . questions a rank-and-filer can grasp as a soul's obligation. Here is where Labor promotes a shared vocabulary that highlights what unites us, what we have in common. Here is where Labor builds a civil society within, and dares to explore its moral center.

Concerned unionists understand what is possible. A character in a Reynolds Price novel cites "six or eight instants when I learned a thing I badly needed to know for survival or when I glimpsed a lone child or adult performing some act of open-hearted grace" (Price). Not to get too soupy about this, but I believe labor traditions, if celebrated with inspiration, can bring us closer to such a state.

CyberUnions will take up anew the challenge of tackling vital, deep-reaching questions, and will draw on computer potentials in ways that will leave the best Cyber Gain unions eager to emulate them.

Six examples can help show the way. The first would have CyberUnions pioneer in offering a "virtual" panorama, dedicated to heightening appreciation of the timeless lessons available in labor lore. The second would have the CyberUnions sponsor a labor museum in cyberspace. The third would have CyberUnions offer a cyberspace calendar. The fourth would have them provide access to labor movies, TV shows, and related "edutainment" resources. The fifth links Internet referrals to Labor's solidarity traditions. And the sixth focuses on K-12 education, and ways in which tomorrow's union members can learn as schoolchildren why Labor counts.

Taken all in all, these innovations can help unionists grasp what the poet William Carlos Williams meant when he taught, "Memory is a kind of accomplishment" (S.J. Miller). CyberUnions will honor and promote such accomplishments, recognizing in them the social glue that helps bind generations, celebrates values, and bolsters solidarity.

Labor Panoramas

Conveying history and traditions early in the twenty-first century will take many new forms, prime among which may be the panoramic format now being revived in cyberspace after over 100 years of neglect.

Already, merely by scanning on their own computer terminals, virtual viewers can "occupy" a seat in a major-league baseball dugout. Or take in the 360-degree view from the peak of Mount Everest. Or explore the Tikal ruins in Guatemala. Or ooh and ah over interplanetary panoramas brought via a NASA Solar System Simulator (Mirapaul).

Much as with the panoramic format used at Disneyland, unionists could be transported to historic scenes of vital significance to a labor organization, as when, 150 years ago, the union was formed. Or 60 years ago, when a major bloody strike was barely won. Or 30 years ago, when the union was instrumental in winning a tight and vital election. Or 10 years ago, when staffers got their first laptops, and began using them in very creative ways. Or five years ago, when members got their "wearables," and this began changing everything. All of this could be seen in a full 360-degree view, complete with engaging sound and music.

CyberUnions, using their learning centers (as explained in Chapter 9), could create a circular enclosure with floor-to-ceiling video displays of moving images. Each lifelike environment could uniquely "teach" much of value about a union's "soul," and its heroes, heroines, setbacks, and successes.

Why would especially bold CyberUnions use this odd format? Because, as an art historian and virtual-reality researcher explains, "forming a physically intimate connection with an image is a very old dream of mankind, so it's no surprise that this idea has come back on a technically developed level" (Grau, in Mirapaul).

Why would they emphasize labor history? Over half of Labor's 14 million members have no adult memory of a labor movement that wasn't in decline. Panoramas can help correct this costly misimpression. One of the major responsibilities we have, as a brother of mine has written in another context, "is to rediscover 'memory' and flesh it out at all levels of integration" (Shostak, 1998). In this way, Labor can pass along empowering and enhancing "memories" to future generations.

What might the panoramas feature? In addition to scenes of direct personal importance to the CyberUnion, 25 of the nation's 2,250 historic landmarks are related to the labor movement, and they would seem fine candidates with which to start. The most recently created National Park Service landmark of relevance, Union Square in New York City, was the site in 1882 of the nation's first Labor Day celebration, and a fine reenactment of that event crowned the 1998 Labor Day march (volunteers dressed like Samuel Gompers, Mother Jones, and Frances Perkins, all in an effort "to remind labor itself of its noble traditions" [Firestone]).

Labor's Virtual Museum

CyberUnions may come together to jointly create a virtual museum, primarily on the Internet.

Modeled on a Guggenheim project completed in late 1998, the labor museum will be much grander than simply another Web site. It will attempt to provide "a boundary-stretching venue that will exist in both digital and real space." Proponents envision an on-line "structure" that could prove a destination unto itself, a popular site for fresh and exciting displays finer than much Labor has relied on to date (Immergut).

The project's real-world component could be housed in a large trailer, a mobile exhibit that moves from labor event to event (including the remarkable annual Union Label and Trades Show) endlessly around the country. The on-line exhibits, in turn, might evoke intense nostalgia for the labor wars and the likes of Road Warriors of the 1920s and 1930s—a brave and bloodied breed whose colorful lives, even now, decades later, hang like smoke in the air of ancient union halls.

Viewers would scroll and click through a shifting collage of digital images and snippets of text, learning all the time much of lasting value about Organized Labor in its many and varied aspects.

As the museum gains experience, its exhibits will change and expand via interaction by visitors to both the van and the site. As well, live public forums may be simulcast through the Internet. All in all, the virtual project has the potential of reaching many "Netters" in an exciting and helpful way, much as museums desire, much as Labor needs.

Cyberspace Calendar

CyberUnions will launch a single pro-traditions calendar in cyberspace to which all will contribute, a calendar that will highlight what occurred on a date in labor history, much as does the IWW nowadays (in hard copy). The CyberUnion labor traditions calendar, however, will take a hypertext approach that will enable users to click on a date and link in depth to the rest of the story, thereby getting as much information about the event as they desire.

Photos and videos will be offered, along with relevant music and the voices of labor historians, current labor leaders, and whenever possible, actual participants in the day's commemorated event(s). Naturally, space will be reserved for the thoughts of any viewer stirred to share a response.

Ethnic, folk, gender, and race-pride festivals, along with labor-related forums, debates, town meetings, and public addresses, will be featured, complete with enticing previews of the event, and engaging coverage of the previous year's celebration. Note will be taken of the high-tech as well as high-touch elements of all such events.

Fortunately, history-valuing unionists are already pioneering this reform, as attested to by this e-mail response to my survey of staffers:

> As "Web master" for our district Web site, I feel rewarded by being able to do a lot of labor history research so that we can have a page concerning important dates in labor history on the site.

CyberUnions will build on this sort of early effort, and create a calendar unionists (and many other Americans) will come to regard as indispensable.

"Edutainment" Resources

CyberUnions will join together in offering in cyberspace access to the many Hollywood films, TV series (*All in the Family,* etc.), radio shows (*The Life of Riley,* etc.), and books and magazines of interest to unionists curious to know how working-class America in general, and labor traditions in particular, have been represented in the mass media over the years.

Otherwise difficult-to-secure films, such as *Blue Collar, Blood Brothers, Harry and Son, Hoffa, Norma Rae,* and *Silkwood,* will be available, along with less well known items, including a wealth of videos made by unions and little known outside the maker's world.

As well, CyberUnions will pool resources to offer workshops in upgrading the representation of union realities. They will take a leaf from Teamster reformers who, on gaining office in 1991, pioneered in revamping the use made of widely distributed union-produced videos.

Up until then, Teamster videos (and unfortunately, those of many like unions) served only the bloated egos of top officers. Workers appeared only as props. They were treated as passive consumers, which served to reinforce a sense of powerlessness. The underlying message was that the leaders were the union, and they alone knew what to do.

Over 24 videos made by the union since 1992 differ in two vital ways. First, they show rank-and-filers taking action and making gains. Second, they try to stimulate discussion that can lead to an action plan. One such video, *Every Member an Organizer,* uses real-life examples "to show how effective volunteer organizers can be and how their efforts benefit union and non-union workers alike" (Witt and Williams, 56). Another video, *It's Your Choice,* acknowledges workers' reasons for not getting more involved in the union, and helps promote constructive rebuttal arguments.

CyberUnions will help activists learn how to make, launch, assess, and improve these empowering forms of "edutainment," especially those that employ cyberspace potentialities.

Providing Referrals

The info glut we have known with printed matter is as nothing compared with the profusion of material on the Internet. Not only are there millions of pages already, but while you are reading these words scores more have been added. The whole thing resembles a big, unindexed overbearing book, and it is far too complicated and inefficient.

Tim Berners-Lee, the Net's founder, envisions a time soon when Web browsers will apply human-style reasoning to search for and apply relevant information, rather than thousands of irrelevant "hits." He also predicts a universal "oh yeah?" button that will tell Web surfers where the information they retrieved came from, thereby enabling them to conduct a quality test of the source (Miller, L.).

CyberUnions will continuously survey rank-and-filers in search of the best e-mail listserves and Web sites known to unionists (Boutin). These will be annotated, categorized, posted, and promoted. Special attention will be paid to outstanding sites, such as the OCAW Web site, which in 1998 offered the only interactive steward-training program on the Net, and also the first Internet job-referral service for those seeking labor staff posts (ujc@unionjobs.com; Union Jobs Clearinghouse). Users will have their job-seeking credentials on-line 24 hours a day, seven days a week, as will unions seeking candidates.

Above all, and in keeping with the solidarity component of labor traditions, CyberUnions will specialize in broadening the horizons of members and forging strategic alliances (see Cyber Source material at close of various chapters, and at the book's close). Rank-and-filers will be encouraged to look at the Web sites of many different groups they may not ordinarily think to visit with, groups that some may initially regard warily (the very poor, those with a different sexual orientation, the physically challenged; the ex-offender, etc.).

Schooling

In addition to working to get school-age children involved in the virtual panorama and labor museum, the nation's CyberUnions will work closely with teacher unions (AFT, NEA, and independents) to substantially upgrade the quality, quantity, and use made of labor traditions materials designed for youngsters.

Teachers will be awarded scholarships to attend short courses and workshops in labor traditions and their value in K-12 schooling. Emphasis will be put on the organic link between labor values and mainstream American goals, along with the critical contribution the labor agenda makes to the nation's well-being.

Contests in essay writing, film-making, mural making, photography, poetry writing, videos, and other such art forms will be run to encourage youngsters to delve into labor lore, and winners will be honored at labor functions. Their handiwork will be featured on the Web sites of various CyberUnions, and sent out via e-mail listserves to many thousands of unionists.

Above all, youngsters will be helped to learn the value of looking back into labor's past, as well as forward, of searching in traditions, as well as in fads, for insights of timeless value.

Reality Check

Even for animated and creative CyberUnions, the challenge here is formidable. The reviving of attention to, and profit from, labor traditions will be difficult to achieve.

Ironically, the prevailing tradition is neglect where labor traditions are concerned. Priorities in union and local budgets (where privilege is protected, and realities are exposed) seldom favor the promotion of traditions, so undervalued are celebrations of the past in these breathless times. Younger union members (Generation "X" and Generation "Y" types alike) appear less available than ever to attend events commemorating history foreign to them. And the steady, inexorable passage of oldsters removes from the scene those who actually helped create the union, and thereby gave a damn about its the Glorious (and often bloody) Past.

Which is only to suggest that goals be modest at the outset. That adequate budgetary resources be secured. And that a long-term perspective be employed. Labor traditions have, do now, and will continue to win the heart-and-soul commitment of stalwarts who will see the struggle through. CyberUnions know this, and will show the rest of the labor movement how to make the most of possibilities here.

Summary

"The past," William Faulkner advised, "is never dead. It's not ever past." Perhaps . . . and especially when activists succeed in linking the present to the very best of the past. CyberUnions intend to do just that, drawing in creative and daring ways on the potential of informatics to celebrate labor traditions (Faulkner).

"Mindsets"—cultural memories and values—are very powerful. They can serve as a reassuring guide, a shield against the continuous disequilibrium ahead. When shaped by labor traditions, when grounded in labor history and lore, they can help move mountains.

For at their very core labor's mindsets, its time-honored traditions, are about forging emotionally committed relationships, "a testimony to the enormity of people sharing their lives." And in the final analysis, "this is all we have to offer one another" (Schnarch, 7). Cyber-Unionists grasp the point, and will strive to make the most of it.

Recommended Resources

Goleman, Daniel. *Working with Emotional Intelligence.* New York: Bantam, 1998. Offers a blueprint for the "emotionally intelligent organization," and contends that emotional intelligence is actually twice as important as IQ and technical intelligence in determining success. Labor could use its computer-boosted traditions to learn much here.

Tannenbaum, Frank. *A Philosophy of Labor.* New York: Columbia University Press, 1951. A forgotten classic that pioneered in a socio-psychological exploration of why unions are created in the first place, and what members really are seeking from them. Links profoundly to labor traditions, and sheds unique light on same.

Zaniello, Tom. *Working Stiffs, Union Maids, Reds, and Riff Raff: An Organized Guide to the Films about Labor.* Ithaca, NY: ILR Press, 1996. Unique, engaging, and discerning guide to obscure and well-known films about the labor movement and its activists and members.

Invaluable is a *Union Songs* Web site reached at http://www.chepd.mq .edu.au/boomerang/unionsong/index.html. It is busy documenting the songs and poems that workers have made in the process of building unions. For labor videos, contact lvpsf@labornet.org

Federations and Unions on the Internet is an extensive list of unions and federations on the Internet, with a special focus on teachers. Available at http://www.osstf.on.ca/www/links/unions.html

For a toolkit to help with use of the 1999 PBS series, "Our Towns," about working people building healthy places to live, see www.pbs.org/livelyhood (or call 510-268-9675).

To help "promote production and use of TV and radio shows pertinent to the cause of Organized Labor and working people," subscribe to UPPNET News (c/o Labor Education Services, University of Minnesota, 321 19th Ave., South, No. 3-300; Minneapolis, MN 55455, or visit their Web site at www.mtn.org/see/uppnet.html

For the view of grass-roots activists, go to UNITED via majordomo @cougar.com

For many great labor links, go to socrates.berkeley.edu/iir/clre.html:, the official Web site of the Center for Labor Research and Education at the University of California, Berkeley, CA.

Reading 10

Bright Future for Unions?

Jim Dator

Jim Dator believes unions are unique among present-day institutions, and offer rewards we urgently need if we are to escape the ravages of capitalism out-of-control. He knows full well the limitations of many unions and locals, but persists nevertheless in hoping Organized Labor will persist in its effort to reinvent itself, an effort he clarifies and bolsters with his remarkable exercise in analysis and prescription.

The conventional wisdom currently says that unions are anachronistic holdovers from an earlier industrial era. If they ever had any value (and perhaps they never did), it is gone in the brave new world of global, entrepreneurial capitalism. Unions will die a slow death. Or else, they should be killed off. They have no positive role to play in the free-spirited world of tomorrow.

Such is the conventional wisdom.

In the face of this, some unions, or union leaders, are merely digging in, holding on, refusing to budge, and willing to die out like dinosaurs, if the good old days cannot be made to return again.

This is understandable. Rapacious, shortsighted, individualistic, global capitalism does seem to be the only ideological game in town. "Transform yourself into a greedy, self-centered global entrepreneur, or die," is the loudest voice I hear wherever in the world I go.

It just emerged again here last week in the recommendations of the Hawaii Economic Revitalization Task Force. According to one headline in Sunday's full-court press, the members of the task force, including apparently your own illustrious leader, went from cynicism, to unanimity, to euphoria. Euphoria, yet! With such delirium, it must be true.

Oh, there may still be some green New Age, or indigenous Hawaiian, voices crying in the wilderness, offering hope of a better, more caring, and communal day, but those voices are made to appear increasingly marginalized and old-fashioned.

Old-fashioned! That is the main thing these guys want to get you to believe: that unions, or concerns about workers generally, are old-fashioned. To be with it, you have to forget workers and turn everyone into a self-centered, endlessly wheeling and dealing, private entrepreneur.

Yet, in spite of this—perhaps because of this—I am here today as a futurist to tell you that there are other possible futures for unions. For more details than I can share today, I recommend that you consider the work of Drexel University futurist Arthur Shostak, if you have not done so already. Shostak has developed very plausible visions of a future in which revived and revised strong unions will exist over the twenty-first century.

Shostak does not assume that global capitalism will go away anytime soon, and he does believe that human labor will still be needed for the foreseeable future. He also argues that unions can and should mimic some of the lean, mean, adaptive, networked, focused forms which some businesses espouse (while also linking together with other unions in order effectively to deal with the global transnational megacorporations which are also emerging as well).

Indeed, I believe it is wrong to assume, as so many business gurus are prophesying, that the most important feature of capitalist structures in the twenty-first century will be small, flexible, temporary electronic-cottage firms of one or two people. There will be many such small firms in the future, I am sure, but the monopolistic logic of capitalism is obviously operating now, and will continue to dominate, so that any successful small firm will either be gobbled up by larger ones or itself gobble up larger ones.

Hence the dominant feature of the future in this regard, in Hawaii and everywhere else, is towards a world in the twenty-first century controlled by a small number of gigantic, diversified, global corporations. Thus, strong, unified, if flexible and networked, unions will still be needed to advance the interests of ordinary people in such a globalized political economy.

But if there can be a bright future for unions generally—if we will need unions in the twenty-first century like never before—what is the future of unions of governmental employees?

Here, the immediate future looks exceedingly grim, as governments everywhere continue irresponsibly to self-destruct in the face of exponentially rising needs for communal infrastructure and services. Privatization seems to be an unstoppable global trend found everywhere.

You know how, every once in a while, some new kind of flu bug arises in some part of the world and then sweeps across the globe, infecting millions and killing tens of thousands, with only a few people staying somehow immune and healthy?

Well, over the years I have concluded that many ideas and fads are also like the flu. They arise somewhere with no clear point of origin, then spread wildly, swiftly infecting millions of people everywhere so that even sensible people begin saying and doing the stupidest things: firing employees, cutting services, and bad-mouthing government workers for no good reason, simply because they are infected by the anti-government bug and just can't help themselves.

As the world eagerly dismantles governments in the name of free market efficiency, we are captured by a sick ideology as weird, powerful, untried, and wrong as the Marxist ideology that Lenin brought to Russia in 1917, infecting that country, and spreading the Red disease worldwide until suddenly, and for no apparent reason, it all died out, everywhere, in 1989 and 1990. The Red Plague abruptly and peacefully came to an end. The Evil Empire, with all its evil emperors everywhere, limply sank to its knees and melted away.

But only to give way to the Blue Plague, a new global disease of even more frightening proportions.

Will it take 70 years of similar suffering before the virulent ideology of free market capitalism is revealed to be equally deadly and empty of life and hope? It may be so, as I look around this community and listen to what so many well-meaning people are saying, advocating, and doing, with such passion and euphoria. Strange. And sick.

Now, it is certainly the case that in the face of such an ideological plague, governmental unions need to become healthy, flexible, efficient, networked, aware, and not be, and not appear to be, stuck in the nostalgic past of big government.

But I am absolutely convinced that the current capitalist ideology is not sustainable, nor do I think the forms and structures which that ideology has created are sustainable.

It is not the case that vigorous capitalism triumphed over diseased communism. Rather, it is the case that neither is a healthy, sustainable way to live, but that communism succumbed first. Capitalism in its current form will also fail because it is based on myths and lies, and not on care or sustainable futures.

While there certainly is a necessary and proper role for free markets, the production of needed goods, and the provision of vital services, diligent labor, and honest advertising, capitalism as it is now organized is none of these things.

It is based on false assumptions about human motivations and preferences (forcing everyone to become greedy and self-centered), false measures of success (such as the GNP or stock market indexes), false premises about the proper role of government (eagerly privatizing decisions and profits while duplicitously socializing losses and damages), and, most dangerously of all, our present economic ideology is concerned only with the immediate pleasures of the here-and-now, acknowledging no responsibility for the impact of current economic activities on future generations, or on the torn and tattered Earth upon which future generations will be forced to try to eke out a living.

When, or rather as, capitalism collapses from its own indulgences and excesses, there will be an urgent need for many kinds of local, community-oriented, helping and caring organizations, such as religious congregations, neighborhood centers, credit unions, local security units such as the National Guard, and labor unions.

While unions must become more flexible and fluid to deal with the present global economic madness, unions also need to retain their communal roots in solidarity, equity, justice, and mutual care.

Of course, as a futurist, I still believe that the long-range future is away from the need or even the possibility of any kind of full employment, or anything even vaguely approaching full employment.

As I have said many times before, human labor, mental as well as manual, is barely needed now, in point of fact, and will rapidly diminish because of automation, artificial intelligence, and the effortless yet sustainable abundance that nanotechnology will bring over the twenty-first century. Unions need to be future-oriented in that respect as well.

The need for human labor is minuscule now, and most jobs are created merely to keep as many people off the streets as possible—not because their labor is needed, but so they can be credit-worthy consumers. Given our global material abundance and overcapacity, what we need now more than anything are consumers, not laborers, but we lack the imagination and will to create a system which accepts and deals fairly with this fact.

Future pressures in this regard will be overwhelming, and we will either respond to them before or after the collapse of our present obsolete economic system.

Thus I conclude that unions need to have three legs to stand on now.

One leg must be firmly rooted in the communal past, enabling unions to continue to do what they were originally set up to do—to ensure that workers receive good pay and other benefits for their labor; to have reasonable assurance that if they work well they will continue to be employed in meaningful jobs and at decent wages; and to see that their workplaces are safe and congenial. This is still a vital leg upon which unions must stand. But that is a rapidly shrinking leg, and it should be allowed, indeed made, to shrink quickly, but humanely.

The second leg is the one which can dance to the contemporary tunes of global capitalism. Unions must recognize that most of the new jobs in the future will be temporary, fluid, global, and increasingly intellectual and symbolic. This leg of unionism should make it one of its highest priorities to guarantee that all persons—and not just a privileged few—are fully educated and motivated to live in this dynamic and knowledge-based world—a very different world from the past.

Unions must also strive to protect the interests of workers in such a world by being themselves truly open, democratic, participatory, fluid, networked, intellectual, aware, and global (and no longer hierarchical, authoritarian, anti-intellectual, bigoted, and parochial, as too many unions still are now).

And the third leg of unionism must be set in the future, helping workers of all kinds prepare eagerly for a world without work, but still a world of material abundance, peaceful interaction, and deep cultural and spiritual, individual and communal, identity and meaning.

It is not only unions which need to have these three legs to stand on. All institutions need them. But I do not see any organization which is able to stand on these three legs now except for unions.

Governments are in confusion, disarray, and often deserve contempt as they cravenly give in to the forces of individual greed and privilege.

Business (as currently organized—it need not be this way) has no soul, and no ability to care about anything beyond its immediate fantasies and desires.

Education doesn't have a clue, paralyzed between the past and the future.

Only unions are built on care, equity, and solidarity.

For unions, or any institutions in the present, to learn also to be intelligent, flexible, fair, and future-oriented is difficult, but it is necessary, and it is possible, I believe. Or at least, so I hope!

Note: This essay is based on a talk given at the HGEA/AFSCME Leadership Conference, October 27, 1997, in the Ala Moana Hotel, Hawaii.

Jim Dator is professor, and head of Alternative Futures Option, Department of Political Science, and director, Hawaii Research Center for Futures Studies, Social Science Research Institute, University of Hawaii, in Honolulu, Hawaii. He was president of the World Futures Studies Federation during the 1980s and early 1990s. He is a union member of the University of Hawaii Professional Assembly. (Jim can be reached via e-mail at Dator@hawaii.edu.)

Part IV

WITH A LITTLE HELP FROM OUR FRIENDS: BUILD IT, AND THEY WILL COME

Never doubt that a small group of individuals can change the world. Indeed, it is the only thing that ever has.
—Margaret Mead, anthropologist
(Warner, *The Last Word,* 1992)

Having tersely scanned the labor-computer scene in Part I, developed a typology of three types of union users of computers in Part II, and advanced my own candidate for twenty-first-century distinction in Part III, it only remains now in this closing section to highlight some key agents whose contributions appear vital if progress is to be made.

Were I not intent on keeping this book brief, I would write at length here about the special role unionists in the telecommunications field could play (as informatics specialists, they can help show the way). I am also intrigued by the unique modeling that labor educators could offer, though at present most are still focusing elsewhere (Medina, et al.). This could change fairly soon, however, as younger Web-farers join the staff of labor education centers, and pre-computer types (like me) retire.

Above all, I am cheered by the auspicious role young unionists are beginning to play, as the computer aficionados among them begin to pressure Labor to "get with it!" A labor educator with a flair for informatics sees the same potential:

> When the next generation starts to get into leadership the control types are going to fade. They are in their 40s, 50s, and 60s, and they don't get it. Young people, they go out and buy their own stuff.

But, space limits preclude anything other than this bare mention of these three potential agents of change.

Instead, I turn in Chapter 11 to five other agents already deeply engaged in the fray, each playing a very special role. The first, the AFL-CIO, is already doing far more than is commonly recognized, but far less than is desirable. The second, international unions, are doing much of value, but few outside their ranks benefit from their example. The third and fourth, City Central Councils and locals, have great variability, and when good, are very, very good . . . but the number of good ones appears very, very, small. And the fifth, women unionists, have in this "startup" stage of computer use by Labor a rare opportunity to advance a "feminizing" reform agenda of value to both sexes, even while aiding Labor to meet the cyberspace challenge.

In Chapter 12, I focus on our union brothers and sisters across the seas, many of whom offer lessons of great value to us. They have pioneered in creating Internet Web sites, listserves, distance-learning projects, and other valuable aids to solidarity, though Americans characteristically know little about any of this.

In Chapter 13, I pose several of the toughest questions my research (still ongoing) has thus far uncovered, questions the answers to which will indelibly shape the near-future record of union uses of computers. Typical is the question of how serious Labor is about helping to close the digital gap between those members with home computers and those now without—this possibly the most serious threat to Labor solidarity going unaddressed today.

Finally, in the book's epilogue I repeat a major cautionary note—computers are no magic wand or silver bullet. Only in combination with better-than-ever strategy, vision, and willpower can further gains from computerization advances help Labor reverse its fortunes, and reinvent itself. Hopeful that unionists recognize how much informatics in general, and computers in particular, offer, I close urging a fair trial for the F-I-S-T–empowered CyberUnion option.

11

Change-Agents: Stateside

No organization can maintain excellence without renewing. No organization can strive for excellence, or even attempt to improve, without the ability to renew.
—Robert H. Waterman, Jr., *The Renewal Factor,* 1987

Five major change-agents, four of which I discuss in the body of this chapter—the AFL-CIO, international unions, Central Labor Councils, and local unions—and another, female union activists, whom I discuss in an essay immediately following—have a major contribution to make if labor is to do more soon with computers. I write in admiration of their present efforts, and with high expectations of what they can go on to accomplish.

AFL-CIO

Having begun in the early 1970s to use mainframe computers to meet standard accounting needs, the Federation is no stranger to these machines. In a most revealing way, however, one that harkens back to Cyber Naught and Cyber Drift mistakes, things did not move quickly after that. Word has it at least one very influential staffer insisted throughout the 1980s that the AFL-CIO did not need to adopt PCs: They were blithely dismissed by this specialist in information technology (and a fan of mainframe use) as merely a "passing fad."

"Disruptive" technologies, like PCs, which threatened to make reliance on familiar equipment obsolete, often rattle bureaucracies (Christensen). This is especially true of organizations where fear reigns and indecision recommends itself to apprehensive decision-(non)mak-ers, mis-leaders who "have been plied with the security of routine and soaked with the fear of action." (Mills, 290). Accordingly, and unfortu-nately, the Federation watched post-mainframe changes from the side-lines (as Cyber Naught unions and locals continue to do today at great cost).

LaborNET

It was not until nearly 20 years later that the AFL-CIO ended its most costly impasse, the sort of failure of imagination and verve that pleases only labor's fervent opponents.

The breakthrough came in 1990 when an Internet service, LaborNET, was founded by the AFL-CIO to exchange information more rapidly with its activists and those of its affiliates. Two years later it was moved to CompuServe to allow greater reliability, flexibil-ity, and support. As explained to me by Blair Calton, its manager, LaborNET serves as a common gateway to information and dialog, an opportunity for 14 million members of affiliates to participate in a larger "electronic labor community."

Specifically, LaborNET offers subscribers access to a remarkable library of resources. Labor graphics, cartoons, charts, and news stories can be downloaded for immediate use in a local's newsletter, and speeches and press releases abound. LaborNET has a message area widely used by far-flung unionists to get and stay in touch. And it has a Conference Section which permits focused, sustained, and timely con-versations among subscribers.

As well, various departments of the Federation offer material of value; e.g., the Union Label Department highlights goods and services made by union brothers and sisters, and urges only their purchase. The Committee on Political Education (COPE) shares the latest political news, poll results, and calls for action. Annotated lists of films, videos, and books available from the Federation help spread the word, as do also announcements of where, when, and why key AFL-CIO leaders are scheduled to speak (along with last-minute changes therein).

At present, plans are being made to move LaborNET to the Internet. Along the way it will be re-engineered into a cutting-edge service complete with Information Agent–like software capable of tracing the interests of each and every individual user. A union subscriber to

LaborNET will complete a profile of what it is he or she wants to keep learning about, the information that is of most interest to their efforts in the labor movement (Boutin). With no further effort on their part, these topics will be constantly researched for them, and e-mail will tell them when (often daily, if not hourly) new information awaits them.

If and when this extraordinary change is achieved, it will propel the AFL-CIO to the forefront of information providers, and make both labor and information tech history.

Other AFL-CIO Moves

In 1995, with the election of the pro-informatics Sweeney administration, a new AFL-CIO publication, revealingly entitled *America@Work,* began to feature a page or more of informatics-boosting material (lists of Web sites of value to unions, examples of bright uses of the Internet by locals, etc.). Every issue since has highlighted valuable cyberspace sources, and in toto, the page says to unionists: "Where the Information Age is concerned, Labor has arrived!"

In 1996, the AFL-CIO held its first major meeting to discuss Labor and the Internet. Between 1996 and 1998 the Federation held two meetings of the information technology officers of key affiliates (and some especially progressive locals). In 1997 it completed its first formal survey of the informatics uses of its affiliates. In 1998 it began to study how to offer an "Intelligent Agent" service to unionists, a remarkably creative and bold stretch for a Federation once thought stodgy and reluctant where information advances were concerned.

Characteristic of newfound flair is a 1998 AFL-CIO Web site which "enables working women to find out how much they have lost—and will lose—from a lifetime of pay inequity. They can enter their current age, salary, and education level, and then get answers to questions such as 'How much will the pay gap cost you?' and 'What could you have purchased with that money? . . . The site (www.aflcio.org/women/equalpay.htm) also guides women in how to fight unequal pay by writing their elected representatives, filling a complaint with the Equal Employment Opportunity Commission, talking to a shop steward, and joining a union" (Anon., *America@Work*).

Timely, informative, energizing, and symbolic, the site is just the sort of cyberspace tool Labor needs.

Similarly, in terms of meeting critical needs, the AFL-CIO has now completed a $20 million-plus rewiring of its entire Washington, DC, headquarters. It is no longer dependent on reels of old-fashioned tapes and an antique, monstrous, room-size mainframe. Instead, it now has PC finesse, a LAN system inside the building, and a fiber optics system capable of handling streaming video and other demanding informatics challenges for many years ahead. For the first time ever, the labor movement has a flagship cyberspace headquarters equal to the challenge.

Reality Check

The Federation is just and only that, a loosely-knit body made up of 74 autonomous affiliates in voluntary membership, with the emphasis put by them on *autonomous*. While open to advice and urgings from the AFL-CIO, the affiliates zealously insist on going their own way. While many may move to match the Federation's Internet advances, some of the more haughty types will continue to do their own thing regardless.

Second, the Federation must remain wary of getting too far ahead in computer uses, lest cyberspace-oriented communications get overly complex and too confusing for certain affiliates. While a drag on progress, this restraint does help guard against undue frustration ("Damn these machines!") from would-be users.

And finally, the Federation has very limited financial resources. Roughly 75 percent of the annual receipts of Organized Labor stay with local unions, and the AFL-CIO gets only about 1 percent (Whitford). This inadequate amount has numerous claimants on it, and as the "new kid on the block," computerization projects must compete with older well-established interests (lobbying, political action, research, public relations, etc.) for every scarce dollar.

Where Next?

As impressive as is this flurry of recent activity, everyone I interviewed or talked to about the AFL-CIO agreed that much more remains to be accomplished.

Office for CyberUnions@Work (OCW)

The Federation, for example, could create an *Office for CyberUnions@Work* (OCW), one that could serve as an R&D center for the promotion of the CyberUnion model. It would hire computerization experts who would scrutinize the literature (hard copy as well as Net material) and represent Labor at conferences on information technologies. They would explore the application to unions of esoteric matters like data warehousing and data-mining, and in 1,001 other ways, help assure that labor stays at the cutting edge in its employ of computer potentialities

OCW and Y2K

One of the first challenges OCW could tackle involves computer glitches that threaten on midnight, December 31, 1999, to wreak havoc with all of Labor's computer systems. A massive effort is necessary to reprogram hundreds of thousands of computers if they are to recognize dates in the new millennium and continue to function.

Business is likely to spend billions trying to fix Year 2000 "bugs," and labor will also have a large repair bill. OCW could promote a greater sense now of urgency and very aggressive approaches, thereby helping to keep the cost of this massive software problem as low as possible.

Labor has a special need here, as its thousands of employee-benefit plans have a fiduciary responsibility to see that the Year 2000 (or Y2K) problem is addressed. As well, unions may want now to anticipate their reactions to possible business slowdowns or shutdowns resulting from data-related system failures. Workable strategies and contingency plans must be put in place, and OCW could help guide just such an urgent national campaign.

OCW and Research

OCW could house a research unit focused on assessing high-tech gadgets and gimmicks hyped by promoters often indifferent to their high touch implications.

Typical is the drive underway to gain widespread use of a chip-based "smart card," a combination identity card and wallet which authorizes access to various facilities and services, and allows purchases to be made with "cash" stored on the chip. Major unions now using affinity credit cards are being invited to convert to this new device. OCW could explore what information the card's use makes available about unionists who use it. To whom does it go, and for what purpose? Is personal privacy protected? Should Labor go along, or insist on certain safeguards?

Another research concern would focus on broad-scale threats from misuses of computers at work. Typical is a new type of software that will enable employers to record every keystroke—which means the Web sites employees browse, and also the programs they use, the memos they prepare, and the content of the e-mail they send and receive. These products let employers use them without employees knowing they are in use. One makes it possible for an employee's daily record to be e-mailed to a supervisor without the employee being aware of any of this.

Proponents claim the new software will discourage employees from wasting the time of the employer. As well, it will provide a record in the event of a post-firing lawsuit by a disgruntled ex-employee.

Critics see a gross invasion of privacy, a blow to trust in the workplace, and a slippery slope which will lead to still greater surveillance abuses. OCW could test the product, and help Organized Labor take an informed and influential stand (Anon., *New York Times*).

Finally, where informatics per se is concerned, pioneering Canadian activist Marc Belanger suggests Labor's research mission should have it "involved in the 'design' of new technologies by being one of its early adopters. Not only do we sometimes then get the lead on employers, but we learn technology-design principles which we can apply to the next round of technological change" (Belanger, in Lee, 63).

OCW and F-I-S-T

Apropos the F-I-S-T model, OCW could scan the literature in futuristics, for example, and interview leading long-range forecasters, represent Organized Labor at meetings of futurists, and help unions and locals learn how to employ forecasting to advantage.

With guidance from OCW, the AFL-CIO could devote an entire page in every issue of *America@Work* to CyberUnion innovations field-proven by a union affiliate and available now for adoption by others. It could highlight such advances at its various meetings, run competitions, and award prizes for outstanding projects. It could pioneer CyberUnion tactics, gadgets, and applications itself, taking care always to promote their employ by its affiliates.

Where services are concerned, OCW, using an e-mail quarterly survey, could ask the Federation's many affiliates and their several thousand locals to report their latest service successes and disappointments. OCW could also function somewhat like Consumers Union in testing novel services before unions and locals involve the membership.

Finally, where tradition is concerned, OCW could study the success of "Bread and Roses," the art and theater project of District 1199-C, and the Annual Labor Arts Festival at the Meany Center, along with similar sources of lessons for bringing along the best of the past into the future. An OCW Web site could be reserved for promoting labor history, legends, and lore, so vital is this to the movement's integrity.

National Labor College

Guided by its OCW, the AFL-CIO could ask its educational unit, the National Labor College of the George Meany Center for Labor Studies (which President Sweeney enjoys calling labor's "War College") to create a degree-granting program in CyberUnion studies. Graduates could be placed with internationals and large locals long ago convinced that they must either secure informatics craft or fall hopeless behind. Similarly, the AFL-CIO could encourage the University and College Labor Educators Association (UCLEA) to begin including CyberUnion material in labor ed programs from coast to coast (Adler).

In recognition of the global nature of this challenge, OCW and the National Labor College could sponsor an annual international meeting of interested laborites from nations hither and yon. Daily high-tech contact among such influentials via teleconferences and e-mail should vastly increase the international exchange of ideas. Nevertheless, annual opportunities for high-touch dialog and hands-on demonstrations will probably long make a uniquely valuable contribution to computer-use progress.

Information Technology Activists

OCW could provide support to ad hoc efforts outside the AFL-CIO framework; e.g., in 1998, an ad hoc committee (which deliberately stayed nameless), made up of 12 information technology officers of especially progressive unions, published a White Paper on making the most of the Internet. It addressed four questions: "Why should Labor be on-line? What should Labor do on-line? How should we get there? What issues will we face in getting and being on-line?" (Anon., *Net News,* 1998).

According to SEIU's Peter Pocock, the convener, "the real point of the exercise was to take a good look at the state of the Internet today; to make some conservative projections about where the technology is headed; and to point at some prospective benefits of the technology for the labor movement and individual unions" (Pocock).

Among its many intriguing points, the White Paper gently urged traditional unionists to broaden their notion of appropriate subject matter for a labor medium: "Our sites . . . should provide all kinds of information not directly related to the union, such as technical help in using the Web, . . . resources for finding kid-friendly sites and helping kids with Internet research, . . . or whatever else will be of interest to our members" (Anon., *Net News,* 13).

Researchers years from now may give the ad hoc group credit for having had a significant impact, especially as its White Paper went to all the presidents of AFL-CIO affiliates, and enjoyed wide circulation and commentary within Labor's ranks.

Despite the singularity and importance of the ad hoc group, it never had a budget, a formal structure, or any resolve to surely meet again after release of its sole product. Everyone worked pro bono, and printing and Web-space costs were donated by Cyber Gain unions. OCW could host further meetings, post the White Paper on its Web site, and promote it via e-mail around the country and the globe.

International Unions as Change-Agents

Certain progressive international unions (IUs) have been showing the way, and seem to grasp a CyberUnion vision of their own. They feature Web sites with at least eight features:

• *Electronic "Union Hall."* Where dues-payers and prospective members can learn much about the union, both from displays and from questions they pose to the union; this often includes a chatroom for unmoderated dialogue;
• *Information on Request.* Anyone can request and receive contract clauses, sample leaflets, the union's constitution and by-laws, facts and figures, etc.;

* *Membership Application and Dues Forms* to enable new members to join in the privacy of their living rooms, and pay via a credit card if their workplace does not withdraw dues from one's paycheck;
* *Announcements and Events Calendar.* The dates, time, place, and purposes of meetings, demonstrations, social events, etc., both of the union and of its many allies in the community; also offers press releases and recent speeches of key officers, the better to help all understand and support union positions;
* *Literature Table* to help gain sales of leaflets, pamphlets, books, bumper stickers, etc., of both the union and its allies;
* *The Union Store* to promote the sale of attractive and useful union-made merchandise with the union logo;
* *The Members' Store* to promote the swapping and selling of attractive and useful union-made goods and services among the membership; and
* *Solidarity Aids* to demonstrate with cross-postings the union's links in solidarity with other worthy causes here and abroad; to urge action-taking on their behalf.

First highlighted at the 1997 LaborTECH Conference in San Francisco, this list is a useful benchmark against which all union and local Web sites can be measured (Hartford).

Another advance worth emulating involves holding computer workshops at district and regional meetings, and at the union's convention. These workshops are growing in number and gaining ever more fans, to judge cautiously from anecdotes I picked up during three years of interviewing for this book.

The best of these gatherings feature many user-friendly machines for actual hands-on use. They use experienced and caring instructors. They have generous hours of access, free software, and a low-key friendly atmosphere. They open a day before the main event (the convention, or whatever) and stay open throughout. Best of all, they repeat event after event, and can therefore be counted on by members who want advice and are well beyond introductory-level material.

Mentoring locals is a powerful boost to everyone involved. The Service Employees International Union (SEIU), for example, has its Ad Hoc Task Force on Technology working in tandem with 20 local union leaders on a study of SEIU in the early twenty-first century. A variety of technologies are being assessed for their ability to support key aspects of SEIU operations (internal and external communications, organizing, etc.).

Where Next?

International unions could focus reform attention on workplace problems directly traceable to soulless computerization processes. A very angry activist urged far more attention to this challenge:

> As if things weren't bad enough, I'm now watching at first hand the steady deskilling of the clerical work we do in the rail industry ... where we once had *proud* people, who were waybill clerks, or rate clerks, or stenographers, or a whole host of other office positions. Now they're basically doing computer input work. Everything is formatted for them; they're closely monitored; they're watched moment by moment, and there's no more think process in their work.
>
> They've become a *disposable* workforce. If I can train somebody to be proficient at data input in two days, then how much will I care about their concerns? If they don't like it, they can get out ... and I'll hire some other 19-year-old to take their place, and train them in two days.
>
> What's the difference, I wonder, between some of my people working on a computer, doing data input day after day, eight hours a day, and my grandmother, as a child, rolling cigars all day in a cigar factory? It's production, production, production!! A new kind of "sweatshop"! We've *got* to do something about this!

Many other interviewees expressed similarly strong feelings about the need to police the impacts computers were having and continue to have at work.

Very helpful here is a rare field-research report that finds workers eager to have their union monitor new computerized equipment. Members want their skill levels protected, and they want assurances that they will get any necessary retraining. They also want any new jobs generated by computer impacts kept in the bargaining unit. The researchers warn in conclusion that "given what we know about the American economy and American employers, we can safely say this: Without the proactive involvement of unions there is little chance that technology will be widely used in a skill-enhancing, pro-worker manner in unionized workplaces" (Malakoff and Kim, 51).

A second major front on which to advance would have international unions spotlight "Best Practice" projects within the ranks. Members who pioneer hardware or software gains for Labor could be featured in the union's Web site and newspaper, called to the platform at convention time, and in other upbeat ways, hailed as models for all.

Along with saluting current members of merit, international unions could add esoteric types to the mix on staff. In 1996, for example, the Steelworkers Union, hired its first (Labor's first?) full-time investment banker as a special assistant to the president. So many high-finance arguments were now coming from corporate management that only in-house expertise would do in response. Naturally, the new staffer required advanced computer modeling and other state-of-the-art informatics aids to do the job, and his use of them dazzled both sides of the bargaining table (while substantially aiding Labor's side [Norton]).

Informatics Group

Little of this will occur unless and until an international hires a full-time information technology specialist (who reports directly to the president). This specialist should be put at the head of an informatics group (IG), a unit closely tied to the union's research department and also its communications department.

IG's highest priority should be collecting e-mail addresses of members who are on-line, reaching out, and welding them into a new cyberspace force; e.g., they can mentor other members thinking of taking the step. They could help rally the troops for a cyberspace torrent of e-mails aimed at a politician. They could exchange reform ideas and report on ideas garned from their Internet surfing. They could help their locals create interactive Web sites, and so on.

Modeled on the OCW explained above, the new informatics group should be spotlighted in the union's publications, on its Web site, and at conventions and like gatherings. Carefully kept free of entanglements in union politics, the group could prove a major element in the union's very survival, to say nothing of its achievement of Cyber Gain status (and later, a still finer life as a CyberUnion).

Reality Check

While money is not the only thing needed, skeptics are correct in arguing that without adequate funds much will not happen here. International unions have got to allocate more resources and money. Even those now on-line (44 of the AFL-CIO's 74 in September, 1998) typically allocate only a portion of one staffer's time to maintaining their Web sites (Cantrell). A full-timer, paid as much as the top-paid service providers (who are commonly better paid than organizers), is indispensable! Until this changes for the better, even the most progressive of the major unions may continue to underachieve in meeting cyberspace possibilities, a prospect Labor can ill afford.

Central Labor Councils

Easily the weakest link in the chain are the Central Labor Councils (CLC) around the country, ironically "the face of Organized Labor in communities where there is still a union presence" (Crouch, 39). Dismissed as unimportant by many internationals because they do not deliver votes for the incumbents, they are commonly short on membership (voluntary) and struggle to get by on bare-minimum funds. Not surprisingly, hardly any are currently players in cyberspace matters. While the AFL-CIO is trying to make membership in CLCs mandatory, the vaunted autonomy of the Federation's affiliates weakens this prospect.

In the best of possible worlds, every CLC would have at least one very able person to create and maintain a citywide Web site. His or her job (or the voluntary effort of a computer enthusiast) would have them rapidly develop an e-mail address database at the city level, and send out regular e-mails and newsletters. They could facilitate political initiatives, "marshal the troops" on short notice, and draw many new users into computer employ. Some might even find the time to tutor eager union learners in computer uses. Best of all, this sort of CLC would offer a modern face to a curious city, quite different from the one now commonly in place.

Locals

As for locals, most already have been using computers for the last several years in their daily business. With only the added cost of a modem, an Internet service provider's monthly charges, and an extra phone line, most union locals can at least have an e-mail address on the Web and send and receive electronic mail.

Locals should go out of their way to nurture their enthusiasts, for unlike CLCs and international unions above them, the locals can draw directly on a wealth of talent in the immediate membership. Typical is this sort of account from an enthusiast:

> I bought a computer for the office, and it has changed my life! I had used somebody else's for about a half-hour on a word-processing program, and I thought that was really a tool that would be nice to have. I convinced the "E" board, maybe three years ago, to buy a computer. And it has turned out to be a tool that has made *all* the difference in the world . . . as far as communications with our members.
>
> I have a regular daily routine. As a computer fanatic I'm trying to make it so that everyone will check in every morning for e-mail messages and such. Every day when I walk into my house I kind of grin at my wife, then I walk into my study where my computer is. I check my "mail."
>
> I've got a route. I hit the local computer bulletin boards first until 6 P.M. I hit the Meany Center board, then the Department of Labor, then the AFSCME board in Washington, DC. I hit NABET or National Association of Broadcasting Engineering Technicians board in Chicago. Then I hit a legal board in Seattle for Supreme Court decisions. Then I relax a bit.
>
> This keeps me up-to-date, especially concerning all the Department of Labor press releases . . . which, by just hitting a button I fax to unions I think might be interested. And it costs only $50 a month for 60 hours of data-transmission phone service.
>
> No one has begun sending me any faxes [of appreciation] back, but people do stop me and say "Oh yeah, I got your fax. Thanks!" I think it helps, and I'll continue doing it.

Acknowledgments, if not expressions of appreciation, go a long way in matters like these.

Locals should try and get a volunteer to monitor cyberspace-covered developments in the industry of direct concern. One such activist offered an explanation of how she came to serve in this way:

> The role I've come to play, a job for the union that is not written anywhere but that I've come to take on, is saying . . . "Here's the global picture of what is going on . . . and we're in deep trouble if we don't figure out how to avoid the technological conflicts ahead!"
>
> I say . . . "Here's something coming down the road, some new piece of gee-whiz tech. I don't understand it. But my intuition says we've got trouble." I then devote time to trying to get some members to work with

me on this. I want to continue to help our people still in the old technologies, the old world, learn how to get into the new world.

I'm hoping to do a lot more with this "advance warning" interest of mine . . . and my knowledge base here has already expanded a hundredfold as I've set out to answer a thousand and more questions. CATV companies, especially those busy now installing a fiber optics network in every community possible, are going to blindside many "sleepy" phone companies at a great cost in jobs to our CWA members . . . unless we think *fast,* act *now,* and somehow get out *ahead* of all of this . . . or, at the very least, give it one helluva good try!

Scores of such technology-savvy types are out there, and enough cannot be done soon enough to take advantage of their far-sighted, early alert contribution.

Summary

Where change-agentry is concerned, much can be expected from the AFL-CIO. Its leaders are no longer stuck on "send," but are now actually open to "receive." While the Sweeneyites have no magical formula for union revival (and there is none to be had), since 1995 things *have* changed for the better, and they continue to improve (naturally with some bumps along the way [Lichtenstein]).

Especially zesty international unions, many locals, and even a few central labor councils also raise bright new expectations, as they are busy employing their computerization finesse to modernize and make valued gains. Hamstrung by budgetary pressures, overworked staff, and problematic relations with employers, these pace-setting organizations nevertheless inspire hope (at least those of the Cyber Gain type do).

In varying degrees, then, these four types of change-agents appreciate the strategic contribution computerization is making, can make, and must continue to make to labor's survival. When they come to also appreciate the further gains possible, *transformational* gains, from the F-I-S-T model, they may help create a new unionism equal to what the twenty-first century portends.

Recommended Resources

Cobble, Dorothy Sue, ed. *Women and Unions: Forging a Partnership.* Ithaca, NY: ILR Press, 1993. More than 40 scholars and activists offer fresh insights into how labor and women can better serve one another. Guidelines are offered for overdue reforms of Organized Labor—many of which would profit from links to the F-I-S-T model.

Heckscher, Charles C. *The New Unionism: Employee Involvement in the Changing Corporation.* Ithaca, NY: Cornell University Press, 1996. An original, provocative argument for "associational unionism," a genuinely new system of representation that rejects the old boundaries between workers and management. Computer networks could make help ensure its success.

Ringle, Willam J. *TechEdge: Using Computers to Present and Persuade.* Boston: Allyn and Bacon, 1998. A reader-friendly, jargon-free, and immediately useful handbook for better use of all the tools associated with informatics. Honest and pragmatic, it can help empower change-agents in many valuable ways.

To stay abreast of AFL-CIO activities, see the AFL-CIO's *"Works in Progress,"* a bimonthly organizing report at wip@aflcio.org

Global Labour Directory. An independent directory of labor directories, serving the trade union movement since 1996. Edited by Eric Lee. Available at http://www.solinet.org/LEE/gldod.html

Labour Telematics Centre supports and encourages trade unions and labor movement organizations in gaining access to, and benefits from, computer-based electronic communications and information technology. Available at http://www.labourtel.org.uk/

Labour Webmasters' Forum. A home on the Web for trade unionists who edit, design, and write Web sites for the labor movement, a forum to discuss technical and nontechnical issues involved in trade union Web site design and maintenance. Available at http://www.labourstart.org/lwf/

Labour Web Site of the Week. A weekly award to a labour Web site of interest, value, and excellence. Available at And http://www.labourstart.org/

Feminist activities are covered at www.igc.apc.org/women/feminist.html

See also the AFL-CIO's *Equal Pay* Web site at www.aflcio.org/women/equalpay.htm

---

Reading 11

Women Unionists: "We Can Do It!"

Arthur B. Shostak
Communications Workers of America,
CWA, Local 189

While everyone has a part to play and a contribution to make, it is just possible that women may be more strategic than men in determining how fast and how well the computerization of unions may continue. Better still, they may be able to leverage their prowess here to extract overdue gains in the age-old struggle to diminish the toll taken by sexism in unions. In any case, the covert dynamics of this new phase in the "Battle of the Sexes" warrants our attention, for the possibility remains that it could yet provide one of the best "win-win" outcomes in recent labor history.

While you might not learn it from conventional volumes of labor history, women have long been decisive in shaping the nature and fortune of Organized Labor. Thanks to new labor histories we now understand, for example, that at a critical juncture in the mid-1880s, when industrialism was reshaping reality, working-class women engaged in lively debate over, and active planning for, the future of unionism and American life.

Labor historian Philip S. Foner believes "it was the militancy and perseverance of woman workers that laid the foundations of trade unionism—this, in the face of the double obstacle of employer-public hostility and the indifference of most male-dominated unions" (Foner, 154).

As full-fledged members of the Knights of Labor, and also of their own Women's Trade Union League, working-class women helped shape Labor's strategies. They confronted employers with historic strikes. They adapted craft-based shop-floor organization to advantage. And they lent special support to the social core of the Knights movement—lectures, entertainments, sociables, and cooperatives. Within the workers' movement women forged a sphere—and a vision—distinctively their own (Levine).

Today, a similar set of opportunities presents itself. Once again a major transformation of reality is under way. Once again women are well-represented among the workforce and its union participants. Once again, thanks to their membership clout (16 percent in 1960; 39 percent today of all unionists, the largest percentage in labor movement history), their AFL-CIO Working Women's Department, and their caucus—the Coalition of Labor Union Women (CLUW)—union women are in a good position to foster lively debate and active planning, this time concerning twenty-first century unionism and anything else they chose to focus on (LRA, Feb. 24, 1998, 4).

As in the 1880s, it will not be easy, and will certainly not go unopposed. Dating back to when the rise of unions first elevated men's work over women's work, male sexism has been a costly aspect of unionism, and its icy grasp has still not been shaken (Hobsbawn). In the 1970s, for example, only two percent of building trades workers were female; after 20 years, with many hard-hat men still in total denial where their sexist ways are concerned, the figure has not yet reached 3 percent (*60 Minutes* TV Show; September 27, 1998).

While the Sweeney "New Voices" team has put more women in more positions of power (officers, executive board members, and staffers) than ever before true of the AFL-CIO, power in the international unions and in their locals is still a prerogative of the "Old Boys Club" than of anybody else.

Women unionists can help reform this situation by teaching lessons in gender equity requirements. A female organizer explained an approach that has her refuse to "do" for men seeking computer aid, but offer instead only to tutor them in doing for themselves:

Women take to computers much better. And I don't know if it is typing skills. I think that has something to do with it. But I also think it is the mentality in our particular office. The men in the office *never* did anything like *that*. Any filing, any kind of typing they wanted done, there were women in the office to do it for them.

So now, we have to educate them—but they're still looking at it from that way. I mean, they'll stand back and ask one of us to turn their computer on and find them what they need, as opposed to doing it themselves. They're not getting much of a response anymore. Me, in particular, I say—"Sit down, I'll show you how to do it." That's what we're doing. We're realizing that the only way it is going to happen is if we don't do it for them.

Refusal to serve, but offers to teach, could go a long way in redefining gender roles for the better, as well as in expanding the number of computer users in a union office.

Women unionists can help with a second, related challenge, that of clarifying the culture that Labor wants to promote with and through its growing reliance on informatics. Close students of their role in labor already ask, "Will the culture and structure of unions alter as more and more women enter their ranks?" (Cobble, 18).

As before, when the AFL replaced the Knights, if certain hard-boiled males have their way, Labor's post-informatics culture will clone today's hard-boiled bureaucratic ethos. A strict hierarchy will continue to stultify nearly everything. Fear will pervade interactions. Politics will take precedence over performance. And a variety of "isms" will covertly control events (sexism, ageism, racism, etc.) (Lester).

Now, when informatics is being introduced, a rare chance exists to alter or even block this cloning process, and replace it with a far healthier culture.

Research suggests that women in organizations prefer far less hierarchy, far less fear, greater emphasis on performance, and the substitution of demonstrated merit for malignant "isms" as a yardstick of worth (Lunneborg). Their political profile appears distinctive, perhaps more distinctive than labor voters in general, but not monolithic (Wilson and King).

Women unionists, in particular, "emphasize the importance of worker involvement, of the necessity of democracy and participation" (Cobble, 18). Typical is the case of the Harvard Union of Clerical and Technical Workers. It has "overcome the bitterness of a hard-fought organizing campaign to establish a highly decentralized, participative, and problem-oriented form of representation, building largely on the energy of the women's movement" (Heckscher, xvi; Shostak 1991, 94–100).

Many I have known over a quarter century of teaching at the AFL-CIO George Meany Center appreciate that computerization can bolster their reform agenda, as in its facilitation of two-way participative "talk" (via e-mail) in the place of yesterday's top-down communications (via snail mail).

Women unionists "indubitably bring new zest and ideas that can help create the essential ferment for change" (Lynch, in Cobble, 421). Accordingly, female computer enthusiasts (and their male allies) might press for (1) free and friendly classes in computer use; (2) payment plans to help needy members (such as single mothers) secure home computers; (3) on-line coverage of all union meetings (especially for homebound child-rearing or child-caring women, etc.); (4) participation gains via e-mail voting for members; and (5) the creation of a listserve of women members, the better to enable women in a local or IU to talk among themselves.

Women nowadays are increasing their presence in the workforce at a much faster pace than men, and are more likely to join unions than are men (Masters, 190). Labor *must* pay far more attention to the preferences of the union activists among them. For "in part it is the ability of Organized Labor to ... transform itself to attract this new work force that will determine whether [non-union] workers opt for paternalistic, individualistic, or collective solutions to their workplace dilemmas" (Cobble, 3).

Reality Check

None of this is to argue that women alone can or will "save" unionism. No silver bullet. No magic wand. Women have too many unrealistic and unreasonable expectations put on them to add still another.

In fact, there is considerable diversity here, and some women may find little to object to in the male-centric bureaucratic model, having long ago made their peace with (and profit off of) it (Hein). There are also women who may have reason to devalue the ability of computerization to promote equality and democracy, as neither goal serves their own self-advancing politics. And there are women who reject anything resembling the "feminization" of labor (a female staffer notes of female-headed locals that "they are not as a group significantly fresher of vision or more solidaristic than those led by men") (Lynch, in Cobble, 418).

While there are character traits common to many (not all) women that promote a revitalized labor movement, "given the seriousness of the crisis confronting Organized Labor in this country, this set of possibilities seems to comprise far too thin a thread on which to hang the movement's future" (Lynch, in Cobble, 420).

It is hard not to agree with this cautionary note. However, the necessity labor has to master the use of computers—along with the edge women may have in helping to accomplish this—gives woman unionists unique leverage, as they can trade their help for substantial gains in taming sexism.

Summary

Attention is owed the rich potential of proactive women unionists to advance on two vital fronts simultaneously—as strategic aids in the computerization of Labor, and as more-effective-than-ever guides in the reduction of sexism in labor. For as AFSME staffer Roberta Lynch explains, "the tasks that are critical to the revitalization of the labor movement cannot be accomplished without the active involvement of women, whose talents and energy must be drawn on to the fullest extent possible. . . " (Lynch, in Cobble, 421).

12

Change-Agents: Overseas

Most crucially, trade unions now accept that, in a global economy dominated by transnational corporations, labour too must organize globally. Without this worldwide dimension, any trade union revival would be outdated and shortlived.
— Arthur Lipow, *Power and Counterpower,* 1996

Wherever I went overseas and interviewed union activists—Jerusalem, London, Montreal, Oslo, Stockholm, Tel Aviv, Toronto, Vancouver, and points in between—and whatever overseas labor movement I contacted via the Internet, the story was much the same: We know what we should be doing, and we are getting to it. While the dream was far more of achieving Cyber Gain status, than anything resembling a CyberUnion, and while there were far more Cyber Naught organizations than I had anticipated, the air crackled with excitement. Change was commonly in the offing, and the activists were in the driving seat.

Getting On with It!

Two related themes dominated dialogue at both the 1997 Labor TECH meeting of informatics enthusiasts that I attended in San Francisco, and the 1998 Labor On-line Conference I attended in New York City. First, that the interactivity made possible by informatics, or specifically, the ability to give voice to an aroused rank-and-file, could substantially aid labor's renewal. And second, that runaway and ominous corporate globalism, if not immediately and effectively countered by Labor's creative use of informatics, could prove labor's undoing (and that of just about everything else of worth).

Corporate globalism, or the steadily growing (and arguably nefarious) influence of transnational firms, is a twenty-first-century challenge of great urgency where Labor is concerned. All the more vital, therefore, are ongoing efforts to use computers to counter this threat, and all the more exciting the progress being made on several fronts.

As well-put by Eric Lee, *the* outstanding student of the subject, ". . . the rise of a global labournet is a long-awaited, long-expected development. . . . It is being created out of necessity, by the changing character of global capitalism, and though it can be slowed down, nothing can stop it. . . . Thanks to the Internet, a century-long decline in [labor] internationalism has already been reversed. For thousands of trade unionists who log on every day, the International has already been reborn" (Lee, E., 1997, 186).

Anyone Out There?

As for whether or not there are enough unionists on-line to make a difference, cyberspace dialogues among unionists around the globe have such quantity and quality nowadays as to suggest a resounding Yes!

To begin with, rapidly growing numbers of average citizens are on-line, and more are joining all the time. In 1998, the top 10 countries in Internet users per 1,000 people were Finland at 244; Norway, 231; Iceland, 227; United States, 203; Australia, 178; Canada, 148; Singapore, 141; United Kingdom, 99; Japan, 63; and Germany, 46 (Anon., *Net News*).

Eric Lee estimates unionists may already account for perhaps 9 of 62 million on-line Americans (almost 15 percent), 2 of 20 million Canadians (10 percent), and 6 of 20 million Europeans (30 percent) for a remarkable total of over 17 million on-line unionists, or 11 percent, around the globe (Lee, March 26, 1998).

As best as can be estimated, by 2001, some 500 million, or 8 percent of humanity, are expected to be on-line (Brown). Given Lee's informed guess that only about 17 million of 102 million on-line types were unionists in 1998, a similar proportion of the 500 million would have about 40 million unionists on-line somewhere around the globe as soon as 2001—a truly mind-boggling possibility!

As for whether or not these anonymous millions mean anything to one another, an American organizer I interviewed who had been eager to demonstrate the meaning of solidarity to a group of potential members offered this anecdote:

> We solicited support on e-mail. I probably got 40 or 50 e-mails from around the world, from London, Rome, Paris. And I gave them to the guys. And it was *very* important to them: "Wow, there is somebody in London who sends their greetings in solidarity."

Many others offered similar tales, all of which were of the "value added" variety.

Swedish Unions Show the Way!

Easily one of the brightest recent developments in global unionism, one rich in lessons for the United States, occurred early in 1997 when 2,200,000 members of the LO, the Swedish bluecollar union federation, were offered top-of-the-line computer systems in a union-initiated purchase deal ($100,000,000) with the Hewlett-Packard company.

When I interviewed LO officials in the summer of 1996, they expressed growing concern that their members were being left behind in the technology race (a concern with which I concurred, after being asked my opinion). So in short order they devised a plan that allowed purchase of a (union-made) PC, modem, color printer, and free Internet access for only $56 a month in toto for 36 months (Moss). Thanks to savings traceable to bulk buying and tax incentives, the price was 30 percent lower than store prices. By June, 1998, the LO deal accounted for more than 30 percent of all PCs being sold for home use in Sweden (Rose and Latour).

Now, the LO has unprecedented interactive contact with hundreds of thousands of far-flung members. It is busy learning how exciting connectivity can be, how challenging, and how zesty. Best of all, the LO has sent a clear message to members, the business community, the government, the media, and the average Swedish citizen, a message that conveys its intent to "compute" in the twenty-first century.

Friendly rivalry, by the way, can play a very constructive role here. I was present in Olso, Norway, in the summer of 1997 when exciting news came that the Swedish LO was arranging with Hewlett-Packard to make high-quality, low-cost PCs available in large numbers to members. Norwegian union leaders I was interviewing moved to leverage the news to advance their drive to do more with computers, and extra time and resources were immediately assigned to the matter at a forthcoming nationwide union meeting.

Transferable Lessons

Leaving to Eric Lee's seminal 1997 book, *The Labour Movement and the Internet,* the story of global Internet-using unionism, I would only highlight below some aspects especially rich in lessons for Americans who would profit from overseas cyberspace efforts.

For example, we are reminded not to think high-tech is more valuable than high-touch. The first-ever labor computer network in the world, one created in 1983 by a Canadian teachers' union, showed that union democracy got a boost from network-wide dialogue among members. That the union could build consensus across great distances, physically and politically. And that committees could work without the expense of meeting here or there. Little wonder, accordingly, that Larry Kuehn, president in 1983 of the British Columbia Teachers' Federation, concluded that "no technology is better than a variety of human commitments it can facilitate" (Kuehn, in Lee, E., 1997, 53).

A second valuable lesson would have us look for rewards from unique research possibilities. Global informatics is especially strong when unions need the kind of data commercial databases often do not provide, the kind that buttresses what in the United States is known as a "corporate campaign."

The 20-million-member ICEM (International Federation of Chemical, Energy, Mine, and General Workers' Unions), for example, offers its 403 union affiliates in 113 countries extraordinary computer-based profiles of relevant companies. These follow a transnational firm's structure, ownership, and performance. Hard-to-get information may be secured on a single plant or a global system's production, industrial relations practices, and collective-bargaining performance—with assurances provided that "all on the network are in possession of this overview" (ICEM, 56).

A third lesson would have us value the first opportunity Labor has ever had to tell the world its story its way at a time of its choosing. Media blackouts and biases have cost Labor dearly, but the Web and the Internet open up whole new dissemination possibilities. The ICEM, for example, believes that "if worldwide electronic networking continues to develop freely, there is real scope for a democratization of the media" (ICEM, 62).

Finally, we can learn to value the ability afforded by unprecedented global links to put pressure on transnational firms to honor global standards, as in health and safety workplace matters. Other standards would have firms refuse to use forced or child labor, and agree that employees can form and join unions. E-mail sped around the planet has been used effectively to put pressure on firms to agree, to applaud those that do, and to damn and boycott the holdouts.

Where Next?

In today's global economy, there is an enormous imbalance of power that grows more ominous daily. There is no adequate instrument to check the worst excesses of transnational corporations. Accordingly, the ICEM, a pioneer in using informatics to fight back, maintains that "the problem for the trade union movement is how to upgrade its response to match the power structures of the late twentieth century" (ICEM, 52). Informatics uses could not be more timely.

Many union activists are busy developing the necessary infrastructure and vision with which to effect change almost instantly in a far-away place; e.g., the Canadian given credit for operationalizing the first national labor network, Marc Belanger, has created an international committee to examine how to launch an International Labour Studies Centre in cyberspace (the world's first town hall and campus of global unionists).

Progress, however, will not come quickly, easily, or without high cost. While you would not know it from the mass media, in 1994, the last year for which data are available, 593 union activists somewhere around the globe were killed for their pro-labor work. Nearly 2,000 were injured. Nearly 70,000 were fired (ICEM, 22).

The struggle goes on, now with the additional aid of a global cyberspace network that can help highlight tragedies of this sort, demand their end, and rally enough pressure to help secure overdue gains for unionists under fire. For unionists confounded by a "race to the bottom" among "free traders" blind to the short-sighted consequences of the acts. And for unionists, like certain Liverpool dock strikers who in 1998 successfully asked via the Internet that a scab-loaded ship from England not be unloaded by American dockers. And for striking Korean labor unions that asked for, and got, an outpouring of e-mail support from unionists everywhere around the globe when it counted.

Computerizing is never easy, and especially not when the labor movements vary so much in level of development, resources, and context. Consider, nevertheless, this sage observation e-mailed to me by Charley Lewis, head of the information technology unit of the Congress of South African Trade Union Congress (COSATU):

> If information computer technologies are the "universal enablers" they're so often trumpeted to be, they can be used to enable trade unions. Certainly, there are massive hurdles and obstacles, particularly in an environment like South Africa's. For instance, it is difficult to chuck on-line conferencing at people who are only beginning to get their heads around the concept of the Web. But unless unions grasp the nettle of technological change, they're likely to be left doggedly organizing the last remaining auto worker, only to find everyone else has moved next door.

Other unionists with whom I met in Europe, the Middle East, and Scandinavia would nod and smile in concurrence. Especially with Lewis's conclusion: "As we are able to show real tangible working benefits from the Internet, we believe our use of it will go from strength to strength."

Summary

American labor leader Richard Trumka, Secretary-Treasurer of the AFL-CIO, explained in 1998 to the millions watching his Larry King TV Show interview, that his union, the Mine Workers, knew it had no choice except to go global:

> Hopefully, out into the future, mine workers in every country will belong to the same organization. They can move us around at the switch of a dial or the punch of a key; the only way we can protect ourselves is if we are linked through international solidarity. I think you'll see more international [labor] organizations. We're loosely linked right now (Trumka 1998, 211).

Global unionism, a social invention with cyberspace distinction, is steadily gaining the technological finesse necessary if labor leaders are to act on a global scale, weld together a far-flung army, preserve its town hall ethos, and assure reasons for the world to take admiring notice.

Humanist Primo Levi would have us understand that "for good or evil, we are a single people: the more we become conscious of this, the less difficult and long will be humanity's progress toward justice and peace" (Levi, 91). An emerging global unionism, drawing unprecedented strength from creative uses of computer power, gives us the best chance we have ever had of achieving a very precious consciousness of oneness, a labor union–promoted global solidarity.

Recommended Resources

Lee, Eric. *The Labour Movement and the Internet: The New Internationalism.* Chicago: Pluto Press, 1997. Indispensable for understanding the background, state of affairs, and enormous potential of global cyberspace unionism. Belongs on every modern unionist's bookshelf.

McChesney, Robert W. et al., eds. *Capitalism and the Information Age: The Political Economy of the Global Communication Revolution.* New York: Monthly Review Press, 1998. Fourteen essays explore the political potential of informatics, and argue that this potential is distorted by the actualities of contemporary capitalism. See especially "Work, New Technology, and Capitalism," by Peter Meiksins.

Sussman, Gerald, and John A. Lent, eds. *Global Productions: Labor in the Making of the "Information Society."* Cresskill, NJ: Hampton Press, 1998. Written by a group of international authors, the essay collection discusses the information society from the perspective of work forces employed within its global electronics factories, back offices, movie lots, TV and animation studios, and telephone service centers—the new international division of labor. Topics addressed include the political economy of communication, the "offshoring" of jobs, worker strife in Silicon Valley, new challenges to Hollywood's labor force, transnationalization of film and TV production, the division of labor in the global animation industry, and the initiatives taken by various industrial, communication, and mass media trade unions.

Wolman, William, and Anne Colamosca. *The Judas Economy: The Triumph of Capital and the Betrayal of Work.* Reading, MA: Addison-

Wesley, 1997. Explains why and how American workers are the victims of a major shift in economic power. Makes a strong case for a new government policy to curb the excesses of the free market.

Corporate Watch: Committed to exposing corporate greed by documenting the social, political, economic, and environmental impacts of the transnationals, and by supporting democratic control of corporations, human rights, and environmental justice. Available at http://www.corpwatch.org/

Directory of On-line Labour Conferences and Communities: Mailing lists, Web forums, live chat, usenet newsgroups, proprietary conferencing systems. Available at http://www.labourstart.org/directory.html

International Confederation of Free Trade Unions (ICFTU): Available at http://www.icftu.org/

International Labour Organisation: The UN agency for the promotion of social justice and internationally recognized human and labor rights. Available at http://www.unicc.org/ilo/

Labour in the Global Information Economy: Staying Alive: Available at http://www.corpwatch.org/internet/globalabor/index.html

The Cyber Picket Line: Arguably the most comprehensive directory of labor on the internet. Available at http://www.cf.ac.uk/ccin/union

The Global Labour Directory of Directories: Descriptions of and links to the top labor directories worldwide. Available at http://www.labourstart.org/gldod.html

Trade Union Advisory Committee: An international trade union organization with consultative status, acting as an interface for labor unions with the OECD and its various committees. Available at http://www.tuac.org/

For more insight from Charley Lewis, contact him at charley@cosatu.org.za. COSATU's Web site is accessible at http://www.cosatu.org.za/ The North American regional office of the International Federation of Chemical, Energy, Mine and General Workers (ICEM) has affiliates which include 15 AFL-CIO unions. See www.icemma.org

13

Choices We Must Make

I am not talking about fault. I'm trying to look for answers.
—Lane Kirkland, President, AFL-CIO,
—David Brinkley TV Show, Labor Day, 1988

Just about every major component of society is finding it difficult to make computing "compute," a fact that helps put the uneven record here of Organized Labor in perspective. For example, 20 or more years after the first PCs arrived on campus, 60 percent of the nation's colleges and universities in 1998 still did not have a curriculum plan or a financial plan for their use, and 70 percent did not have a plan for using the Internet in their distance-learning initiatives (Green). Similarly, the *Wall Street Journal* reported in November, 1998, that "the Internet commerce boom is posing a tormenting challenge for many of America's biggest companies. . . . Anything different is a threat to their corporate culture—and next quarter's earnings" (Anders).

This said, the fact remains that Organized Labor has more than its share of difficulties. Although labor's use of computers has been under way since the 1970s, it has far to go before delivering on its promise. A few unions and locals even pretend it's not a big deal, which it is. Others agree there is something to it, but they'll be damned if they know what—and until they stop drifting, they will . . . be damned, that is.

Happily, a small but growing number of unions and locals (and possibly even a Central Labor Council or two) gain on the rest. They no longer settle for computer data management alone, but insist on "pushing the envelope." If and when they also adopt their own variation of the F-I-S-T formula laid out in Part III, they are likely to command far more respect, power, and allegiance than ever before.

Further progress may hinge on resolving several tough questions computerization continues to pose, questions that lead reasonable unionists to respectfully disagree with one another. Consider, for example, the five below, alternative resolutions of which would take Organized Labor in very different directions.

Access for All?

Computer use by Labor is still so novel that many in the ranks lag far behind others. It is widely understood that "the major factor expected to change everyday life in the twenty-first century is the personal computer, and the rapidity of that change is reflected in the recent spurt in the number of homes that have computers" (Robinson and Godbey, 154). This notwithstanding, access to computer technology and computer literacy is very unequally distributed. The resulting gap, or "Digital Divide," between Information Haves and Have-Less types, is arguably the greatest threat posed now to union solidarity in specific, and to democracy in general (Mazepa).

Least-connected Americans are disproportionately found among the rural poor, rural and central-city minorities, female-headed households, and households headed by people younger than 25—all types of Americans that Labor seeks to organize and help (Hall). African Americans and Hispanics badly trail non-Hispanic whites and Asian Americans in PC ownership, and the gap between blacks and whites (22 percent) appears to have actually widened between 1994 and 1997 (Poope).

Unionists know these facts at first hand, as witness these thoughts from a frustrated organizer in the Deep South:

> I always ask workers, do they have a computer? And do they have e-mail? It is very seldom. I was thinking that everybody had a PC. But a lot of workers that I've gone after don't. The people we're trying to organize—the low-income people—still can't afford it.

Similarly, a high-level staffer worries aloud:

> If the labor movement does not do something to equalize the balance of computer usage, the work force will likely become so divided by the

year 2005 that the term "Organized Labor" will apply—once again—
only to one [white] segment of the population . . . "Justice for Janitors"
and "America Needs a Raise" are great slogans, but so too is "Internet
Access for Everyone!"

Fragmentation and polarization threaten a future none of us desire.
Unless and until Labor can help solve this problem, it runs the risk of
having its use of computers inadvertently favor the Haves, sideline the
Have-Less types, and exacerbate already costly divisions between the
two in the union (Robinson and Godbey, 166).

While I recognize the merit of alternative claims (as by organizers)
on scarce union funds, I side with those unionists who want funds
earmarked to help Have-Less members secure home computers.

CyberUnions can help by "cutting deals" that should lower computer purchase or lease costs. They can also negotiate favorable
time-purchase plans, ample loans, and even generous subsidies.
Stunning price breaks nowadays make computer purchase or lease
less and less expensive. One company, Apple, explicitly initiated a
payment program in 1998 targeted to people earning down to
$15,000 a year. Indeed, experts expect that 1999 may be the first
year when low-income households ($35,000 or less) become the
leading source of first-time home computer purchasers (Richtel,
September 17, 1998).

Coming next are Internet-compatible laptop-sized machines that
start up instantly, rarely crash, and weigh less and cost less than full-
fledged portable PCs in the late 1990s (Mossberg). Still further along
are "simplified network" computers that do less, but do it far better,
and cost very much less (Wildstrom).

CyberUnions, through both leveraging labor's buying power for private purchases, and working with public libraries to set up computer
corners for more public access, can and should facilitate rapid catch-up
achievements.

Democracy—by Fiat?

Computerization is still so novel that some specialists busy helping
labor get "with it" would boost democracy in unions by imposing it
as part of their implementation deal. Critics lambast this sort of
"democracy by fiat" as an inane oxymoron. Advocates insist it is a

legitimate strategy, one for which the "window of opportunity" is so small as to require immediate moves.

Typical is the challenge I heard a leading East Coast Web site creator dramatically put to attendees at the Labor TECH'97 conference. Unless a union or local was willing to have him design its Web site for wide-open interactivity, that is, unless the power-holders were willing to give every rank-and-filer a chance to say what they wanted to—even harsh things about the power-holders—he would not help that union or local launch its site. Computerization, he insisted, must serve grass-roots democracy, and union power-holders must be forced by computer gurus to agree to this.

Other TECH attendees, many comparably proficient, rejected the speaker's stance as high-handed, the imposition of an outsider's ideology on elected union leaders who should be left free to work out their Web-site philosophy in context (preferably through dialogue with the rank-and-file). Some others felt that pro-democratic institutional forms or creations were an expression of an organization's organic culture, and should therefore not be imposed from "on high." They feared that if Web gurus required democratic practices as the price for their help, many union power-holders would say the hell with the entire matter . . . and thereby fate their organizations to more years in what I call a Cyber Naught limbo.

New research underlines how difficult it is going to be to use computer tools (teleconferences, distance-learning courses, etc.) to alter old habits and achieve a truly participative democratic culture in unions and locals wary of such a culture (Mazepa). The question remains: Is this early stage of initiating computer applications a rare chance to compel electronic democracy? Or is the very notion an oxymoron, and is it instead a matter rightly for members and their elected officers to resolve?

Use It or Be Used?

Computer applications are still so novel that a real risk remains some unionists may forget why they started to use them to begin with. That is, the unionists may become slavish users, rather than stronger unionists. Computers can tempt one into patterns of reliance and dependency through which lives can be indirectly and irrevocably reshaped, not necessarily in the best interest of the labor movement (Rochlin, 7).

Typical of the concerns about losing direction that are already being felt are these thoughts from two pioneering and far-sighted users:

> You have to be careful that your computer does not get between you and the people you are trying to organize. It could happen. When you start staying in your office, and depending on that, and taking the information that you get or don't get from your computer, it's absolute. And you can become a person who's so into that computer that you don't turn it off and go out to see workers. I think you really have to watch out!

> There is definitely a tendency to get lost in it. The information is so free and accessible. You have a tendency to resolve issues from behind your desk, and spend a lot less time at the site. This can damage Labor's image. People always have concerns about how we are spending their money. So when we use the computer at the site, they tease us and say, "So, this is where our money is going!" We talk a lot about this at our training sessions.

Still another troubled staffer volunteered similar qualms in a somewhat formal e-mail to me:

> Without a concerted effort to retain certain "high-touch" features of unionism, the communal nature of our movement could be replaced by "electronic relationships" which lack the element of humanity. Convenience may replace bonding, and software applications may replace instinct in our desire to keep pace with the latest technology.

Over and again I heard unionists ask how they were to strike a healthy balance here, a task made all the more difficult by the absence of good modeling from above or sound precedents.

Firmer yet was a thought offered by a young West Coast activist whose advocacy of a "high-touch" emphasis was quite common among those I interviewed:

> To bastardize the NRA slogan, machines don't build unions, people build unions. The impersonality of the medium renders it secondary to direct contact. It is no more helpful than the telephone in building relationships. No one would suggest that unions can organize using phonebanks instead of organizers, and we should be cautious not to assume the computers are capable of building community.

Similarly, a close student of global unionism insists that Organized Labor should never confuse cyberspace with real space:

> The Internet, e-mail, CNN, faxes, voice mail, cell phones, pagers; each of these things contributes to the illusion that we are capable of knowing intimately what it is like to live in another place . . . we cannot, we do not, we will not gain this understanding until we move away from our nests of "virtual reality" and get out into the world (F.W. Lee).

Many with whom I spoke voiced similar misgivings, believing as they did that "the rapid accumulation of change is not always progress, and forward motion is not always an advance" (Weiner, 126).

So the question and challenge in front of Organized Labor asks: How do we keep in touch with our high-touch responsibilities while also realizing our high-tech possibilities? How do we stay in charge, and keep on guard against certain seductive aspects of computerization that threaten to make us servants of the machine?

Accept or Assess?

Computerization is still so novel that standards of use by unions and locals leave much to be desired. An exasperated labor educator complained that standards were unacceptably low:

> Eighty percent of the educational stuff now on the Web is completely trivial. The content is zero, junk. If unions *really* want to do it right, they have a perfect opportunity to do it. Nobody's thought about educational basics and design. What they think about is, "Gee, that looks great! Let's change that color." And, turn pages over and over again.
>
> These people wouldn't know an educational objective if they fell over it at night. They just use it as a delivery mobility. That's *not* going to work! Labor has to rely on people who understand this educational work from an instructional and theoretical point, and make it happen. But that's not what you're getting up to this point.
>
> You look at the international Web pages up to now. Some are very nice, and a lot has gone into them. They've done an incredible job on them. Some offer a lot of information. But I doubt if they have gotten a lot of visiting. I'm a member of XXX for 29 years, and I've never bothered to go to its Web page, I've had no reason to. Today it's all top-down. It's also not at the level where people are, and they're not interested.

Others with whom I raised the issue of standards had similar complaints, often in more colorful language.

Two choices beckon: Insist that quality is nobody's business but the sponsor's, whether it be the Federation, the unions, or the locals. Alternatively, insist that the rank-and-file deserve only the best. In which case some sort of advisory standards-setting committee should be established by the AFL-CIO to offer free advice, give valued awards annually for outstanding computer-utilization work, clarify the related job standards, and, in other diplomatic ways, nurture finer material "from an instructional and theoretical point."

The question remains: Given the fierce individualism of the autonomous unions in the Federation, and the like autonomy of many of their locals, can any standardization of high quality, and any criteria for the relevant staffers, soon be established? And if not, how can the costs to labor be minimized?

Drift or Direction?

Finally, computer utilization is still so fresh that problems can be traced to what would otherwise be regarded as a major strength, namely, a union's gritty hard-boiled culture. Many such organizations lack over-arching goals and an appealing vision beyond what conventional thinking would recommend, a vision capable of rallying support and mobilizing adequate action toward its achievement. Nor do they see how choices they make in their uses of computers might help them improve this situation.

Typical is a revealing response from the president of an East Coast steelworkers local admired far and wide for informatics prowess:

> You ask if we have a vision or blueprint? No. Not really. I think we operate on a "practical use" basis. We look at what's out there. We look at what we're doing and ask what can the technology do to help us. Where it can, we go and get it and we use it. . . . Information technology changes so quickly that it really doesn't make much sense to do long-range planning . . . because you don't know what your capacity is going to be further out.

This stance helps reduce the highest achievement of the day, the Cyber Gain model, to little more than an improved means to an unimproved end.

The question remains: Can activists come soon to appreciate and promote the vision-enhancing possibilities in computerization, as in its facilitation of F-I-S-T realities? Can activists come soon to appreciate that computerization without a guiding vision is computerization sorely handicapped, for vision can lend soul and grace.

Summary

No one ever said it was going to be easy, and it has not been. Incorporating mainframe uses in a union's standard office practices shook things up in the 1970s, and it has only gotten more turbulent since. Nowadays, with desktop PCs giving way to laptops, laptops to palmtops, and palmtops possibly soon giving way to "wearables," the uncertainties are greater than ever. We have watched the capacity of a memory chip go up by a factor of 4,000 since 1968, and we know more dazzlement is coming (Rochlin, 221).

All the more reason to seek resolution soon of five significant challenges the use of computers poses for Organized Labor, namely, finding the right ways to subsidize access, to relate to union democracy, to protect against technological tyranny, to establish high standards, and to promote vision-aiding possibilities in computer use. All five pose hard choices, though choosing is made a little easier when F-I-S-T realities are brought to mind. CyberUnions will be stronger and finer for working through these choices, for to paraphrase the poet E.E. Cummings, always the wise answer who asks a wiser question yet.

Recommended Resources

Adler, Lee. "Informating, Communicating with, and Mobilizing Our Members Through the Internet." Available from Lee at the School of Industrial and Labor Relations, Cornell University, 308 ILR Conference Center, Ithaca, NY 14853-3901 (607-255-7992).

Greenbaum, Joan. *Windows on the Workplace: Computers, Jobs, and the Organization of Office Work in the Late Twentieth Century.* New York: Monthly Review Press, 1995. Thoughtful analysis of changes in the culture of office information systems since the 1950s. Indicts employers for zealous and clumsy pursuit of ever-greater control over employees, and notes ongoing union efforts to curb computer-use abuses of the office work force.

Herzenberg, Stephen et al. *New Rules for a New Economy*. Ithaca, NY: Cornell University Press, 1998. Offers advice to counter economic anxiety and job insecurity. Particularly good in proposing aids for workers, as through new craft-type unions which would cut across companies in an industry. Rejects technological determinism, and emphasizes the indispensability of making informed policy choices.

Mantsios, Gregory, ed. *A New Labor Movement for the New Century*. New York: Monthly Review Press, 1998. Twenty-eight contributors, including Elaine Bernard, Steve Early, Bill Fletcher, Jr., George Koupias, Tony Mazzocchi, John J. Sweeney, and Kent Wong, explore the possibilities for a more creative, democratic, and inclusive labor movement.

Cafe Progressive: A one-stop interactive resource for the progressive political and educational community. Available at http://come.to/cafeprogressive

LaborOnline was established in early 1998 by progressive labor educators, trade unionists, and technicians to help organize, educate, and mobilize the labor movement through using the Internet and interactive technologies. Its activities include training and educating workers and trade unionists on the use of the Internet, researching the union movement's use of the Internet, and conferences for academics and union leaders. Contact Professors Immanuel Ness and Joseph Wilson of the Brooklyn College Political Science Department and the Graduate Center for Worker Education 718-966-4014, or info@laboronline.org

Loka Institute Post: The site for an occasional series on the democratic politics of research, science, and technology. Sponsors on-line forum on these subjects. Promotes gains by citizens' organizations, environmental groups, local governments, etc. E-mail address: Loka@amherst.edu

PubliCations (sec): The personal Web page of activist Paul Johnston, where he publishes columns and articles about citizenship, the new

labor movement, and participatory sociology. Web site: http://
mail.cruzio.com/johnston/

Reading 13

Virtual Corporations and American Labor Unions: So Many Unknowns, So Much Potential

Arthur B. Shostak

*An especially sound reason to peer into the future is to better pre-
pare, and where virtual organizations are concerned, Organized
Labor cannot begin to prepare soon enough. I try in the brief essay
below to model the kind of informed speculation with which a serious and sustained exercise in preparation might begin. I am confident CyberUnions will adopt some such model of anticipatory
discussion, and will prove equal to the virtual organization
challenge, and then some.*

*. . . the virtual organization is built around trust and cooperation. Those
who cannot accept this new reality risk becoming superfluous. Union
leaders face the same challenges as do their long-time antagonists in
management.*
　　　　—William H. Davidow and Michael S. Malone, *The Virtual
　　　　Corporation: Structuring and Revitalizing the Corporation
　　　　for the 21st Century,* 1992

What are the implications for America's 16 million unionized workers of the likely arrival soon of the virtual workplace? How are the
AFL-CIO and its 74 constituent international unions likely to react?
What are the major problems here for Organized Labor? And what
opportunity does this pose for improving labor-management relations tomorrow?

Implications for Organized Labor

What lies ahead where virtuality in the workplace is concerned is anything but clear this early in the innovation process. The likelihood appears good, however, that many resulting business organizations will resemble a film production company:

> A film is produced at a specific location by a "unique" combination of people with different skills who come together utilizing various technologies and techniques to produce a film. Once the product is completed, the crew disbands only to reassemble again to produce a new film, with different people, technologies, and techniques (Roberts 1995, 205).

Unionists challenged to imagine relating to more and more such models of workplaces early in the twenty-first century wince at the thought, but regain composure and hope when reminded that many American film crews at present are thoroughly unionized.

A virtual corporation, with its ephemeral organizational structures, its far-flung dispersion of resources, and its culture of high-speed change, will probably set Organized Labor challenges unlike any it has thus far confronted. To judge very cautiously from speculative literature and the very few prototypes available today, much of what unions are conventionally about may be turned upside down, on its side, and inside out.

Where the traditional unionized workplace, for example, valued the stability a labor contract could help assure, a unionized virtual corporation is likely to value instead an amorphous culture, one whose roles, rights, and responsibilities are constantly shifting.

Where Labor and management once considered the situation in hand if routine dominated matters, the unionized virtual organization will probably enmesh the parties in "continuous, unremitting, almost unendurable transformation" (Davidow and Malone 1992, 7).

The concept of a definable job could give way to continuous mixing and matching of employees with unique skills. Where the worker was traditionally protected by unions from regimentation, exploitation, and/or dehumanization, Labor's new problems will probably derive from unpredictability, lack of a comfortable structure, and more responsibility than certain workers desire.

Another highly probable change on the shop floor involves the greatly increased allocation of corporate resources to employee training in consensus building, group dynamics, and problem solving. Labor will be expected to help develop a cooperative workplace culture, and this may leave unionists confused about the remaining utility of their traditional skills in conflict management (Chapin 1995).

As if this was not enough, a virtual organization will probably rely on massive outsourcing, a downsizing strategy strenuously opposed by labor. It may reward speedy employ of labor-displacing equipment. It may induce ever more efforts to capture the skill and experience of craftsmen in computer software. It may, in short, exacerbate tensions between Labor and management on more fronts than any will find comfortable.

Labor has long depended on organizational stability to underwrite the credibility of its multi-year contracts. It has long depended on the compactness of a worksite to support the role of its shop stewards in workplace co-governance. Similarly, it relies on its skill in conflict management to keep both sides on their toes. And it seeks to keep its dues-payers on a respectable and predictable company payroll.

Virtuality would seem to undermine these mainstays of union well-being, the traditional "way things are done around here."

This is no trivial matter for a social movement whose survivability has always been problematic in a social order regretfully known for the highest degree of anti-union animus among all advanced industrial nations. Plainly, then, if Organized Labor is to survive the shift to what some virtuality enthusiasts insist is an economic necessity, it must make major changes in its culture and behavior.

Reaction of Organized Labor

Much of labor's response will hinge on what it perceives to be the real motivation, the basic intent of the corporate sponsor. Labor has very little trust in corporate America, given the dark history of labor-management relations.

As well, Labor expects that management abuses will continue to drive aggrieved employees toward union organizers; e.g., a leading futurist contends that "corporate abuses are relentless, continuing, and growing—and will ultimately lead to pressures for redress . . . in the form of the revival of unions." (Coates 1992, 29; see also Craver 1983, 78).

At the same time, however, a new mood is apparent, one that has more and more union influentials open to taking a (guarded) chance on selected management innovations, lest the payroll of an entire stateside industry steadily go overseas, or in some related way fall victim to global competition. Accordingly, Organized Labor is now helping progressive companies that meet it halfway, and this could probably be expanded to include experiments in virtual-organization formats.

Typical of such cooperation is a Philadelphia coalition of building trade union locals known as Built-Rite, a forum that sponsors four task forces: Productivity and Cost Effectiveness; Communications and Training; Safety and Health; and Public Policy, Research, and Public Information. Each is made up of three traditional adversaries: business contractors, the users of large-scale construction projects (such as hotel chains or mall developers), and union locals.

Each of the task forces reviews all proposed work contracts and resolves worksite problems before they materialize. They assess which (once-rival) locals should do what job. They discuss project budgets. They clarify the quality of work that is expected. They review health and safety guidelines. They agree to a regular schedule of problem-solving meetings throughout the duration of a building project. And they exchange traditional defensiveness and posturing for the freest flow of communications ever known in the building industry.

Above all, in project after project the parties are able to boast they finished ahead of schedule, below budget, without accidents, and without a single work stoppage . . . claims that help union builders beat out the non-union competition for the next big job.

At the national level, large-scale experiments exist that validate the payoff in a cooperative "win-win" approach . . . one sensitive to research finding that "successful employee involvement in the long run requires that the workers' collective bargaining power not decline" (Levine 1995, 68). The Painters Union, for example, has recently joined forces with progressive unionized companies to "bring fresh thinking and business practices to the changing construction industry."

Specifically, a Finishing Industry (union-management) Alliance promises to lower total project costs, reduce workers' compensation costs, and promote innovative applications of new technologies—all pro-employment gains uniquely available at a unionized worksite. This is the sort of far-sighted labor-management cooperation that could substantially aid a virtual corporation—provided both Labor and management were adult enough to give it a chance.

Union Possibilities

All forms of a twenty-first-century virtual corporation will have to rely on better-than-ever relations between employees and employer. Union advocates insist that trust and cooperation require the shield of due process protections provided by a written labor-management contract, a formal union grievance process, and the on-the-spot availability of a shop steward—none of which they consider anti-management, and all of which they believe an asset to a well-managed workplace.

Accordingly, such union influentials are sanguine about Organized Labor's prospects in a world of virtual business organizations. Provided, that is, that the historic animus of business toward Labor—and vice versa—is soon replaced by an experimental and far more collaborative mindset (Chaison and Rose 1991).

Progressive union leaders offer their corporate counterparts a fresh start at labor-management collaboration, believing as they do that this win/win option is worth all the attendant risks. These unionists understand that only in this way will a significant number of influential Americans ever agree that unions promote otherwise unattainable and invaluable gains in productivity (Freeman and Medoff 1984; Kelly and Harrison 1992; Bluestone and Bluestone 1992).

Summary

Organized Labor could join with progressive business organizations to shape a distinctive value-added social invention, one that could assure a competitive edge for this country, namely, a virtual workplace co-designed, co-managed, and collaboratively hailed by Organized Labor and management alike. As the future of our organizations, our "organic ways of being and doing together," rests in our collective hands, achieving such a cooperative work scene would be a giant step forward (Lipnack and Stamps, xx).

Note: A much longer version appears in *The Virtual Workplace,* Magid Igbaria and Margaret Tan, eds. Hershey, PA: Idea Group, 1998, pp. 360–367.

References

Adler, Glenn, and Doris Suarez, eds. 1993. *Unions Voices: Labor's Responses to Crisis.* Albany, NY: State University of New York Press.

Beaumont, P.B. 1987. *The Decline of Trade Union Organization.* London: Croom Helm.

Bell, Daniel. 1958. "The Capitalism of the Proletariat? American Trade Unionism Today." *Encounter* (February): 40–46.

Bluestone, Barry, and Irving Bluestone. 1992. *Negotiating the Future: A Labor Perspective on American Business.* New York: Basic Books.

Broad, William J. 1993. "Broad Remodeler of a Drifting Agency." *New York Times,* December 21, p. C-1.

Chaison, Gary N., and Joseph B. Rose. 1991. "The Macrodeterminants of Unions' Growth and Decline." In *The State of the Unions,* George Strauss, et al., eds. Madison, WI: IRRA, pp. 3–46.

Chapin, Vince. 1995. "Knowledge at Work: Human-Centered Machining Technology." In *Re-Shaping Work: Union Responses to Technological Change,* Christopher Schenk and John Anderson, eds. Ontario: Ontario Federation of Labour, pp. 163–198.

Coates, Joseph F. 1992. "Five Strategic HR Issues of the 1990s and Beyond." *HR Horizons* (Autumn): 25–30.

———, and Jennifer Jarratt. 1989. *What Futurists Believe.* Bethesda, MD: World Future Society.

Craver, Charles B. 1983."The Future of the American Labor Movement." *The Futurist* (October): 70–76.

Davidow, William H., and Michael S. Malone. 1992. *The Virtual Corporation: Structuring and Revitalizing the Corporation for the 21st Century.* New York: HarperCollins.

Freeman, Richard B., and James L. Medoff. 1984. *What Do Unions Do?* New York: Basic Books.

Geoghegan, Thomas. 1992. *Which Side Are You On? Trying to Be for Labor When It's Flat on Its Back.* New York: Plume.

Goldfield, Michael. 1987. *The Decline of Organized Labor in the United States.* Chicago: University of Chicago Press.

Kelley, Maryellen, and Bennett Harrison. 1992. "Unions, Technology, and Labor-Management Cooperation." In *Unions and Economic Competitiveness,* Lawrence Mishel and Paula B. Voos, eds. Armonk, NY: M.E. Sharpe, pp. 112–120.

Krannich, Ronald L., and Caryl Rae Krannich. 1992. *The Best Jobs for the 1990s and into the 21st Century.* Manassas Park, VA: Impact.

Levine, David I. 1995. *Reinventing the Workplace: How Business and Employees Can Both Win.* Washington, DC: Brookings Institution.

Lipnack, Jessica, and Jeffrey Stamps. 1994. *The Age of Network: Organizing Principles for the 21st Century.* New York: John Wiley and Sons.

Pizzigati, Sam, and Fred J. Solowey, eds. 1992. *The New Labor Press: Journalism for a Changing Union Movement.* Ithaca, NY: ILR Press.

Puette, William J. 1992. *Through Jaundiced Eyes: How the Media View Organized Labor.* Ithaca, NY: ILR Press.

Roberts, Bruce. 1995. "From Lean Production to Agile Manufacturing: A New Round of Quicker, Cheaper, and Better." In *Re-Shaping Work: Union Responses to Technological Change,* Christopher Schenk and John Anderson, eds. Ontario: Ontario Federation of Labour, pp. 197–213.

Salvatore, Nick. 1992. "The Decline of Labor: A Grim Picture, A Few Proposals." *Dissent* (Winter): 86–92.

Shostak, Arthur B. 1991. *Robust Unionism: Innovations in the Labor Movement.* Ithaca, NY: ILR Press.

———. 1994. "America's Labor Movement: Sociological Models and Futuristic Scenarios." *IRRA Spring Meeting Proceedings, 1994.* Madison, WI: IRRA.

———. 1995. "Applied Sociology and the Labor Movement: On Bargaining Mutual Gains." *Journal of Applied Sociology* (Winter): 11–27.

———. 1995. *For Labor's Sake: Gains and Pains as Told by 28 Creative Inside Reformers.* Lanham, MD: University Press of America.

Tarpinian, Greg, ed. 1992. *The Future of Labor.* New York: Labor Research Association.

———. 1993. "Union Trends." *Trade Union Advisor,* March 16, p. 4.

———. 1995. "Wages/Unions." *LRA's Economic Notes* (February): 4.

———. 1996. "Union v. Nonunion." *LRA's Economic Notes* (July–August): 7–8.

Epilogue

Under Construction

Vision without action is a daydream,
Action without vision is a nightmare.
—Japanese proverb

Thanks to a half-century development of computer uses, and especially the last 20 years of personal computer advances (the Internet, the World Wide Web, Web-TV, etc.), a far-reaching revolution in organizational and social reality is in process, arguably one of the most thoroughgoing changes in information processing in modern times. The span of applications "now ranges from international fund transfers to supermarket checkouts, from spacecraft controls to automobile warnings . . ." (Rochlin, xi).

With mind-boggling speed the so-called Age of Information has engulfed Labor in a world not of its own making, and one rife with migraine-inviting confusion.

This notwithstanding, many gains have been won, gains of which Organized Labor has much reason to be proud. Consider this account from a very computer-savvy research director of a major international union:

> I've saved thousands of jobs, thousands! We come into bargaining knowing more about the company than they do, by far. We've researched everything, I mean everything—their return on investment, their philanthropy profile, their executive profit-sharing payout . . . like, I mean, everything!
>
> When they say they can't afford this or that, we come right back and show them how they can—and we show them what they will gain if

they do. We give them a better analysis of their ability to pay than they ever thought possible. And when we've got the contract we were after, we sell it to our members, and begin to prove to the company they were right all along to go along.

Similarly, an activist with whom I talked after I gave a workshop on union and computer possibilities proudly explained his own situation:

> Does it help? You bet it does! I've got my entire office in this little machine, all of my data decks. I can help a member right on the spot, no waiting, no fuss. They really are impressed, and I feel good about it. Heck, I've been a computer nerd since the 1970s, and I keep upgrading my stuff, so it's easy for me now. I can't remember how it was before I took this way, but it couldn't have been good enough.

Labor's record to date, put as a bumper sticker, might read: "Extraordinary possibilities under development."

Problems persist, of course, what with only a small minority of unionists on-line, and even fewer clicking on Web sites other than that of their local or union. Too many such Web sites are dull, static, top-down billboards, and too many leaders (and large numbers of members) are comfortable with that. Deep-reaching questions abound, as in this thought from the sage head of a very impressive computer-using local:

> Part of what's happened is that the labor movement hasn't really decided how it wants to be, or what it want to look like. And so, it has a hard time setting up computer support systems. Because it is not sure what it wants to be.

Far more, in short, is required if Organized Labor is to soon maximize the potential of computer use, an adoption on which its survival may partially hinge.

Fortunately, a new generation of Web-faring activists are eager to get on with it. Labor's "digerati" types (those eager to expand and improve creative uses made of computers) have lives steeped in Information Age technologies, and are living ever more effectively in a "networked" world. Forward-thinking and visionary, these techno-savvy men and women have a hefty dose of indefatigable optimism. Unlike many of their Cyber Naught or Cyber Drift peers, their expectations concerning the renewing of Organized Labor are almost without limits.

When such activists envision the years ahead, they expect computers to soon secure unprecedented access of everyone in Labor to everyone else. They expect rapid polling of the membership. Galvanizing of rallies or e-mail protests. Spotlighting of models worth emulating, and of wrongs for the righting. Libraries put at a unionist's beck and call, along with valuable arbitration, grievance, and mediation material. Open chat rooms and bulletin boards for the creation of a high-tech electronic (virtual) "community" to bolster high-touch solidarity among real folk.

As if this was not enough, the vision of labor's digerati includes a quantum increase soon in the collective intelligence of "global village" unionists in a global international. They expect unprecedented cooperation across national borders, and thereby, the first effective counter to transnational corporate behemoths. Going out a year or two further, they envision Intelligent Agent software housed in computer wearables, empowering unionists as never before.

Examples of such thinking are available in the volume's "from-the-trenches" essays. Brown explains telecommuter possibilities for staffers. Breedlove applauds courses in Windows already part of journeyman upgrading programs. Cantrell offers a computer-aided plan for organizing new members. Dator insists that high-touch matters. Evon links high-tech/high-touch progress to prior gains in union democracy. Giljum imagines a virtual union reality. Laskonis points to computer-aided political options that work. Pinnock outlines a futurizing process that works. Rodgers sees job jeopardy ahead, and does not flinch. And me, I urge more appreciation for futuristics course offerings, for the contribution women activists can provide, and for the unique role unions can play as virtual organizations. In all, the ten of us share our confidence that Labor can and will "compute" early in the third millennium, can and will help us preserve lives that honor us all.

At the end of the day, if my confidence in labor falters, I reread these essays and take heart. I remember Breedlove advising, "We must stop thinking in terms of tomorrow, but in terms of years, because tomorrow is too late to prepare for change." And I remember Laskonis urging us to "think of the possibilities the labor movement has in the future, provided we use the Internet to its fullest potential."

Guided by this growing cadre, labor can soon move more unions and locals into Cyber Gain status. And thereby invigorate the membership. Draw in new members. Intimidate opponents. Intrigue vote-seekers. Meet the aspirations that union "netizens" have for the Labor movement. And in other valuable ways, significantly bolster Labor's chances of moving especially advanced unions and locals up to CyberUnion status early in the twenty-first century.

Which, however, is *not* the same thing as saying that computers can or will save Organized Labor (to deliberately repeat a cautionary note struck elsewhere in the volume). *Computerization is no magic wand.* It is costly, complex, and demanding, only as reliable and effective as the humans in charge. It works best when aiding such high-touch efforts as "one-on-one" organizing, "shoe leather" vote-getting, "buttonhole" lobbying for labor law reform, and so on. It works best when kept as an accessory and an aid, rather than allowed to become a confining and superordinating system. It would be a costly mistake to expect too much from it, almost as costly as present-day underutilization.

Similarly, it would be wrong to take a "one-size-fits-all" approach to the CyberUnion model espoused throughout this book. Every union and local has a unique history, culture, and vision. While all could benefit from some application of the F-I-S-T model, each will want to preserve the best of its uniqueness and make its own path to CyberUnion status. Those that give the F-I-S-T model a chance should evolve toward a more nuanced and supple existence.

Students of planned change commonly agree that "it is extremely difficult for organizations to reinvent themselves." (Heckscher, xiv). Fortunately, more and more activists seem to grasp the pro-labor potential of computer use, and to judge cautiously from my field research, many are eager to help realize it. They know the task is daunting, but they are energized, rather than intimidated, by the challenge.

Unless and until labor makes more creative use of computer and cyberspace possibilities, its long slide into irrelevance may not be reversed. Murray Kempton, one of the most insightful writers about unionism, wistfully notes of seemingly appealing reforms, "One sees at once that here is the way to get at the thing, and wonders why, with the sign painted this plain, the road has been so seldom followed" (Kazin).

It is time to heed signs pointing toward the CyberUnion, and give this Information Age labor organization a twenty-first-century trial.

Recommended Resources

Nadler, David A., and Michael Tushman. *Competing by Design: The Power of Organizational Architecture.* New York: Oxford University Press, 1997. Two management consultants contend that organizations cannot hope to flourish in the twenty-first century if based on a nineteenth-century design. Explain how to achieve new winning capabilities.

Schuler, Doug. *New Community Network: Wired for Change.* New York: Addison-Wesley Longman, 1996. The definitive book on the nonprofit movement to bring computers to low-income Americans, one with which Labor could do more. A promising and inspiring example of socially responsible computing.

Zohar, Danah. *Reviving the Corporate Brain.* San Francisco: Berrett-Koehler, 1997. Makes a good case for transforming organizations to thrive on uncertainty, deal creatively with rapid change, and release the full potential of leaders and members alike.

Computer Mediated Communications, an on-line magazine, offered in its November 1996 issue several articles concerning use of the Internet by the labor movement around the world. Accessible at www.december .com/cmc/mag/1996/nov/toc.html

Computer Professionals for Social Responsibility offers guidelines on behalf of a sounder cyber society. Available at www. cpsr.org

ENODE is a monthly column about the Internet, one that pays special attention to issues of democracy, policy, labor, and other progressive matters. Available at enodelist@garnet.berkeley.edu

Michael Moore, film maker and author, offers no-holds-barred commentaries on labor and almost everything else. Accessible at www.dogeatdogfilms.com/

SAWS (Scholars, Artists, and Writers for Social Justice), an outgrowth of pro-union campus teach-ins, can be reached at www.sage.edu/html/SAWS, or, sawsj@1vc.umass.edu

Sources

The educated person is someone who knows how to find out what he doesn't know.

—Georg Simmel, *Pearls of Wisdom,* 1987

Adler, Lee H. "Informing, Communicating with, and Mobilizing Our Members Through the Internet." NY: ILR Conference Center, 1998 (unpublished paper).

Agel, Jerome, and Walter D. Glanze, eds. *Pearls of Wisdom: A Harvest of Quotations from All Ages.* New York: Harper and Row, 1987.

Anders, George. "Discomfort Zone: Some Big Companies Long to Embrace Web, But Settle for Flirtation." *Wall Street Journal,* November 4, 1998, pp. A-1, A-14.

Anon. "Why the Internet Matters to Organized Labor." Washington, DC: Ad Hoc Committee of Information Technology Staffers, 1998. Unpublished.

———. "Union Membership Stayed Flat in '97 at 12.9 Million." *Wall Street Journal,* January 30, 1998, p. A-4.

———. "Profile of the Electorate." *Los Angeles Times,* June 4, 1998, p. D-5.

———. "New Surveillance Devices." *New York Times,* August 27, 1998, p. G-3.

———. "National Rankings in Internet Users." *Net News,* September 9, 1998 (on the Internet).

———. "New from the AFL-CIO." *America@Work,* October 1998, p. 23.

Aronowitz, Stanley. *From the Ashes of the Old: American Labor and America's Future.* New York: Houghton Mifflin, 1998.

Aronowitz, Stanley, and William DiFazio. *The Jobless Future.* Minneapolis, MN: University of Minnesota Press, 1994.

Atkins, John, and David Spooner. "Harnessing the Potential Benefits of Computer Communications: Telematics for Workers' Organizations." *Labour Education* (1994): 1–7.

———. "Have Modem, Will Bargain." *New Statesman Guide to Trade Unions and the Labour Movement,* 1995, pp. 40–41.

Bailey, Keith E. Commencement Speech, University of Tulsa. *New York Times,* May 27, 1998. p. B-9.

Barr, James, and Theodore Barr. "The Pentium Bug War Ends PR as We Know It." Omegacon, Inc., 1994. Cited in *The Digital Economy: Promise and Peril in the Age of Networked Intelligence.* Don Tapscott. New York: McGraw-Hill, 1996, p. 93.

Baugh, Robert, and Jane M. Pines. "Taking the Road Less Traveled: Workers, Welfare, and Jobs." *Social Policy* (winter 1997): 37–43.

Beeler, Duane, and Harry Kurshenbaum. *Roles of the Labor Leader.* Chicago: Union Representative, 1976.

Belanger, Marc. In Eric Lee, *The Labour Movement and the Internet,* Chicago: Pluto Press, 1997, p. 63.

Bell, Daniel. "Into the 21st Century, Bleakly." *New York Times,* July 26, 1992, p. E-17.

Bell, Wendell. *Foundations of Futures Studies: Human Science for a New Era.* Volume 1: *History, Purposes, and Knowledge.* New Brunswick, NJ: Transaction Press, 1997.

Bennett, James T., and John T. Delaney. "Research on Unions: Some Subjects in Need of Scholars." *Journal of Labor Research* 14 (1993): 95–110.

Bollen, Peter. *A Handbook of Great Labor Quotations.* Lynnfield, MA: Hillside Books, 1983.

Boren, James H. "Arcane and Proud of It." *New York Times,* June 4, 1998, p. A-27.

Boulding, Kenneth. "Presidential Address." *American Economic Association Proceedings,* 1978, p. 165.

Boutin, Paul. "Answer Man." *WIRED,* February 1999, p. 45.

Brecher, Jeremy, and Tim Costello. "The Challenge Ahead." *The Nation,* September 21, 1998, pp. 11–17.

Brier, Steven E. "Smart Devices Peep into Your Grocery Cart." *New York Times,* July 16, 1998, p. G-3.

Brin, David. *The Transparent Society: Will Technology Force Us to Choose Between Privacy and Freedom?* Reading, MA: Addison-Wesley, 1998.

Brock, Terry. "Send Your Web Site to Top of the Hit Parade." *Philadelphia Business Journal,* July 3–9, 1998, p. 14.

Brokaw, Tom. *NBC Nightly News,* October 27, 1998.

Brown, Lester. *Vital Signs 1998.* Washington, DC: WorldWatch Institute, 1998, p. 3.

Brunner, John. *The Shockwave Rider.* New York: Harper and Row, 1975, p. 1.

Bulkeley, William M. "Kaplan Plans a Law School via the Web." *Wall Street Journal,* September 16, 1998, p. B-1.

Burkins, Glenn. "Number of Workers in Labor Unions Grew Last Year." *Wall Street Journal,* January 26, 1999, p. B-2

Cairncross, Frances. "A Connected World." *The Economist,* September 13, 1997, p. 86.

Cantrell, Carl D. "Unions on the Web." Senior Paper prepared for the National Labor College (NLC) of the AFL-CIO George Meany Center for Labor Studies, Silver Spring, MD, Fall 1998.

Chapman, Gary. "Taming the Computer." In *Flame Wars: One Discourse of Cyberculture,* edited by Mark Dery. Durham, NC: Duke University Press, 1994.

Christensen, Clayton M. *The Innovator's Dilemma: When New Technologies Cause Great Firms to Fail.* Boston: Harvard Business School, 1997.

Coates, Joseph F. et al., *2025: Scenarios of US and Global Society Reshaped by Science and Technology.* Greensboro, NC: Oakhill Press, 1997.

Cobble, Dorothy Sue, ed. *Women and Unions: Forging a Partnership.* Ithaca, NY: ILR Press, 1993.

Cohen-Rosenthal, Edward, ed. *Unions, Management, and Quality: Opportunities for Innovation and Excellence.* Chicago: Irwin, 1995.

Connell, Mike. "Avoid Cyberspace Ripoffs: Political Campaigns through the Internet." *Campaigns and Elections* (June 1998): 48.

Corn, David. "Union Dues, Political Don'ts." *The Nation,* May 18, 1998, pp. 16–20.

Covey, Stephen R. *The 7 Habits of Highly Effective People.* New York: Simon and Schuster, 1989.

Coyle, Diane. *The Weightless World: Strategies for Managing the Digital Economy.* Boston: MIT Press, 1998.

Crossette, Barbara. "A New Measure of Disparities: Poor Sanitation in Internet Era." *New York Times,* May 12, 1998, p. A-11.

Crouch, Mark. "A Change of Image Is Not Enough." *Labor Studies Journal* (Winter 1998): 31–42.

Dertouzos, Michael L. *What Will Be: How the New World of Information Will Change Our Lives.* San Francisco: Harper, 1997.

Eisenscher, Michael. "Beyond Mobilization: How Labor Can Transform Itself." *Working USA* (March/April 1998): 36–38.

Eisner, Michael. *Work in Progress.* New York: Random House, 1998.

Faulkner, William. *As I Lay Dying.* New York: Random House, 1950, p. 116.

Feng, DaShuan. "E-mail Report." May 22, July 15 and 16, 1998 (unpublished).

Finder, Alan. "Now, Continuing Education for Lawyers." *New York Times,* September 17, 1998, p. B-3.

Firestone, David. "A Life's Work: Honoring Those Who Labored." *New York Times,* September 4, 1998, p. B-2. The quote is from Dr. Debra E. Bernhardt, Labor Archivist.

Fletcher, Bill. Transcript of a Speech given to the UCLEA/AFL-CIO Meeting, May Day 1998, San Jose, California.

Foner, Philip S. "Women and the American Labor Movement: A Historical Perspective." In *Working Women: Past, Present, Future,* Karen S. Koziara, et al., eds. Washington, DC: Bureau of National Affairs, 1987.

Gates, Jeff. *The Ownership Solution: Toward a Shared Capitalism for the 21st Century.* Reading, MA: Addison-Wesley, 1998.

Geenen, Jon. "Unions and Information Technology." Silver Spring, MD: National Labor College, 1998. Unpublished Independent Study Paper.

Gelernter, David. "The Computer of the Future." *Wall Street Journal,* October 26, 1998, p. A-22.

Geoghegan, Thomas. *Which Side Are You On? Trying to Be for Labor When It's Flat on Its Back.* New York: Plume, 1991.

Gittlen, Ike. Speech, Labor Day, Harrisburg, Pennsylvania, Central Labor Council, September 8, 1998.

Gleckman, Howard. "A Rich Stew in the Melting Pot." *Business Week,* August 31, 1998, p. 76.

Glover, Mike. "A U.S. Ballot on Women for President." *Philadelphia Inquirer,* September 25, 1998, p. A-26.

Goleman, Daniel. *Working with Emotional Intelligence.* New York: Bantam, 1998.

Goodman, Susan. "She Lost It at the Movies." *Modern Maturity,* March–April, 1998, p. 14.

Grau, Oliver, as quoted in Mirapaul. "World-Wide Views on the World Wide Web." *Wall Street Journal,* September 3, 1998. p. A-20.

Green, Kenneth C. *Campus Computing Survey, 1998.* Encino, CA: Campus Computing, 1998. (cgreen@campuscomuting.net)

Greenbaum, Joan. *Windows on the Workplace: Computers, Jobs, and the Organization of Office Work in the Late Twentieth Century.* New York: Monthly Review Press, 1995.

Greenhouse, Steven. "Despite Efforts to Organize, Union Rosters Have Declined." *New York Times,* March 15, 1998, p. 33.

———. "Unions, Growing Bolder, No Longer Shun Strikes." *New York Times,* September 7, 1998, p. A-12.

———. "Republicans Credit Labor for Success by Democrats." *New York Times,* November 6, 1998, p. A-29.

———. "Union Membership Rose in '98, but Unions' Percentage of Work Force Fell." *New York Times,* January 26, 1999, p. A-20.

Grimsley, Kristin D. "Beep Her the Fax About the Voice Mail on Her E-Mail." *Washington Post,* June 1, 1998, p. 30.

Hall, Mike. "First We Mobilized Members. Then We Registered Them. Now It's Time to Vote." *America@Work* (October 1998): 9.

Hall, Royce T. "Blacks, Hispanics Still Lag Behind Whites in Level of PC Ownership, Internet Access." *Wall Street Journal,* July 29, 1998, p. B-12.

Hannigan, Thomas A. *Managing Tomorrow's High-Performance Unions.* Westport, CT: Quorum, 1998.

Harmon, Amy. "Access to Clinton Data Abets E Pluribus Unum, '90s Style." *New York Times,* September 20, 1998, p. A-16.

Hart, Peter. "AFL-CIO Labor 2000." Washington, DC: Peter D. Hart Research Associates, 1997; "A Survey Conducted for the AFL-CIO Among Union Members; February 1999.

Hartford, Bruce. "Unions and Computers: Notes for the LaborTECH '97 Conference." Unpublished paper. San Francisco: NWU, UAW Local 1981. (nwu@nwu.org)

Harwood, John, and Jackie Calmes. "Midterm Exam." *Wall Street Journal,* November 5, 1998, pp. A-1, A-11.

Heckscher, Charles C. *The New Unionism: Employee Involvement in the Changing Corporation.* Ithaca, NY: Cornell University Press, 1996 ed.

Heim, Pat. *Hardball for Women: Winning at the Game of Business.* Los Angeles: Plume, 1993 ed.

Hill, G. Christian. "Cyber Servants," *Wall Street Journal,* September 27, 1994, pp. A-1, 12.

———. "Adult Net User," *Wall Street Journal*, December 11, 1997, p. A-11.

Hobsbawn, Eric. *Uncommon People: Resistance, Rebellion, and Jazz.* London: New Press, 1998.

Holcomb, Henry J. "Labor Is Training for the Future." *Philadelphia Inquirer,* September 7, 1998, pp. D-1, D-3.

Howe, Irving, as quoted in "Sisyphus in the Basement." George Packer. *Harper's Magazine,* July 1998, p. 71.

ICEM (International Federation of Chemical, Energy, Mine and General Workers' Unions). *Power and Counterpower: The Union Response to Global Capital.* Chicago: Pluto Press, 1996.

Illingworth, Montieth M. "Workers on the Net, Unite!" *Information Week,* August 22, 1994, pp. 26–36.

Immergut, Debra Jo. "The Gallery: Guggenheim in CyberSpace." *Wall Street Journal,* September 10, 1998, p. A-20.

Jasen, Georgette. "Business Bulletin." *Wall Street Journal,* September 24, 1998, p. 1.

Johnson, Malcolm. *Crime on the Labor Front.* New York: McGraw-Hill, 1950.

Johnston, Paul. *Success While Others Fail: Social Movement Unionism and the Public Workplace.* Ithaca, NY: ILR Press, 1994.

———. "Re: LaborTalk Re: Organizing: Better Training? or Better Vision?" In "PubLabor Digest," 1398 (Listserve; September 13, 1998).

Jones, Glenn R. *Cyberschools: An Education Renaissance.* Boulder, CO: Jones International, 1997.

Joyce, Amy. "Please Don't Call Them Grease Monkeys." *Washington Post Weekend Edition,* August 31, 1998, p. 20.

Karlgaard, Rich. "The Web Is Recession-Proof." *Wall Street Journal,* July 14, 1998, p. A-18.

Karr, Albert R. "Work Week." *Wall Street Journal,* June 2, 1998, p. A-1.

Kazin, Alfred. "Missing Murray Kempton." *New York Times Book Review,* November 30, 1997, p. 35.

Keller, John J. "Streamlined." *Wall Street Journal,* June 2, 1998, pp. A-1, A-6.

Kelly, Kevin. *New Rules for the New Economy: 10 Radical Strategies for a Connected World.* New York: Viking, 1998.

Kempton, Murray. *Part of Our Time: Some Monuments and Ruins of the Thirties.* New York: Delta ed., 1967.

King, Larry. *Future Talk.* New York: Bantam, 1998.

Lee, Eric. *The Labour Movement and the Internet: The New Internationalism.* Chicago: Pluto Press, 1997.

———. "How Many Unionists Are There on Line?" Global Labournet (an online newletter), March 26, 1998.

Lee, Francis W. Excerpt from Graduation Speech, Roanoke College. *New York Times,* May 27, 1998, p. B-9.

Lee, Richard A. "Ageist and Arrogant." *American Demographics* (April 1996): 59. The expert cited is Cheryl Russell.

Lester, Richard. *As Unions Mature: An Analysis of the Evolution of American Unionism.* Princeton: Princeton University Press, 1958.

Levi, Primo. *The Mirror Maker: Stories and Essays.* New York: Schocken Books, 1989.

Levine, Susan. *Labor's True Woman: Carpet Weavers, Industrialization, and Labor Reform in the Gilded Age.* Philadelphia: Temple University Press, 1984.

Levy, Steven. "Technomania." *Newsweek,* February 27, 1995, p. 26.

Lewis, Michael, "The Little Creepy Crawlers Who Will Eat You in the Night." *New York Times Magazine,* March 1, 1998, pp. 40–48, 58–60, 62, 79–81.

Lewis, Robert. "Boomers to Reinvent Retirement." *AAUP Bulletin* (June 1998): 1, 16.

Lichtenstein, Nelson. "Roll the Union On: Rebuilding the Labor Movement." *In These Times,* October 18, 1998, pp. 18–20.

Lincoln, Abraham. As quoted in *Power Quotes.* Daniel B. Baker. Detroit: Visible Ink, 1992, p. 305.

Lohr, Steve. "Even Amid a High-Tech Revolution, Evolution Is the Norm." *New York Times,* October 25, 1998, p. BU-4.

LRA (Labor Research Association). "Another Slip in Membership." *Economic Notes* (February 1998): 5.

———. "Who Belongs to a Union?" *Trade Union Adviser,* February 24, 1998, p. 4.

———. "How Much Do We Need to Organize?" *Trade Union Adviser* March 1998, p. 8.

———. "Organizing Up Significantly in 1997." *Economic Notes* (July/August 1998): 5.

———. "Unions' Urge to Merge Will Accelerate." *Trade Union Adviser,* August 18, 1998, p. 1.

———. "Union Friendly Skies." *Economic Notes* (September 1998): 6.

Lund, John. "Using Microcomputer Spreadsheets to Teach Industrial and Labor Relations Applications." *Labor Studies Journal* (summer 1995): 22–27.

Lunneborg, Patricia. *Women Changing Women.* New York: Greenwood, 1990.

Lynch, Roberta. "Comments." In *Women and Unions: Forging a Partnership.* Dorothy Sue Cobble, ed. Ithaca, NY: ILR Press, 1993, pp. 414–421.

McChesney, Robert W., et al., eds. *Capitalism and the Information Age: The Political Economy of the Global Communication Revolution.* New York: Monthly Review Press, 1998.

McCollum, Kelly. "'Yahoo!'s Magazine Selects Dartmouth as the 'Most Wired' College." *Chronicle of Higher Education,* April 24, 1998, p. A-37.

McWilliams, John-Roger, and Peter McWilliams. *Life 101.* Los Angeles: Prelude Press, 1991.

Madrick, Jeffrey. "Computers: Waiting for the Revolution." *Challenge* (July–August 1998): 42–65.

Malakoff, Walter, and Dong-One Kim. "Computerized Technology, Jobs and the Union's Role: The Views of Union Members in a Skilled Craft Industry." *Labor Studies Journal* (winter 1996): 39–51.

Mandel, Michael J. "You Ain't Seen Nothing Yet." *Business Week,* August 31, 1998, pp. 60–64.

Markoff, John. "Taking a Step Toward Converting the Home into a Supercomputer." *New York Times,* July 15, 1998, p. A-1.

Martin, James. *Cybercorp: The New Business Revolution.* New York: American Management Association, 1996.

Martin, Judith. "Proper Answers to Improper Questions." *Sunshine,* September 27, 1998, pp. 9, 11.

Masters, Marick F. *Unions at the Crossroads: Strategic Membership, Financial, and Political Perspectives.* Westport, CT: Quorum, 1997.

Mazepa, Pat. "The Solidarity Network in Formation: A Search for Democratic Alternative Communication." M.A. thesis, Carleton University, Ottawa, Ont., 1997. (pmazepa@alfred.ccs.carleton.ca)

Medina, Kim et al., eds. *Faculty Work: Inspiring Activism and Supporting Working Families.* Washington, DC: AFL-CIO Organizing Institute, 1998.

Miller, Leslie. "Web Father Says System Needs More." *Philadelphia Inquirer,* September 6, 1998, p. D-3.

Miller, Susan J. *Never Let Me Down: A Memoir.* New York: Holt, 1998, See the opening epigram.

Mills, C. Wright. *The New Men of Power: America's Labor Leaders.* New York: Houghton-Mifflin, 1947.

Mirapaul, Matthew. "World-Wide Views on the World Wide Web." *Wall Street Journal,* September 3, 1998, p. A-20.

Moore, Geoffrey, Paul Johnson, and Tom Kippola. *The Gorilla Game.* New York: HarperBusiness, 1998.

Moore, Michael. *Downsize This! Random Threats from an Unarmed American.* New York: Crown, 1996.

Morin, Richard. "The Move to 'Net News.' " *Washington Post Weekly Edition,* June 1998, p. 34.

Mort, JoAnn, ed. *Not Your Father's Union Movement.* New York: Verso, 1998.

Moss, Nicholas. "Bulk Buys and Tax Breaks Boost PCs." *The European,* March 23, 1998, p. 14.

Mossberg, Walter S. "Computing Got Easier Last Year, But It Still Has a Long Way to Go." *Wall Street Journal,* October 8, 1998, p. B-1.

Mount, Ian. "Vcall Gives Investors the Corporate Word via Internet." *Philadelphia Inquirer,* September 7, 1998, p. D-10.

Nadler, David A., and Michael Tushman. *Competing by Design: The Power of Organizational Architecture.* New York: Oxford University Press, 1997.

Naik, Gautam. "Prepaid Plans Open Up Cellular-Phone Market." *Wall Street Journal,* September 16, 1998, p. B-1.

Naisbitt, John. *Megatrends.* New York: Warner Books, 1982.

Narisetti, Raju. "Now You Can Cook Your Books and Dinner at the Same Time." *Wall Street Journal,* September 10, 1998, p. B-1.

Negroponte, Nicholas. *Being Digital.* New York: Alfred A. Knopf, 1995.

Norton, Ernie. "From Investment Banker to Union Man." *Wall Street Journal,* January 23, 1996. pp. B-1, 8.

Ogden, Frank. *Navigating in Cyberspace: A Guide to the Next Millennium.* Toronto: Macfarlane Walter and Ross, 1995.

Orwell, George. *Down and Out in Paris and London.* London: Harper and Brothers, 1933.

Packer, George. "Sisyphus in the Basement." *Harper's Magazine,* July 1998, pp. 67–72, 74.

Paul, Gregory S., and Earl D. Cox. *Beyond Humanity: CyberEvolution and Future Minds.* Rockland, MA: Charles River Media, 1997.

Pentland, Alex. "Information Technology." *Business Week,* October 20, 1997, p. 42.

Peter, Kristyne. "Labor on the Internet." *WorkingUSA* (May/June 1997): 82–87.

Petzinger, Thomas, Jr. "Chris Langton Wants to Give Executives a Living Computer." *Wall Street Journal,* July 24, 1998, p. B-1.

Pocock, Peter. E-mail, August 28, 1998.

Polman, Dick. "Prosperity." *Inquirer Magazine,* September 20, 1998, p. 10.

Poope, David. "Blacks and Hispanics Are Trailing Other Groups in Computer Ownership." *Philadelphia Inquirer,* August 6, 1998, p. F-2.

Prelinger, Rick. "Living Better Digitally." *New York Times Book Review,* March 30, 1997. p. 26.

Price, Reynolds. *Roxanna Slade.* New York: Scribner, 1998.

Puette, William J. *Through Jaundiced Eyes: How the Media View Organized Labor.* Ithaca, NY: ILR Press, 1992.

Quick, Rebecca. "Web's Robot Shoppers Don't Roam Free." *Wall Street Journal,* September 3, 1998, p. B-1.

Quintanilla, Carl. "Work Week." *Wall Street Journal,* September 15, 1998, p. A-1.

Raney, Rebecca F. "Voting on the Web: Not Around the Corner, But on the Horizon." *New York Times,* September 17, 1998, p. G-8.

Raskin, A.H. "New Directions for the AFL-CIO." *New Management* (Winter 1996): 12–13.

Rathke, Wade. "No More Mourning in America: A Forum." *The Nation,* September 21, 1998, p. 17.

Rawlins, Gregory J.E. *Slaves of the Machine: The Quickening of Computer Technology.* Cambridge: MIT Press, 1997.

Reich, Robert. "The Company of the Future." *FAST Company* (November 1998): 138.

Richardson, Charley. "Avoiding the Tricks and Traps of Involvement: Developing a New Model for Powerful Bargaining in a Changing Workplace." *New Labor Forum* (spring 1998): 104–113.

Richtel, Matt. "Technology." *New York Times,* September 7, 1998, p. C-2.

Rifkin, Jeremy. "News Watch." *New York Times,* September 17, 1998, p. G-4.

———. *The End of Work.* New York: G.P. Putnam's Sons, 1995.

Ringle, William J. *TechEdge: Using Computers to Present and Persuade.* Boston: Allyn and Bacon, 1998.

Robinson, John P., and Geoffrey Godbey. *Time for Life: The Surprising Ways Americans Use Their Time.* University Park: Pennsylvania State University Press, 1997.

Rochlin, Gene I. *Trapped in the Net: The Unanticipated Consequences of Computerization.* Princeton: Princeton University Press, 1997.

Rogers, Joel. "A Strategy for Labor." *Industrial Relations* 34 (1995): 367–381.

Rose, Matthew, and Almar Latour. "Hewlett's PC Deal with Swedish Union Gets Enthusiastic Response by Workers." *Wall Street Journal,* June 2, 1998, p. 2.

Rosen, Saul. "One Stop on the Road to Full Employment." *Social Policy* (winter 1997): pp. 26–30.

Safire, William. "Hang in There." *New York Times,* September 10, 1998, p. A-33.

Schiesel, Seth. "A Cuisinart of Phone Technology Fails to Whip Up Enthusiasm." *New York Times,* June 3, 1998, p. D-1.

Schnarch, David. *Passionate Marriage.* New York: Henry Holt, 1998.

Schuler, Doug. *New Community Network: Wired for Change.* New York: Addison-Wesley Longman, 1996.

Sebastian, Pamela. "Business Bulletin." *Wall Street Journal,* July 16, 1998, p. A-1.

Sheth, Jagdish N. *InfoVisions: Visions of the Information Age: The ComForum Report.* Chicago: National Engineering Consortium, 1994.

Shostak, Arthur B. "2000: A Futurist's View." *Insight* (Winter 1990): 2–4.

————. *Robust Unionism: Innovations in the Labor Movement.* Ithaca, NY: ILR Press, 1991

————, ed. *For Labor's Sake: Gains and Pains as Told by 28 Creative Inside Reformers.* Lanham, MD: University Press of America, 1995.

————, ed. "Impacts of Changing Employment: If the Good Jobs Go Away." *The Annals,* March 1996.

Shostak, Arthur B., and David Skocik. *The Air Controllers' Controversy: Lessons from the PATCO Strike.* New York: Human Sciences Press, 1986.

Shostak, Stanley. *Death of Life: The Legacy of Molecular Biology.* London: Macmillan Press, 1998, p. 210.

Sixty Minutes. September 27, 1998.

Smart, Tim. "A Corporate Perspective on the New World Order." *Washington Post,* June 11, 1998, pp. C-1, 4. Interview with George David, CEO of United Technologies.

Solomon, Norman. "What If We Didn't Need Labor Day?" E-mail material, MODEM Listserve, September 5, 1998.

Standage, Tom. *The Victorian Internet.* New York: Walker, 1998.

Stern, Andy. In "Andy Stern's Mission Impossible." Aaron Bernstein. *Business Week,* June 19, 1996, p. 73.

Stone, Brad. "The Keyboard Kids." *Newsweek,* June 8, 1998, p. 72.

Sussman, Gerald, and John A. Lent, eds. *Global Productions: Labor in the Making of the "Information Society."* Cresskill, NJ: Hampton Press, 1998.

Takahashi, Dean. "Behind the Boom." *Wall Street Journal,* June 15, 1998, p. B-4.

Tapscott, Don. *The Digital Economy: Promise and Peril in the Age of Networked Intelligence.* New York: McGraw-Hill, 1996.

Taylor, Jeff. "The Continental Classroom: Teaching Labour Studies On-Line." *Labor Studies Journal* (Spring 1998): 19–38.

Toffler. Alvin. *The Third Wave.* New York: William Morrow, 1980.

Trillin, Calvin. *Uncivil Liberties.* New Haven: Ticknor & Fields, 1982.

Trumka, Richard. "Keynote Address." AFL-CIO Information Technology Conference, 1996 (VCR Tape, AFL-CIO), pp. 211–12.

————."Interview." In *Future Talk,* Larry King, ed. New York: Bantam, 1998.

Vitez, Michael. "AARP Reaches Out to New Generation." *Philadelphia Inquirer,* June 7, 1998, p. E-3.

Voos, Paula B., ed. *Proceedings of the Fiftieth Annual Meeting,* Volume 1. Madison, WI: Industrial Relations Research Association, 1998.

Wade, Nicholas. "From Ants to Ethics." *New York Times,* May 12, 1998, p. F-6.

Wald, Matthew L. "In Computers, Fast, Faster, and Fastest." *New York Times,* October 28, 1998, p. C-6.

Walker, Tom. Internet communiqué, FutureWork Listserve, August 12, 1998.

Warner, Carolyn. *The Last Word.* Englewood Cliffs, NJ: Prentice-Hall, 1992, p. 15.

Waterman, Peter. *International Labour Communication by Computer: The Fifth International?* The Hague: Institute of Social Studies, 1992.

Weber, Roy P. "Infotech." In *InfoVision: Visions of the Information Age—The ComForum Report.* Chicago: National Engineering Consortium, 1994.

Weiner, Jonathan. *The Beak of the Finch.* New York: Knopf, 1994, p. 126.

Whitford, David. "Labor's Lost Chance." *Fortune,* September 28, 1998, pp. 177–180.

Wildstrom, Stephen H. "The Last Days of the Home PC?" *Business Week,* November 9, 1998, p. 34.

Wilson, Margaret Gibbons, and Judith L. King. "Power, Politics, and the Union Woman." *Labor Studies Journal* (Spring 1998): 52–73.

Wind, Jerry Y., and Jeremy Main. *Driving Change: How the Best Companies are Preparing for the 21st Century.* New York: Free Press, 1998.

Witt, Matt, and Gaye Williams. "Labor Video: Organizing Is the Message." *WorkingUSA*, July/August 1998): 54–59.

Wolman, William, and Anne Colamosca. *The Judas Economy: The Triumph of Capital and the Betrayal of Work.* Reading, MA: Addison-Wesley, 1997.

Wysocki, Bernard Jr. "Internet Is Opening Up a New Era of Pricing." *Wall Street Journal,* June 8, 1998, p. 1.

Yahoo (www.yahoo.com/Business-and-Economy/Labor), as cited in Jim Young, and Ike Gittlen, "From Potential to Reality: Labor Online and the Local Union." Unpublished paper, 1998 (made available at the Labor Online Conference, New York City, 1999).

Zaniello, Tom. *Working Stiffs, Union Maids, Reds, and Riff Raff: An Organized Guide to the Films about Labor.* Ithaca, NY: ILR Press, 1996.

Zohar, Danah. *Reviving the Corporate Brain.* San Francisco: Berrett-Koehler, 1997.

Cyber Sources

What was beyond the grasp of imagination yesterday, except for the fertile minds of futurists and fiction writers, has already happened today.
                                    —Jacques Attali, *Millennium*, 1991

Chapter 1: Using Computers as a Servicing Aid

Learning On Line University is located at Znet's Web site, which is www.zmag.org/znet.htm. Although they do have an e-mail address, which is sysop@zmag.org, this is usually used for technical assistance or requests for information about Znet.

Noam Chomsky's e-mail address is Chomsky@mit.edu, but another way to communicate with him is through Znet forum boards, which is at Znet's Web site at the address above.

As for political listserves, two labor forum boards are available at Znet.

See also CAP Web, A Guide to the U.S. Congress. Contact: policy.net/ capweb/congress.html

Favorite listserves of Charles Laskonis include MODEM, at cherylm@soltec.net, and *PubLabor,* which is at publabor@relay. doit.wisc.edu (for unions in the public sector primarily, but not exclusively).

Democracy University is kind of a "melting pot" of people who think the little guy does not have the voice that is due him/her in America's political process. It is at democracyu@makelist.com

Helpful is E-The People, which describes itself as "America's Interactive Town Hall," and resides in cyberspace at www.e-thepeople.com. You can sign a petition already posted on the site, create a new petition, or write a letter to government officials (the e-mail addresses of whom will be provided).

Global Trade Watch is at listproc@essential.org

Corporate Watch is a listserve that brings together news, analysis, diverse viewpoints, and networking resources for activists addressing the role corporations play in economic, social, and political issues. It is at corp-watchers@igc.org.

Focus on the Corporation is a moderated listserve which distributes the weekly column "Focus on the Corporation," co-authored by Russell Mokhiber, editor of *Corporate Crime Reporter,* and Robert Weissman, editor of *Multinational Monitor* magazine. Focus on the Corporation scrutinizes the multinational corporation—the most powerful institution of our time. Once a week, it reports and comments critically on corporate actions, plans, abuses, and trends. To subscribe to Corp-Focus, send an e-mail message to listproc@essential.org with the following all in one line: subscribe corp-focus <your name>.

Safety problems are addressed at an OSHA site (www.osha.gov).

Chapter 2: Organizing

The National Labor Relations Board (www.nlrb.gov) offers help through its Internet Web site.

Arbitrators can be found by accessing the National Mediation Board (www.nmb.gov) or the Federal Mediation and Conciliation Service Web sites (www.fmcs.gov).

Helpful is up-to-date socioeconomic analysis from the Economic Policy Institute; contact it at: www.epn.org/epi.html, or, epi@epinet.org

The Center to Protect Workers Rights can be reached at: www
.cpwr.com

Chapter 6: Innovations

On the Guggenheim virtual museum, see www.guggenheim.org, the
umbrella site of the Guggenheim organization.

Chapter 7: Services

For the Union Jobs Clearinghouse, go to ujc@unionjobs.com. It offers
an alphabetical listing of all the groups posting job announcements.
When you click on "Staffing Positions" to leave the first page, you
next see a page with all the states (at least 19 and DC turned on
currently, and growing). At the top of the next page, just under the
words "STAFFING POSITIONS" is the sentence, "To view union
positions by alphabetical order, click here." Click there and you go to
the index. Operated by Gary Cortes: Union Jobs Clearinghouse,
http://www.unionjobs.com

On tomorrow's jobs (Bureau of Labor Statistics), see: http://stats
.bls.gov/oco/oco2003.htm

On jobs growing the fastest and having the largest numerical increase
in employment from 1994 to 2005, by level of education and training:
http://stats.bls.gov/oco/ocotjt1.htm

For the latest developments in labor law, see a service provided by
Law Professor Ross Runkel: labor-emp@willamette.edu.

Chapter 11: Change-Agents: Stateside

See "Janet's IBEW Page," an unofficial site that offers IBEW the
skinny on what is going on in the locals.

On visionary projects, see http://www.awakeningearth.org. The sponsor offers a Millennium Project that promotes a "reflective/living-sys-
tems perspective." This emphasizes conscious consumption, personal
growth and community, fair competition, personal responsibility for

the well-being of the world, and a "spaceship earth ethic in global relations."

For insightful commentary, see listproc@mcfeeley.cc.utexas.edu to subscribe to a listserve that forwards copies of Gary Chapman's published articles, including his column "Digital Nation" in the *Los Angeles Times*.

The best source for links to Labor and other progressive sites may be IGC's membership list. Available at: http://www.igc.org/igc/members/members.f2p.html

Also helpful is a site entitled *Unions and Other Organizations on the Information Highway*. Available at: http://www.igc.org/igc.ln/feature/961115 2155/feature.html

Appendix: Survey

Dear reader: Could you please send me YOUR answers to the questions below (please identify ANY answers you would rather stay anonymous)—and, circulate the survey to other unionists who might also help.

1) How do you profit as a unionist from your use of a computer?

_____

_____

2) What are the problems you find in your use of it?

_____

_____

3) What effort is your local and/or international making to promote more use of the computer?

_____

_____

How effective is this?

_____

_____

4) Looking out five years ahead, how do you think unionism will be any different for its new uses of the computer? Please discuss POSITIVE and also NEGATIVE possibilities.

_____

_____

_____

5) What can be done NOW to promote the best of these uses? To block the worst of these uses?

_____

_____

_____

_____

6) What are your favorite listserves and web sites—in your role as a unionist? Why?

A._____

B._____

C._____

D._____

What aspect(s) of this topic have I overlooked with the questions above, and what can you help me understand about it?

_____

_____

_____

_____

_____

MANY thanks, fraternally, Art Shostak, Labor Educator (523 Dudley Ave, Narberth, PA 19072 (215-895-2466). Please e–mail your reply to SHOSTAKA@DREXEL.EDU

Index

About the Author

Arthur B. Shostak is a professor of sociology at Drexel University, Philadelphia, Pennsylvania (1967 to date). He previously taught at the Wharton School of Finance and Commerce, University of Pennsylvania (1961–67). Shostak is also an adjunct sociologist on the faculty of the National Labor Relations College at the AFL-CIO George Meany Center for Labor Studies, Silver Springs, Maryland (1975 to date). In 1998 he was appointed Director of the Drexel Center for Employment Futures (DCEF^{TM}), a university-based think tank devoted to exploring frontiers in tomorrow's world of work.

Shostak holds a B.S. in Industrial and Labor Relations from the New York State School of Industrial and Labor Relations at Cornell University (1958), and a Ph.D. in Sociology from Princeton University (1961). A consultant for many unions, he has conducted workshops for a dozen of the largest labor organizations in America. Shostak is also a member of Workers Education Local 189, CWA.

Shostak's homepage is at http://httpsrv.ocs.drexel.edu/ faculty/ shostaka and also at http://www.futureshaping.com/shostak/. His e-mail address is Shostak@drexel.edu, and he welcomes hearing from you, especially if you have material he can use in an improved second edition of this book.

Also by Arthur Shostak:

Impacts of Changing Employment: If the Good Jobs Go Away (1996; ed.)

Private Sociology: Unsparing Reflections, Uncommon Gains (1996; ed.)

For Labor's Sake: Gains and Pains as Told by 28 Creative Inside Reformers (1996; ed.)

Guidelines from Gomberg: No-Nonsense Advice for Labor and Management (1992; ed.)

Robust Unionism: Innovations in the Labor Movement (1991)

The Air Controllers' Controversy: Lessons from the PATCO Strike (1986; co-authored with David Skocile)

Men and Abortion: Lessons, Losses, and Love (1984; co-authored with Gary McLouth and Lynn Serg)

Blue-Collar Stress (1980)

Our Sociological Eye (1977; ed.)

Putting Sociology to Work (1974; ed.)

Privilege in America (1974; co-edited with Jon Van Til and Sally Bould VanTil)

Modern Social Reforms (1974)

Sociology and Student Life (1971; ed.)

Sociology in Action (1966; ed.)

Blue-Collar Life (1969)

Blue-Collar World (1965; co-edited with William Gomberg)

America's Forgotten Labor Organization (1963)